Interpretive Lenses in Sociology

Series editors: **Thomas DeGloma**, Hunter College, City University of New York, and **Julie B. Wiest**, West Chester University of Pennsylvania

---

The *Interpretive Lenses in Sociology* series provides a unique forum for scholars using a wide range of interpretive perspectives to explore their approaches to uncovering the deep meanings underlying human actions, events and experiences.

Forthcoming in the series:

Interpreting the Authoritarian Turn
Cultural, Emotional and Psychosocial Causes Of a Global Phenomenon
Edited by **Lynn Chancer** and **Neil McLaughlin**

Interpreting Identity
Dimensions of Power, Presence, and Belonging
Edited by **Wayne Brekhus** and **Susie Scott**

Out now in the series:

Interpreting Contentious Memory
Countermemories and Conflicts over the Past
Edited by **Thomas DeGloma** and **Janet L. Jacobs**

Interpretive Sociology and the Semiotic Imagination
Edited by **Andrea Cossu** and **Jorge Fontdevila**

Interpreting Religion
Making Sense of Religious Lives
Edited by **Erin Johnston** and **Vikash Singh**

Find out more at
bristoluniversitypress.co.uk/interpretive-lenses-in-sociology

International advisory board:

Jeffrey C. Alexander, Yale University, US
Marni A. Brown, Georgia Gwinnett College, US
Giuseppina Cersosimo, University of Salerno, Italy
Lynn S. Chancer, Hunter College, City University of New York, US
Erica Chito-Childs, Hunter College, City University of New York, US
Manase Kudzai Chiweshe, University of Zimbabwe, Zimbabwe
Jean-François Côté, University of Montreal, Canada
Emma Engdahl, University of Gothenburg, Sweden
Veikko Eranti, University of Helsinki, Finland
Emily Fairchild, New College of Florida, US
Gary Alan Fine, Northwestern University, US
Stacey Hannem, Wilfrid Laurier University, Canada
Titus Hjelm, University of Helsinki, Finland
Annemarie Jutel, Victoria University of Wellington, New Zealand
Carol Kidron, University of Haifa, Israel
Krzysztof T. Konecki, University of Lodz, Poland
Joseph A. Kotarba, Texas State University, US
Donileen Loseke, University of South Florida, US
Eeva Luhtakallio, University of Helsinki, Finland
Lisa McCormick, The University of Edinburgh, Scotland
Neil McLaughlin, McMaster University, Canada
Beth Montemurro, Pennsylvania State University, Abington, US
Kylie Parrotta, California Polytechnic State University, US
Laura Robinson, Santa Clara University, US
Andrea Salvini, University of Pisa, Italy
Susie Scott, University of Sussex, UK
Cristine G. Severo, Federal University of Santa Catarina, Brazil
Xiaoli Tian, University of Hong Kong, Hong Kong
Vilna Bashi Treitler, Northwestern University, US
Hector Vera, National Autonomous University of Mexico, Mexico
Gad Yair, The Hebrew University of Jerusalem, Israel
J. Patrick Williams, Nanyang Technological University, Singapore
Eviatar Zerubavel, Rutgers University, US

Find out more at
bristoluniversitypress.co.uk/interpretive-lenses-in-sociology

INTERPRETING SUBCULTURES

Approaching, Contextualizing, and Embodying Sense-Making Practices in Alternative Cultures

Edited by
J. Patrick Williams

First published in Great Britain in 2025 by

Bristol University Press
University of Bristol
1-9 Old Park Hill
Bristol
BS2 8BB
UK
t: +44 (0)117 374 6645
e: bup-info@bristol.ac.uk

Details of international sales and distribution partners are available at bristoluniversitypress.co.uk

© Bristol University Press 2025

British Library Cataloguing in Publication Data
A catalogue record for this book is available from the British Library

ISBN 978-1-5292-1861-9 hardcover
ISBN 978-1-5292-1862-6 paperback
ISBN 978-1-5292-1863-3 ePub
ISBN 978-1-5292-1864-0 ePdf

The right of J. Patrick Williams to be identified as editor of this work has been asserted by him in accordance with the Copyright, Designs and Patents Act 1988.

All rights reserved: no part of this publication may be reproduced, stored in a retrieval system, or transmitted in any form or by any means, electronic, mechanical, photocopying, recording, or otherwise without the prior permission of Bristol University Press.

Every reasonable effort has been made to obtain permission to reproduce copyrighted material. If, however, anyone knows of an oversight, please contact the publisher.

The statements and opinions contained within this publication are solely those of the editors and contributors and not of the University of Bristol or Bristol University Press. The University of Bristol and Bristol University Press disclaim responsibility for any injury to persons or property resulting from any material published in this publication.

Bristol University Press works to counter discrimination on grounds of gender, race, disability, age and sexuality.

Cover design: blu inc
Front cover image: Pexels/ Thiago Matos

Contents

Series Editors' Preface: Interpretive Lenses in Sociology—   vii
    On the Multidimensional Foundations of Meaning in Social Life
Notes on Contributors   xii
Acknowledgments   xvi

PART I   Approaching Interpretive Practice

1. Making Sense of Subcultures: Interpretive Practice and/in Subcultural Theory   3
J. Patrick Williams
2. Subculture, Scene, Lifestyle, or Movement? Conceptualizing Straight Edge from Insider and Academic Perspectives   21
Ross Haenfler
3. Ghosts in the Machine: (Post)subculture and the 'Problem' of Contemporary Youth   41
Andy Bennett and Daniel Bennett

PART II   Contextualizing Interpretive Practice

4. No More Heroes: Portuguese Punk and the Notion of Subculture in the Global South   59
Paula Guerra
5. Still Crazy After All Those Years: A Trajectory of Discourses on Youth Subcultures in Korea, from Exclusion to Recognition to Legitimization   75
Hyunjoon Shin
6. Interpreting Chinese Punk: From Doing Nothing to Hermit Lifestyle   93
Jian Xiao and Xinxin Dong
7. The Dynamic Meaning of Subculture among DIY Indonesian Musicians   107
Oki Rahadianto Sutopo

PART III Embodying Interpretive Practice

8	"That's Not Punk!" Authenticity, Older Punk Women, and the 'Doing' of Punk Scholarship *Laura Way*	127
9	"Let's All Be Friends": Emotional Labor and Insider Research in Punk Subculture *Stanislav Vysotsky and Donna Manion*	150
10	Intimacy, Exchange, and Friendship as Sensitizing Concepts: Interpreting and Teaching Subcultures through Ethnographic Fieldwork *Shane Blackman and Laura Barnett*	168

PART IV Conclusion

11	Approaching, Contextualizing, and Embodying Interpretive Practice in Subcultural Studies *J. Patrick Williams and Samuel Judah*	189

Index   205

Series Editors' Preface: Interpretive Lenses in Sociology—On the Multidimensional Foundations of Meaning in Social Life

Thomas DeGloma
(Hunter College and the Graduate Center, CUNY, USA)

Julie B. Wiest
(West Chester University of Pennsylvania, USA)

Sociology is an interpretive endeavor.[1] Whatever the approach taken to study and explain an aspect of social life—qualitative or quantitative, micro or macro—sociologists work to interpret their data to reveal previously unseen, or to clarify previously misunderstood, social forces. However, within the broad field of sociology, and under the purview of its kindred disciplines, there are many scholars who work to unpack the deep structures and processes that underlie the *meanings* of social life. These interpretive scholars focus on the ways that social meanings constitute the core structures of self and identity, the ways that individuals negotiate meanings to define their shared situations, and the collective meanings that bind people together into communities while also setting any given group or context apart from others. From this perspective, meaning underscores social mindsets and personal orientations in the world, as well as the solidarities and divisions that define the dynamics and mark the boundaries of our social standpoints and relationships. Furthermore, such scholars are concerned not only with how the individuals and groups they study actively make and remake the definitions that are central to their lives, as well as how those understandings influence their behaviors, but also how they seek to impact the world with their meaning-making processes. In this regard, meaning is of paramount significance to both the extraordinary moments and the routine circumstances of our lives.[2]

In their efforts to illuminate the deep social foundations of meaning, and to detail the very real social, political, and moral consequences that stem from the ways people define and know the world around them, interpretive scholars explore the semiotic significance of social actions and interactions, narratives and discourses, experiences and events. In contrast to those who take a positivist or realist perspective and see the world—or, more precisely, argue that the world can be known—in a more direct or literal light,[3] they use various approaches and draw on different interpretive traditions to decipher their cases in order to better understand the deep social, cultural, and psychic foundations of the phenomena they study. From such interpretive perspectives, a fundamental part of any social phenomenon is not directly evident or visible. Rather, the core foundations of meaning underlying the cases scholars study need to be unpacked, analyzed, and interpreted—and then rearticulated—to comprehend their deeper essences.[4] And they do this work of interpretation from various angles and perspectives, using different 'lenses'. It is with such interpretive lenses, in sociology and beyond, that we concern ourselves here. How do the people we study make sense of the world? How do they cooperate with others to construct shared understandings, and how do such actors define their situations for various audiences? Furthermore, how do scholars understand their sense-making processes and interpret their actions and experiences? How do they get at the deep social forces, culture structures, and relationships underlying the topics and themes they study?[5] Finally, how do their interpretations allow scholars to construct new and powerful explanations of social phenomena? How do they 'possess explanatory torque' with regard to various topics of widespread significance (Reed, 2011, p 11; see also Garland, 2006, pp 437–438)?

This is the perspective from which we organized a unique conference, *The Roots and Branches of Interpretive Sociology: Cultural, Pragmatist, and Psychosocial Approaches*, in Philadelphia, Pennsylvania, in August 2018. From this endeavor, we learned that many scholars were excited by our call to bring them to the table to discuss their interpretive lenses with one another. Many almost intuitively grasped the distinctions we made among traditions and camps in the field (the cultural, the pragmatist/interactionist, the psychosocial, and others) that could be gathered under the umbrella of a broader 'interpretive' agenda in sociology. And why not? We make such distinctions between different camps, with their various theoretical and methodological traditions, when we teach. This is how we organize many of our journals, our professional societies and their sections, and other scholarly institutions. We also often use such categories to explain our scholarly identities. In line with these distinctions, qualitative interpretation has developed simultaneously along different paths and among a field of factional communities, and the proponents of these different camps make various claims to distinguish their respective approaches from others.

However, despite the fact that we use such distinctions to delineate our disciplinary field, they rarely sync neatly with the work scholars actually do when they interpret the cases, communities, and issues they study. Rather, in their practices of social research and in their acts of interpretation, scholars combine and integrate elements of different traditions and programs in various ways that help them to focus on and make sense of their experiences as scholars. In other words, the process of interpretation comes alive in the practice of research and, more particularly, in research situations that demand a range of theoretical and methodological tools to illuminate and articulate the social foundations of meaning central to the case at hand.[6] Thus, over the course of their work, scholars develop interpretive lenses that help them find answers to the questions that drive them. While this may not come as a surprise to many readers, we rarely interrogate or compare the nuances of these lenses explicitly.

The purpose of this series is to interrogate, explore, and demonstrate the various interpretive lenses that scholars use when they engage their areas of interest, their cases, and their research situations. Each volume is centered on a substantive topic (for example, religion, the body, or contentious memories) or a particular interpretive-analytic method (for example, semiotics or narrative analysis). The editors of each volume feature the work of scholars who approach their central topic using different interpretive lenses that are particularly relevant to that area of focus. They have asked each author to explicitly illustrate and reflect on two dimensions of interpretation in their work, and to explore the connections between them. First, they asked authors to address how the individuals and communities they study assign meanings and achieve shared understandings with regard to the core topic of their volume. In doing so, authors address the social and cultural forces at play in shaping how people understand their identities, experiences, and situations, as well as how they frame their accounts, motivations, and purposes while acting, communicating, and performing in the world. Second, volume editors asked contributing authors to explicitly reflect on their interpretive processes and approaches to unpacking the meanings of the social phenomena they study. Some authors present new material while others provide a reflexive overview of their research to date, but all illustrate and discuss the work of interpretation and the central significance of meaning. Such conscious reflection on our interpretive traditions and lenses—on how they shape our analytic foci (in terms of what cases we explore, at what levels of analysis, and with regard to which social actors) and the ways we find meaning in our cases—can illuminate under-recognized or unspoken choices we make in our work. Furthermore, it can expose blind spots and suggest new frameworks for dialogue among scholars. This reflexive dimension, along with the diversity of lenses featured together in each volume, is what makes this series unique. In this vein, and to these ends, we hope the volumes of this series will present arrays of interpretive lenses that readers can use while working to make sense of their own cases and to develop new perspectives of their own. In the process, we also hope to advance the dialogue about interpretation and meaning in the social sciences.

In this volume, J. Patrick Williams presents a fascinating collection of chapters that advances the study of subcultures in several important ways, most generally by highlighting underexplored dimensions of interpretation and analysis. With an overarching emphasis on 'the process of conceptualizing and articulating subculture', regarding both the ways that participants in subcultural communities comprehend their lived experiences and the ways that scholars make sense of what their subjects do, how they think, and how they feel about their lives in relation to others, this volume sheds much needed light on a diversity of cases and methodological topics. Dealing with a variety of groups and communities from different parts of the world, the scholars featured in this book offer numerous insights that are masterfully tied together in the volume's introductory chapter, which both explains and contextualizes the evolution of the sociological analysis of subcultures while offering a cogent discussion of the challenges and possibilities of interpretive scholarship in this broad and evolving area of study.

The 15 scholars featured in this volume apply various combinations of analytic perspectives and standpoints to their studies of subculture while also addressing a wide variety of important issues and themes, including those related to age, sex and gender, nationality, emotion and affect, legitimation and authenticity, aesthetics, lifestyle, and more. In addition, all of these scholars purposefully illustrate and reflect on their particular interpretive lenses, considering how they allow us to understand subcultures and subcultural lives in various contexts and situations. In the process, these authors offer us interpretive tools with which to conduct research on subcultural groups and communities around the world. Thus, with this collection, Williams leads the way in demonstrating how paying explicit attention to interpreting and analyzing subculture can help researchers grasp the complex meanings of communities and lifestyles, both at the level of everyday existence and with regard to the ways that such meanings and new understandings emerge in the scholarly process. All of the scholars featured here raise and address many important issues that move the interpretive analysis of subcultures in new and illuminating directions. We are thrilled to feature this important book as part of our *Interpretive Lenses in Sociology* series.

Notes

[1] An extended series introduction is available for open access download at bristoluniversitypress.co.uk/interpretive-lenses-in-sociology. Shorter and slightly modified versions of this introduction appear as prefaces to the different volumes of this series.

[2] On the centrality of meaning in interpretive social analysis, see Reed's (2011) important work on interpretation and knowledge, especially his discussions of the 'interpretive epistemic mode' (pp 89–121) and the 'normative epistemic mode' (pp 67–88).

[3] See Reed (2011), especially on the 'realist semiotic and the illusion of noninterpretation' (p 52).

[4] Indeed, this is what Clifford Geertz (1973) meant when he called for 'thick description' in ethnographic analysis.

[5] Alfred Schütz (1967 [1932], pp 205–206; 1970, p 273) recognized the layers of interpretation we point to here when he argued that '[t]he thought objects constructed by the social scientist ... have to be founded upon the thought objects constructed by the common-sense thinking of [people], living their daily life within their social world. Thus, the constructs of the social sciences are, so to speak, constructs of the second degree, namely constructs of the constructs made by the actors on the social scene'. Geertz (1973, p 9) made a similar distinction when he argued 'that what we call our data are really our own constructions of other people's constructions'. Also see Reed (2017, pp 29–31) on 'interpreting interpretations'. Such a distinction also informs the fundamental premises of psychoanalysis, as the analyst is always in the business of interpreting interpretations and unpacking layers of symbolism.

[6] See also Tavory and Timmermans (2014), who advocate engaging the process of research and interpretation armed with 'multiple theoretical perspectives' (p 35).

References

Garland, D. (2006) 'Concepts of Culture in the Sociology of Punishment', *Theoretical Criminology*, 10(4): 419–447.

Geertz, C. (1973) 'Thick Description: Toward an Interpretive Theory of Culture', in *The Interpretation of Cultures*, New York: Basic Books, pp 3–30.

Reed, I.A. (2011) *Interpretation and Social Knowledge: On the Use of Theory in the Human Sciences*, Chicago: University of Chicago Press.

Reed, I.A. (2017) 'On the Very Idea of Cultural Sociology', in C.E. Benzecry, M. Krause and I.A. Reed (eds) *Social Theory Now*, Chicago: University of Chicago Press, pp 18–41.

Schütz, A. (1967 [1932]) *The Phenomenology of the Social World*, Evanston: Northwestern University Press.

Schütz, A. (1970) *On Phenomenology and Social Relations*, Chicago: University of Chicago Press.

Tavory, I. and Timmermans, S. (2014) *Abductive Analysis: Theorizing Qualitative Research*, Chicago: University of Chicago Press.

Notes on Contributors

Laura Barnett is Lecturer in Higher Education at the University of Surrey, Guildford, UK. She obtained her PhD in Cultural Studies at Canterbury Christ Church University. Her thesis was an ethnographic study of youth, alcohol, and binge drinking in the UK. Laura's research interests relate to the sociology of higher education, inequalities in education, and alcohol and drug studies. She is a Senior Fellow of the Higher Education Academy (AdvanceHE).

Andy Bennett is Professor of Cultural Sociology in the School of Humanities, Languages and Social Science at Griffith University, Australia. He is a Faculty Fellow of the Yale Centre for Cultural Sociology, an International Research Fellow of the Finnish Youth Research Network, a founding member of the Consortium for Youth, Generations and Culture, and a founding member of the Regional Music Research Group. He is co-founding editor of the journal *DIY, Alternative Cultures and Society* and co-founder/co-convenor of the biennial Keep It Simple, Make It Fast (KISMIF) conference.

Daniel Bennett attended Silkwood School in Queensland, Australia. He also gained high distinction in a Headstart course on song-writing and music production at the University of the Sunshine Coast. He is now completing an apprenticeship at Toyota on the Gold Coast.

Shane Blackman is Professor of Cultural Studies at Canterbury Christ Church University, UK. He received his PhD (1990) at the Institute of Education, University of London with a scholarship from the ESRC, supervised by Professor Basil Bernstein and Professor Phil Cohen. He is an editor of the *International Journal of Youth Studies* and an editor of *YOUNG: The Nordic Journal of Youth Research*. His most recent article is: Blackman, S. (2023) 'Black Ethnographic Activists: exploring Robert Park, Scientific Racism, the Chicago School, and FBI Files – through the black sociological experience of Charles S. Johnson and E. Franklin Frazier', Special Issue: *Symbolic Interaction, Forgotten Interactionists of Color* (2023).

Xinxin Dong is a doctoral student at the College of Media and International Culture, Zhejiang University, China. She is concentrating on Urban Studies and Digital Culture Studies.

Paula Guerra is Professor of Sociology at the University of Porto, Portugal, and Researcher at the Institute of Sociology of the same university. Paula is Adjunct Associate Professor at the Griffith Centre for Social and Cultural Research. She is the founder/coordinator of All the Arts: Luso-Afro-Brazilian Network. Paula is the founder/coordinator of Keep It Simple, Make it Fast (KISMIF; kismifconference.com and kismifcommunity.com). Paula is a member of the board of the Research Network of Sociology of Art of ESA and chair of the Portuguese branch of the International Association for the Study of Popular Music (IASPM). She is editor-in-chief (with Andy Bennett) of SAGE's new journal *DIY, Alternative Cultures and Society*.

Ross Haenfler is Professor of Sociology at Grinnell College, USA. His courses and research revolve around subcultures, lifestyle movements, and critical masculinity studies. Ross is the author of *Subcultures: The Basics* (2023); *Goths, Gamers, & Grrrls: Deviance and Youth Subcultures* (2010); and *Straight Edge: Clean-Living Youth, Hardcore Punk, and Social Change* (2006). He has published in a variety of journals and presented work on subcultures and social change around the world.

Samuel Judah is a graduate student in sociology at Nanyang Technological University, Singapore. His research interests are in music subcultures, youth culture, social media studies, digital society, and the sociology of emotions. Currently, he is studying emo subculture and the subcultural framing of emotion through interaction with music videos and social media.

Donna Manion teaches Sociology of Gender, Sociology of Race, Sociology of Family, Diversity, Social Problems at SUNY Polytechnic Institute in Utica, New York, where she is an adjunct lecturer. She has researched, studied, and written on sexism in the punk scene for the last 16 years. She has been an anarcho-punk since 1985 and organized the feminist punk Combatting Latent Inequality Fest in Richmond, Virginia. Donna is also very passionate about feminism and social justice issues.

Hyunjoon Shin is Professor in the Faculty of Social Sciences and the Institute for East Asian Studies at Sunkonghoe University, Korea. Having received his PhD with a thesis on the transformation of the Korean music industry at Seoul National University, he has carried out broader studies on popular culture, international migration, and urban space in Korea and East Asia. He was a visiting scholar at National University of Singapore,

Leiden University in the Netherlands, Leuven University in Belgium, and Duke University in Durham, USA. He is currently a member of the international advisory editorial board of *Popular Music* and a member of the editorial collective of *Inter-Asia Cultural Studies*. His papers have appeared in *Positions: East Asia Cultures Critique*, *Popular Music*, *Inter-Asia Cultural Studies*, *City, Culture and Society*, and others. He has been directly or indirectly involved in the indie music scene in Hongdae, Seoul since its inception in the mid-1990s.

Oki Rahadianto Sutopo is Associate Professor of Sociology and Director of Youth Studies Centre at the Faculty of Social and Political Sciences, Universitas Gadjah Mada, Indonesia. His research interests include youth studies, cultural studies, and sociology of art. He has published his works in *Journal of Youth Studies*, *Perfect Beat*, *Sociological Research Online*, *Asian Music*, *Continuum and Crime*, and *Media, Culture*. He was visiting scholar at the School of Social and Political Sciences, University of Melbourne in 2019.

Stanislav Vysotsky is Associate Professor of Criminology at the University of the Fraser Valley, Canada. Dr Vysotsky's research on the militant antifascist movement and the relationship between threat, space, subculture, and social movement activism has been published in a number of academic journals and the book *American Antifa: The Tactics, Culture, and Practice of Militant Antifascism* (2020). He has also published research on far-right movements in scholarly journals as well as several edited volumes. His current research continues to look at far-right cultural practices and mobilization as well as the culture, strategy, and tactics of antifascist movements.

Laura Way is Research Fellow at the University of Lincoln, UK. She is a feminist sociologist and qualitative researcher with research interests and experience primarily concerning punk (particularly punk pedagogies, punk and marginalized identities), subcultures and gender/ageing, and family research (particularly young fatherhood). She is the author of *Punk, Gender and Ageing: Just Typical Girls* (2020).

J. Patrick Williams is Associate Professor of Sociology at Nanyang Technological University, Singapore. He has published widely on the interactions and experiences of people who self-identify as subcultural and is particularly interested in the social construction of subcultural authenticities. He is an associate editor of the journal *Deviant Behavior* and an editorial board member of the journal *DIY, Alternative Cultures and Society*. He has authored and/or edited seven books, including *Gaming as Culture: Essays in Social Reality, Identity and Experience in Fantasy Games* (2006), *Authenticity* *in Culture, Self, and Society* (2009), *Subcultural Theory: Traditions and Concepts* (2011), and *Studies on the Social Construction of Identity and Authenticity* (2020).

Jian Xiao is Associate Professor in the College of Media and International Culture, Zhejiang University, China. Her research is focused on urban politics, new media, and cultural studies. She has published in many journal articles and authored the monograph *Punk Culture in Contemporary China* (2018).

Acknowledgments

This book was conceived in the late summer of 2019, when there was no real hint of what was to come in early 2020. The COVID-19 pandemic had immediate and long-lasting effects around the world, including on the development and progress of this book. My own work and family life were turned upside down as the Singapore government instituted a set of lockdown and isolation-oriented policies from 2020 until 2022 to prevent the spread of the virus in the country. I found working from home to be hard. Around the world, contributors struggled with their own problems as they also sought to maintain and/or balance their work, family, and personal lives amid the crisis. Multiple authors who had agreed to contribute chapters in 2019 were ultimately unable to do so. Despite the loss of those scholarly contributions, the book managed to see the light of day thanks to the dedication of a number of people. I would like to first thank series editors, Tom DeGloma and Julie Wiest, for their immediate and continued enthusiasm for the project after I verbally proposed it at the 2019 annual meeting of the Society for the Study of Symbolic Interaction. Their feedback has been decisive in shaping the project. A sincere thanks to Samuel Judah, who joined the book project as managing editor while undertaking his MA degree in sociology, writing on social media and emo subculture. Not only did he help manage day-to-day issues with the book, he became a great sounding board for my own ideas regarding subcultural theory and interpretative practice. Anna Richardson and the team at Bristol University Press were also continuously helpful and supportive throughout the entire process, from proposal to cover design. Finally, thanks to all the contributors, who joined from around the world to turn a collective and reflexive gaze back on interpretive practice in subcultural studies.

PART I

Approaching Interpretive Practice

1

Making Sense of Subcultures: Interpretive Practice and/in Subcultural Theory

J. Patrick Williams

Distinct, non-normative, Do-It-Yourself (DIY), and marginal cultures, often encapsulated under the umbrella term 'subcultures', continue to be popular topics across a variety of social science and humanities disciplines and empirical research areas. Building on academic trajectories rooted in the Chicago School of sociology and the Birmingham School of cultural studies, the consistent publication of research that uses the subculture concept attests to the sustained scholarly interest in, and relevance of, theoretical and empirical examinations of a diverse range of phenomena using the concept as an interpretive lens. Despite such interest, however, no prior book has assembled a set of contributions that intentionally explore the interpretive practices through which subcultural phenomena are conceptualized—that is, made real by scholars and by social actors in everyday life. In the chapters that follow, scholars from around the world discuss in various ways their own research to show the reader how interpretive practices connect to the sociological concept of subculture. By explicitly focusing on interpretation as a process that has profound influence in our understandings of social and cultural phenomena, this introduction begins by bringing meaning-making to the foreground of subcultural studies.

The process of conceptualizing and articulating subculture is part of the larger process of conceptualizing reality. For a theory of reality, we can go at least as far back as ancient Greece and Plato's concept of 'forms', which suggested that if people want to understand what something is, they should begin by considering what it should be, that is, to imagine the phenomenon in its ideal form. Plato (and ancient Greek philosophers more generally) argued that everything had an ideal or essential form that was created by the gods—a perfect version that might or might not exist in lived reality. What Plato was theorizing philosophically was the nature of the relationship among reality, language, and knowledge. While a variety of scholars over the centuries have come to various conclusions about the nature of reality, the important point for this volume on interpretive practice is that beliefs about a pure, abstracted, gods-given version of things has been largely rejected within the social sciences. Most sociologists, for example, agree that reality exists obdurately, but that the meanings that are created and negotiated by people turn that reality into a social and cultural world. One important outcome of this way of thinking is that 'currents of thought are *strategic*; they originate in group experience and collective action' (McCarthy, 1996, p 3, italics in original) as people strive to make sense of things going on around them, often in ways that will satisfy or support their own desires, beliefs, values, or interests. This is true of academic as well as lay understandings of reality (Harker, 2015) and means that subculture doesn't have a single meaning. Rather, people make subculture meaningful in ways that work for them. This follows from Baldwin et al's (2006, p 4) argument that there is no singular definition of culture more broadly: culture 'is a sign, an empty vessel waiting for people—both academicians and everyday communicators—to fill it with meaning. But, as a sign in the traditional semiotic sense, the connection between the signifier (the word "culture") and the signified (what it represents) shifts, making culture a moving target'.

The moving target analogy is clear in the variety of theoretical and analytic approaches taken toward subculture, as well as the empirical focus of such research. Certainly, subculture has not *meant* the same thing to everyone. Even within academic fields and circles, variation and difference are obvious. I use italics here to emphasize that *meaning* is a key aspect of this discussion. We are not talking about whether or not subcultures exist in any real sense, or whether there are right and wrong ways of theorizing the term. Rather, in taking a reflexive interpretivist approach to the concept, this volume functions as a space in which we can continue to ask questions about the relative analytic power that subculture possesses and what that means for scholarship. Therefore, while comprehensive accounts of subcultures and subcultural theory exist (see Jenks, 2004; Gelder, 2007; Williams, 2011), my interest in assembling this volume was to focus attention on the interpretive practices through which subculture becomes conceptually meaningful. In this first chapter, I want to set the stage for the chapters that follow by looking back at how sociocultural phenomena have been approached as subcultural. I will start by expanding the ideas from the opening paragraphs into a larger statement about interpretive practice. Next, I will review the history of subcultural theory, keeping interpretive practice as a focal point. Finally, I will introduce the rest of the volume, which contains contributions from scholars around the world studying phenomena that have often been characterized as subcultural, either by participants within those cultures, by scholars, or by both.

Interpretation and interpretive practice

The purpose of the social sciences is to organize understandings of the social world, whether in terms of person, culture, society, and so on. Social scientists go about their work in a diverse number of ways and hold a variety of assumptions regarding the nature of reality (ontology), what and how people know about reality (epistemology), and how reality can or should be studied (methodology). Yet, regardless of assumptions, all scholars rely on concepts, which are abstract ideas generalized from the practice and details of lived human experience. As with all knowledge and culture, concepts are rooted in language, through which human understandings are created and communicated. The sociology of knowledge informs us that 'language is both the foundation and the instrumentality of the social construction of reality' and that from language we build all of our 'interpretative schemes ... value systems and, finally, theoretically articulated "world views" which, in their totality, form the world of "collective representations"' (Berger, 1966, pp 108, 109). Through their research within scientific communities, scholars work collaboratively to construct understandings and representations of reality, which for our purposes includes things that come to be called subcultural.

Among the many types of social science, interpretivism is a paradigm in which scholars believe that reality is multilayered and that phenomena can have multiple meanings or interpretations. While a lot of sociological research is conducted formally using 'scientific' principles (for example, operationalized variables, a value-neutral stance, and an interest in generalizability-*cum*-predictability), interpretive research gives primacy to the *meanings* people attribute to reality/realities and phenomena. Further, such work is done through the study of how people think, feel, and/or act *in everyday life* rather than through the study of quantified macro-level data or contrived experimental conditions. A large proportion of what can be assembled under the umbrella of subcultural studies is interpretivist in orientation, though not all subcultural scholars recognize their work as interpretivist *per se*. Many may be trained to study cultural phenomena, for example, but not readily recognize the differences between emic and etic perspectives. Some may never have turned an intentionally reflective eye to their own scholarly practices in order to unpack the oftentimes taken-for-granted logics and processes through which knowledge of the subcultural is created, negotiated, and shared.

The idea of turning a reflective eye back onto our interpretive practices was the impetus behind this volume. I was exposed to two quite different theoretical approaches to subcultures during my own graduate studies in two separate disciplines. In sociology, I read Chicago School ethnographic sociology, symbolic interactionism, and deviance studies. In cultural studies, I encountered the Birmingham School's work on youth subcultures as part of a larger focus on critical theory and social justice. Later, as I followed debates in the 2000s about whether or how subculture might still be a useful concept, I perceived real fervor as scholars positioned themselves in relation to the concept. I had learned to see subcultures from multiple perspectives but had also developed my own preferences for how to utilize the concept in my work. Because of this, it always remained clear to me that subculture did not have to hold a single meaning. I use subculture as a concept to sensitize myself to certain empirical phenomena. I recognize that not just anything can or should be labeled as subcultural, but that the term does continue to operate as a meaningful concept and can be used in a variety of ways (Williams and Kamaludeen, 2017; Williams, 2019).

Still, some will ask questions about whether this or that constitutes a subculture, or what 'exactly' the term refers to. To answer such questions, it is worth considering Wittgenstein's maxim: 'Don't look for the meaning, look for the use' (Rorty, 1961, p 198). Generating some basic statistics via Google Scholar provides some initial insights into the use of subculture over time. First, we can look at disciplinary use (see Figure 1.1) across the humanities and social sciences. We cannot see *how* it has been used, only that the concept appears to have been used more widely in some disciplines than others.[1]

Second, we can look at other terms that co-occur with subculture. Figure 1.2 suggests that class and resistance have been frequently used in connection with subculture, while terms such as delinquent and deviant have been used less often.[2] Sex has also been used frequently alongside subculture, yet even a cursory glance through the results reveals a wide variety of uses, from analytical distinctions (male versus female subculturalists) to sexual practices defined as leisurely or criminal (for example, BDSM or prostitution) to marginal or oppositional identity-based collectives (for

Figure 1.1: Google Scholar results for 'subculture' and '[_____]'

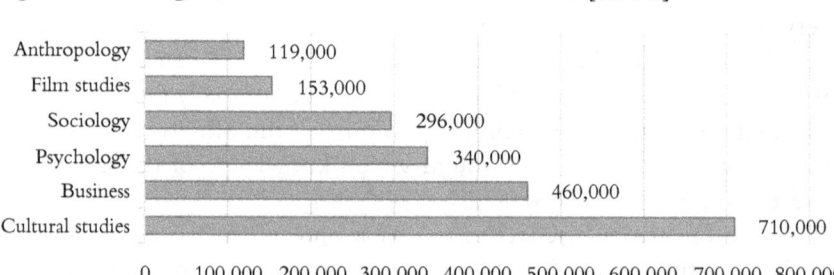

Figure 1.2: Google Scholar results for 'subculture' and '[_____]'

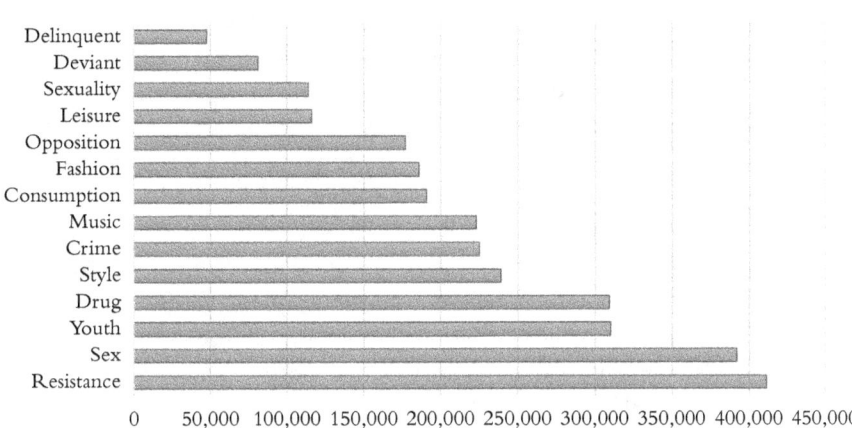

example, LGBTQIA+ subcultures). Further, many of the early results categorized under 'subculture and sex' appear to frame sexual practices and identities as deviant or delinquent, which would shift the pattern visible in Figure 1.2 if we engaged in an interpretive qualitative analysis of the results rather than simply rely only on Google Scholar's quantified output. Nevertheless, what these graphs usefully highlight are the varied interpretive uses of subculture. This kind of variety has led to claims that 'there continues to be no generally accepted definition of subculture or standard analytical criteria for applying the concept' (Atkinson, 2003, p 92). To understand why this is, let us review two 20th-century schools of subcultural scholarship that have their own interpretive traditions and practices, keeping in mind that the term holds academic, popular, and personal significances that may not align.

A brief history of subcultural theory as interpretive practice

The brief space allotted for this introductory chapter prevents a comprehensive review of the development of subcultural theory, but relevant histories can be found elsewhere (see Blackman, 2005; Gelder, 2007). Here I want to focus on the interpretive practices that constitute the concept of subculture within academia. In doing so, I also want to highlight and distinguish the concept from what it refers to when scholars use the term. Tolson (1990) argued that the *notion* of subculture (but not the concept itself) emerged in the journalistic work of Henry Mayhew in Britain in the 1830s. Elsewhere its origins have been suggested to go back as far as English rogue literature from the mid-16th century (see Williams, 2014). There are two points worth making in regard to thinking about the history of the term vis-à-vis interpretive practice. First, the origins of subcultures have been produced retrospectively from the present. Scholars have looked back at historical people and practices—including fictional and non-fictional written accounts of marginal or peripheral classes and groups—and, based on contemporary understandings, interpreted those historical phenomena as subcultural. Second, these have been academic, *etic* interpretations, disconnected from the historical phenomena themselves and from the people whose beliefs, values, languages, or practices may or may not have formed the *emic* basis for subcultural understandings. This is not to suggest that such histories are wrong, but merely to highlight that they are interpretations rather than facts (Williams, 2020).

Blackman (2014) and Barmaki (2016) describe the subculture concept entering sociological parlance via Chicago School sociology in the 1920s, as evidenced in Vivien Palmer's (1928, p 73) textbook reference to 'subcultural groups which display variations in the prevailing culture of the land' and whose 'clear-cut variations in customs, attitudes and behavior patterns are disclosed through scientific investigation'. Early studies such as those by Anderson (1923), Thrasher (1927), and Cressey (1932) exemplify the Chicago School's early focus on naturalistic inquiry and methods through which pragmatic understandings could be drawn from the everyday lifeworlds of those being studied (Prus, 1997). The Chicago School's early work laid the foundation for an American sociological version of subcultural theory that was primarily ameliorative in nature, and sociology's early functionalist concerns correlated with the building of formal concepts and generalizable theories that could help solve modern social problems. By mid-century, there were notable examples of American subcultural theory, such as Gordon's (1947) classificatory conceptualization of subcultures as sub-components of a larger national culture based on a unique combination of demographic characteristics (race, class, region, and so on) and Cohen's (1955) social-psychological conceptualization of subcultures as inversions of mainstream culture predicated on the strains that marginalized individuals experienced in complex modern societies. In this tradition, subculture was used to label lower-class minority youths, identifying them as potential victims of psychological and cultural strain (Merton, 1938).

American criminology emerged during the early-to-mid 20th century and used the term extensively to conceptualize so-called delinquent, deviant, or other individuals and practices deemed to be problematic by mainstream society (Cohen, 1955; Bell, 2010). However, there has been opposition toward the use of subculture as a pejorative label in recent decades, as is clear in the field of cultural criminology (Ferrell, 1999; Williams, forthcoming). Elsewhere, sociologists such as Yinger (1960; 1984) developed the concepts of contraculture and counterculture to focus interpretive attention on the oppositional politics of certain marginalized groups that arose after mid-century, while Fine and Kleinman (1979) developed a version of subcultural theory that avoided any reliance on notions of strain, deviance, or opposition vis-à-vis mainstream culture, instead proposing a conceptualization rooted in interactions and shared meanings among members of particular networks.

In the United Kingdom, there were also scholars developing subcultural theory outside of then-dominant sociological and criminological traditions. Largely rejecting interpretivist and interactionist sociologies and instead drawing upon the work of continental neo-Marxists such as Gramsci, Lévi-Strauss, Barthes, and Althusser, 'new subcultural theory' at the University of Birmingham's Centre for Contemporary Cultural Studies' (CCCS) engaged in ideological analyses of youths' cultural styles. According to the CCCS, there was something unique about the postwar years. Namely, the growing purchasing power of working-class youth thanks to a booming economy and the expansion of media and consumer industries clashed with the rigidity of a class system in which working-class youths had traditionally been excluded from conspicuously consumptive lifestyles. Similar to Merton's (1938) notion of strain, Clarke et al (1976) saw working-class youths as attempting to solve the problems associated with living between working-class and bourgeoise cultural realities. Much of the CCCS work was semiotic in nature and thus very different from the Chicago tradition. Rather than studying the meanings that specific styles and practices had for those who embodied them, it instead framed those styles and rituals within abstract systems of signification rooted in power and ideology. As a result, subcultural styles and rituals were seen as impotent or 'magical' attempts to solve working-class youths' problems. So, whereas American subcultural theories had often focused on deviant behaviors *arising from* psychological strain, the CCCS focused on how stylistic behaviors *represented* ideological strain. Despite this major distinction, it can be fairly said, however, that subculture in both traditions developed within an overarching frame in which youths were 'symbols of trouble' (Cohen, 1980) and thus objects for surveillance (Hebdige, 1988) in need of protection or reform.

In the 1990s, another wave of innovative conceptualizations of youth and subculture coincided with the broad spread of postmodernist theories in the social sciences. Interest in youth cultural practices around styles and rituals related to things such as music, clothing, and/or media remained, but there was a shift away from presumptions about the (homogeneous) nature of subcultural formations and the (ideological) meanings they allegedly symbolized. Unlike some of the more distanced, semiotic work such as Clarke's (1976) or Hebdige's (1979), studies by Thornton (1995), Widdicombe (Widdicombe and Wooffitt, 1995), and Muggleton (2000) are noteworthy in their collection and analyses of data rooted in the everyday words, practices and meanings of those who self-identified as insiders in the cultures being studied. Such studies were indicative of the bridges continually being built between the empirical field of youth studies and various social-science perspectives, as well as the shift in focus away from opposition and resistance toward consumption and hedonism. Thornton integrated American sociological and British cultural studies traditions in her research on British club cultures, while Muggleton synthesized early 20th-century Weberian sociology with postmodernist conceptions of fashion and identity. Meanwhile, Widdicombe went around subcultural theory altogether, bringing together social psychology and ethnomethodology to create new empirical insights into how young people identified themselves and others vis-à-vis subcultures.

By the end of the 20th century, there were searches for a new conceptual vocabulary that might better articulate the changing nature of youth cultures, identities and practices. Following the claim that subculture was no longer a useful or sufficient analytic term, alternatives such as scene, lifestyle, neo-tribe, and figuration began circulating as (particularly British and Commonwealth) scholars sought to escape the limiting connotations attached to the British/CCCS framing of the subculture concept (Bennett, 1999; Miles, 2000; Wilson, 2002; Atkinson, 2003).[3] The study of 'post-subcultures' trended in the early 2000s (Muggleton and Weinzierl, 2003; Bennett, 2004), even as other researchers continued to develop subcultural theory relevant to contemporary social contexts (for example, Wheaton, 2000; O'Connor, 2003; Jensen, 2006; Shildrick and MacDonald, 2006; Williams, 2006), sometimes by explicitly integrating it with other theories and concepts (for example, Berzano and Genova, 2015; Stahl, 2003, pp 21–26).

Now well into the 21st century, subcultural scholarship has spread well beyond its early American and British contexts. Buttigieg et al (2015, pp 1–2) argue that 'subculture—as a term, as a research tradition, as a framework—underlies and drives so much of the contemporary work in Australian youth culture studies', for example. The concept is increasingly used as an interpretive frame for research in non-anglophone countries and contexts, whether used to study a Western subculture such as bikers in a non-Western context like India (Romy and Dewan, 2021), a non-Western religious subculture like Jihad within a European context (Jensen et al, 2022), or to make sense of unique instantiations of cultural phenomena in Asia, such as Chinese youths' reactions to feelings of alienation from governmental discourse about how young people ought to be (Tan and Cheng, 2020). Likewise, 'subculture' has spread across disciplines and is used in business, marketing, psychology, and sport sciences (among others) to frame distinct but patterned ways of thinking or behaving (for example, Moshier et al, 2012; Coulter et al, 2016; Ulusoy and Fırat, 2018; Koch and Sauerbronn, 2019). In some of this recent (inter)disciplinary research, subculture has been returned to a more neutral, functional analytic usage.

This volume does not attempt to cover the full breadth of subcultural scholarship suggested in Figure 1.1. None of the contributors take a psychological, business, or criminological approach, for example. Rather, the volume maintains a more targeted focus on subcultural studies by scholars who (implicitly or explicitly) draw on both the Chicago and Birmingham Schools *in the study of youth, music, and meaning*. The reader may notice that several of the chapters feature research on punk or similar DIY/resistance-based music scenes. That would be a fair observation, and one that fits well with the CCCS's empirical interests on style-driven youth subcultures (see Hall and Jefferson, 1976). In fact, all the chapters deal in one way or another with youth and/or music, and it is in this way that all the contributions share a common reliance on the British tradition of subcultural studies. More importantly, however, the contributions do not conceptualize subcultures as homogeneous, nor do they rely reductively on class, resistance, or style as analytic frames. Rather, they focus explicitly on the interpretive methods developed and later championed by Chicago School sociology, namely naturalistic inquiry involving reflexive data collection and analytic strategies (Prus, 1996). It is this *interpretive lens* that sets the book apart from general introductions to subcultural studies (for example, Brake, 1985; Haenfler, 2023). The scholarship presented in the chapters ahead is not intended to be read primarily for its empirical data (although the chapters contain a wealth of empirical data and insight) but rather in terms of how each author—with their unique biographies, geographies, and perspectives—goes about interpreting data as subcultural or otherwise.

Contributions to the volume

Collectively, the chapters that follow effectively communicate the significance that interpretation plays in contemporary subcultural scholarship. Some chapters draw attention to professional and academic interpretive practices; others highlight the interpretive practices of subculturalists or the interplay between scholarly and lay practices; still others apply and exemplify interpretive practices through the analysis of data. In other words, interpretation play a variety of roles in and for subcultures and subcultural studies. I have organized the book to take this variety into account.

Part I, 'Approaching Interpretative Practice', focuses on overarching issues or meta-concerns related to the interpretation of subcultural phenomena today; namely, how scholars have approached and labeled sociocultural phenomena as subcultural (or not) and then how scholars have developed and deployed concepts that support, expand, or move beyond subcultural theory. In this first chapter, I have sought to set the stage by explicating the significance of interpretive practice and by looking back at how the subculture concept developed across time, place, and discipline. My point has been that the paradigms within which scholars work influence their approaches to cultural phenomena, both conceptually and methodologically. Scholars focusing on relatively mainstream (or at least, non-deviant) youth cultures, for example, have been more critical of a subcultural approach to contemporary youth phenomena (Bennett, 1999; Miles, 2000), while those focusing on marginalized or non-normative cultures have been more likely to defend or update its relevance (Hodkinson, 2004; Blackman, 2005).

The other chapters in this section approach interpretive practice in ways that highlight how listening to cultural insiders' voices can affect how we build our theories and concepts. Yet, the differences in the authors' areas of expertise and interest also influence how they value the subculture concept. As a scholar trained in new social movements theory (Buechler, 1995), Ross Haenfler has a longtime interest in youth committed to positive social change. In Chapter 2, he considers the relevance of subculture, movement, scene, and lifestyle by analyzing how self-identifying 'straight edgers' utilize such terms in their everyday lives. As he notes, paying attention to what members of cultural groups *mean* when they use such terms can sensitize us to the 'connections and disjunctions' between academic and lay conceptualizations of (sub)cultural realities. As his data demonstrate, members of contemporary straight edge see themselves as participating in a subculture, a scene, a lifestyle, *and* a movement. In Chapter 3, Andy Bennett assesses the concepts of subculture and post-subculture vis-à-vis his long-term interest and expertise in popular youth cultures, style, and music. He reflects first on his own engagement with notions of subculture and youth culture from his school days in 1970s Britain through to his academic career in the UK and then in Australia. Along the way, he notes how subcultural and post-subcultural scholarship has been affected both by ageing academics with subcultural careers, and by the rise of digital and social media. Bennett draws reflexively on backstage conversations with his son and co-author Daniel Bennett to come away with the growing belief that neither subculture nor post-subculture are particularly relevant terms for describing youth cultures today. This position is enmeshed with the authors' interest in *popular* rather than marginal or non-normative youth cultures. At the same time, their insights into the reorganization of contemporary youth cultures and experiences through social media practices, and the implicit idea that such reorganization is affecting more than just mainstream youths, is just as relevant to those who identify/are identified as subcultural.

Part II, 'Contextualizing Interpretive Practice', draws us further into contemporary subcultural theory by bringing together a set of authors who embody subcultural interpretive practices from further afield, so to speak. Whereas the authors in Part I are all white males born, trained and working in anglophone countries that have long sociological traditions, the authors in Part II come from and work outside that Northern/Western 'cultural center'. It is no surprise then that these authors offer a variety of critiques of and responses to traditional Western subcultural theory. In Chapter 4, Paula Guerra draws attention to how punk in Portugal is in some ways (mis) aligned with both the CCCS-subcultural and post-subcultural frameworks. Like Bennett (Chapter 3), Guerra notes how the rise of the internet and social media have reshaped sociocultural configurations, including communication channels and modes of engagement and activism. She also argues that Portuguese punk needs to be interpreted through a *contextual* lens that takes account of the country's history of authoritarianism, where ideas such as 'resistance' were lived out very differently than in the UK. More than 40 years on from the subculture's origins, social media have enabled Portuguese punks to articulate collective resistance and identity, but also fluidity and cosmopolitanism as they connect themselves with other activist-oriented people and cultures around the world.

In Chapters 5–7, both context and focus shift away from the West entirely and onto subcultures in East and Southeast Asia. In Chapter 5, Hyunjoon Shin offers two distinct contributions to the discussion of interpretive practice. First, he describes the importation of 'subculture'—as both an English-language word and an Anglo-sociocultural concept—into Chinese, Japanese, and Korean languages and societies. Second, he considers the messy process of using the Western term to make sense of East-Asian youth cultures since the 1970s. The concept has not simply been transposed from the West and then applied in analyses of Asian contexts. Rather, East-Asian scholars have had to unpack its interpretive baggage to effectively study a wide swathe of the youth-cultural terrain, from Japanese *otaku* to Korean political activism. Likewise in Chapter 6, Jian Xiao and Xinxin Dong reflect on using a CCCS conception of subculture to study punk—a subculture imported from the West—within the contemporary Chinese context. While some of Xiao's published work on punk has relied on Western subcultural concepts such as 'authenticity' and 'resistance' (Xiao, 2016; Xiao et al, 2022), this chapter offers a new interpretive lens—namely, using the Chinese philosophical conceptions of 'doing nothing' and 'hermit lifestyle'—as part of a decolonizing intervention alongside the broader globalization of punk culture (Bestley et al, 2021).

Like in Chapter 4, Oki Rahadianto Sutopo (Chapter 7) takes both subcultural and post-subcultural perspectives to task though his study of the developing careers of male Indonesian DIY musicians. It has been previously argued that 'the range of interpretations that youth make at different times in their subcultural careers, and the diverse ways that similarly located youth understand their "shared" experiences are only sometimes examined in studies of youth subculture' (Wilson, 2002, p 376). Sutopo uses ethnographic data, contextualized within the modern Indonesian nation-state and focused through a biographical lens, to show musicians' reflexive understandings of themselves and their participation within music scenes over many years. On the one hand, he finds that resistance and class—cornerstones of CCCS subcultural theory—do not offer useful insight into their everyday lived experiences. On the other hand, their identities and practices as DIY musicians are not nearly as fluid or ephemeral as post-subcultural theory would lead us to expect. Rather, their identities and practices develop within and are sustained by subcultural careers. Collectively, the contributions in Part II work to decenter the hegemony of traditional, particularly CCCS, subcultural theories by highlighting how the study of contemporary subcultural phenomena demands attention to contextual—historic, political, economic, and/or technological—dimensions of everyday life. Deciding which of these dimensions may be significant in any particular study remains something that researchers must take on in their own projects, based on their research questions and goals.

This last point brings us to Part III, 'Embodying Interpretive Practice', which provides a window through which to view how interpretive practices are embedded within researcher roles and relationships. Each chapter highlights how scholars can use 'sensitizing concepts' (Blumer, 1954; van den Hoonaard, 1997) to not only build a richer understanding of subcultural milieux, but of their own interpretive practices as well. In Chapter 8, Laura Way utilizes a feminist methodology to explore how the subcultural identities of older punk women are interpreted by herself as the researcher, by themselves as ageing female punks, and by other punks in the scene. Using authenticity (Williams and Schwarz, 2021) as a sensitizing concept, she explores the oftentimes taken-for-grantedness of punk identity, describing along the way how both lay and scholarly interpretations of authenticity are tied to assumptions about what counts as meaningful membership. Way not only calls out some younger male subculturalists for exclusionary practices, but also reflects on how her own research interests and study design resulted in marginalizing or excluding certain kinds of participants within the research context. Chapter 9 also deals with the intersection of identity and interpretive practices as Stanislav Vysotsky and Donna Manion—longtime members of anarcho-punk scenes—reflect on the difficulties they encountered while conducting research. Turning a reflective eye toward their own 'positionalities' (Rose, 1997) and relationships within the subculture, the authors use the concept of emotional labor to reinterpret many unpleasant moments they experienced as insider researchers during the period when their academic identities were emerging during graduate school alongside their punk identities. As with Way's (Chapter 8) research, unpleasant experiences were to some degree counterbalanced by the depth of insight they were able to generate through embodied interpretive research strategies. As such, both chapters offer important cautionary tales about the strains associated with studying one's own subculture.

The significance of emotional and relational work in research is also visible in Chapter 10, wherein Shane Blackman and Laura Barnett discuss their teaching of ethnographic methods to tertiary students studying youth cultures and subcultures. Beginning with the Chicago School's ethnographic tradition, the authors then share a series of embodied and reflexive vignettes from their own research projects to illuminate how research relationships are bound up in issues of intimacy, exchange, and friendship. Identifying these three concepts, they argue, is an important step in linking subcultural research to effective teaching practice, and in particular to sensitizing students to the significance of researcher roles and how they shape interpretive practice. Together, the chapters in this section serve as exemplars of interpretivist subcultural research that should encourage readers to reflect on their research interests, study designs, and interpretive practices.

In the concluding chapter, Samuel Judah and I take a sample of ten peer-reviewed publications from 2018 to 2022 and analyze them alongside the chapters in this volume in terms of how they approach, contextualize, and embody interpretive practice in the study of subcultural phenomena more generally. Whereas the chapters in this volume focus on youth and music culture, the selected articles represent research from a broader range of disciplinary perspectives and empirical topics as represented in Figures 1.1 and 1.2. By closing out the book in this way, we invite readers to reflect once more on the practices of interpretation. Is the focus on youth and music, or on DIY or resistance, sufficient, or do we need to broaden our horizons to account for what constitutes subcultural studies today? This is an important question because, as DeGloma and Wiest point out:

> Whatever the topic of analysis may be ... a shared interpretive endeavor provides an important framework for dialogue and debate among scholars working from different analytic perspectives in the field of study, a foundation upon which an overall understanding of the substantive themes, salient moral and political issues, and significant events and experiences central to their area of concern may be built. (2022, p 3)

Notes

[1] I do not take these numbers as objectively accurate, not least because the process through which Google assigns values is not transparent. Rather, I'm using them here only to suggest some disciplinary variation.

[2] This list of terms is not exhaustive. Quite the contrary, it was the result of my own decisions about what to search for. Searching for deviance instead of deviant, for example, returned much fewer results, as did searching for sexuality instead of sex (though the results for sexuality seemed more coherent than for sex).

3   I contend that most such terms miss the analytic mark by conflating social and cultural concepts. *Social* refers broadly to relationships among individuals or groups, while *cultural* refers to sets of meanings or meaning-making practices that individuals or groups share. In other words, a subculture is not a social, but rather a cultural concept, and may be used alongside social terms—for example, a 'subcultural scene'.

References

Anderson, N. (1923) *The Hobo: The Sociology of the Homeless Man*, Chicago: University of Chicago Press.

Atkinson, M. (2003) *Tattooed: The Sociogenesis of a Body Art*, Toronto: University of Toronto Press.

Baldwin, J.R., Faulkner, S.L., Hecht, M.L., and Lindsley, S.L. (2006) *Redefining Culture: Perspectives Across the Disciplines*. Mahwah, NJ: Lawrence Erlbaum Associates.

Barmaki, R. (2016) 'On the Origin of the Concept of "Deviant Subculture" in Criminology: W I Thomas and the Chicago School of Sociology', *Deviant Behavior*, 37(7): 795–810.

Bell, A. (2010) 'The Subculture Concept: A Genealogy', in S.G. Shoham, P. Knepper, and M. Kett (eds) *International Handbook of Criminology*, New York: Routledge, pp 179–210.

Bennett, A. (1999) 'Subcultures or Neo-Tribes? Rethinking the Relationship between Youth, Style and Musical Taste', *Sociology*, 33(3): 599–617.

Bennett, A. (2004) *After Subculture*, London: Palgrave Macmillan.

Berger, P. (1966) 'Identity as a Problem in the Sociology of Knowledge', *European Journal of Sociology/Archives Européennes de Sociologie*, 7(1): 105–115.

Berzano, L. and Genova, C. (2015) *Lifestyles and Subcultures: History and a New Perspective*, New York: Routledge.

Bestley, R., Dines, M., Guerra, P. and Gordon, A. (eds) (2021) *Trans-Global Punk Scenes: The Punk Reader* (vol 2), Bristol: Intellect.

Blackman, S. (2005) 'Youth Subcultural Theory: A Critical Engagement with the Concept, its Origins and Politics, from the Chicago School to Postmodernism', *Journal of Youth Studies*, 8(1): 1–20.

Blackman, S. (2014) 'Subculture Theory: A Historical and Contemporary Assessment of the Concept for Understanding Deviance', *Deviant Behavior*, 35(6): 496–512. doi: 10.1080/01639625.2013.859049.

Blumer, H. (1954) 'What Is Wrong with Social Theory?', *American Sociological Review*, 19(1): 3–10. doi: https://doi.org/10.2307/2088165.

Brake, M. (1985) *Comparative Youth Culture: The Sociology of Youth Culture and Youth Subculture in America, Britain, and Canada*, London: Routledge and Kegan Paul.

Buechler, S.M. (1995) 'New Social Movement Theories', *Sociological Quarterly*, 36(3): 441–464.

Buttigieg, B., Robards, B. and Baker, S. (2015) 'Introduction: Youth Culture Research in Australia', in S. Baker, B. Robards and B. Buttigieg (eds) *Youth Cultures and Subcultures: Australian Perspectives*, Farnham: Ashgate, pp 1–20.

Clarke, J. (1976) 'Style', in S. Hall and T. Jefferson (eds) *Resistance through Rituals*, London: Routledge, pp 175–191.

Clarke, J., Hall, S., Jefferson, T. and Roberts, B. (1976) 'Subcultures, Cultures and Class', in S. Hall and T. Jefferson (eds) *Resistance through Rituals: Youth Subcultures in Post-war Britain*, London: Hutchinson, pp 9–74.

Cohen, A.K. (1955) *Delinquent Boys: The Culture of the Gang*, Glencoe, IL: Free Press.

Cohen, S. (1980) *Folk Devils and Moral Panics*, London: Routledge.

Coulter, T.J., Mallett, C.J. and Singer, J.A. (2016) 'A Subculture of Mental Toughness in an Australian Football League Club', *Psychology of Sport and Exercise*, 22: 98–113.

Cressey, P.G. (1932) *The Taxi-Dance Hall: A Sociological Study in Commercial Recreation and City Life*, Chicago: University of Chicago Press.

DeGloma, T. and Wiest, J.B. (2022) 'On the Multidimensional Foundations of Meaning in Social Life: An Invitation to the Series Interpretive Lenses in Sociology', *Bristol University Press*, https://bristoluniversitypress.co.uk/asset/11003/de-gloma-wiest-series-editors-article.pdf

Ferrell, J. (1999) 'Cultural Criminology', *Annual Review of Sociology*, 25: 395–418.

Fine, G.A. and Kleinman, S. (1979) 'Rethinking Subculture: An Interactionist Analysis', *American Journal of Sociology*, 85(1): 1–20.

Gelder, K. (2007) *Subcultures: Cultural Histories and Social Practice*, London: Routledge.

Gordon, M.M. (1947) 'The Concept of the Sub-Culture and Its Application', *Social Forces*, 26(1): 40–42.

Haenfler, R. (2023) *Subcultures: The Basics* (2nd edn), New York: Routledge.

Hall, S. and Jefferson, T. (eds) (1976) *Resistance through Rituals*, London: Hutchinson.

Harker, D. (2015) *Creating Scientific Controversies: Uncertainty and Bias in Science and Society*, Cambridge: Cambridge University Press.

Hebdige, D. (1979) *Subculture: The Meaning of Style*, London: Methuen & Co.

Hebdige, D. (1988) *Hiding in the Light: On Images and Things*, London: Routledge.

Hodkinson, P. (2004) 'The Goth Scene and (Sub) Cultural Substance', in A. Bennett and K. Kahn-Harris (eds) *After Subculture: Critical Studies in Contemporary Youth Culture*, London: Palgrave Macmillan, pp 135–147.

Jenks, C. (2004) *Subculture: The Fragmentation of the Social*, Thousand Oaks: SAGE.

Jensen, S.Q. (2006) 'Rethinking Subcultural Capital', *Young*, 14(3): 257–276.

Jensen, S.Q., Larsen, J.F. and Sandberg, S. (2022) 'Rap, Islam and Jihadi Cool: The Attractions of the Western Jihadi Subculture', *Crime, Media, Culture*, 18(3): 430–445.

Koch, E.S. and Sauerbronn, J.F.R. (2019) '"To Love Beer above All Things": An Analysis of Brazilian Craft Beer Subculture of Consumption', *Journal of Food Products Marketing*, 25(1): 1–25.

McCarthy, E.D. (1996) *Knowledge as Culture: The New Sociology of Knowledge*, New York: Routledge.

Merton, R.K. (1938) 'Social Structure and Anomie', *American Sociological Review*, 3(5): 672–682.

Miles, S. (2000) *Youth Lifestyles in a Changing World*, London: McGraw-Hill Education.

Moshier, S.J., McHugh, R.K., Calkins, A.W., Hearon, B.A., Rosellini, A.J., Weitzman, M.L. and Otto, M.W. (2012) 'The Role of Perceived Belongingness to a Drug Subculture among Opioid-Dependent Patients', *Psychology of Addictive Behaviors*, 26(4): 812–820.

Muggleton, D. (2000) *Inside Subculture*, Oxford: Berg.

Muggleton, D. and Weinzierl, R. (2003) *The Post-Subcultures Reader*, New York: Bloomsbury USA Academic.

O'Connor, A. (2003) 'Punk Subculture in Mexico and the Anti-Globalization Movement: A Report from the Front', *New Political Science*, 25(1): 43–53.

Palmer, V.M. (1928) *Field Studies in Sociology: A Student's Manual*, Chicago: University of Chicago Press.

Prus, R.C. (1996) *Symbolic Interaction and Ethnographic Research: Intersubjectivity and the Study of Human Lived Experience*, Albany: SUNY Press.

Prus, R.C. (1997) *Subcultural Mosaics and Intersubjective Realities: An Ethnographic Research Agenda for Pragmatizing the Social Sciences*, Albany: SUNY Press.

Romy, A. and Dewan, M. (2021) 'The Bikerni: An Ethnographic Study on Women Motorcyclists in Modern India', *Journal of Tourism and Cultural Change*, 19(6): 868–883.

Rorty, R. (1961) 'Pragmatism, Categories, and Language', *The Philosophical Review*, 70(2): 197–223.

Rose, G. (1997) 'Situating Knowledges: Positionality, Reflexivities and Other Tactics', *Progress in Human Geography*, 21(3): 305–320.

Shildrick, T. and MacDonald, R. (2006) 'In Defence of Subculture: Young People, Leisure and Social Divisions', *Journal of Youth Studies*, 9(2): 125–140.

Stahl, G. (2003) 'Tastefully Renovating Subcultural Theory: Making Space for a New Model', in D. Muggleton and R. Weinzierl (eds) *The Post-Subcultures Reader*, pp 27–40.

Tan, K. C. and Cheng, S. (2020) 'Sang Subculture in Post-reform China', *Global Media and China*, 5(1): 86–99.

Thornton, S. (1995) *Club Cultures: Music, Media, and Subcultural Capital*, Cambridge: Polity Press.

Thrasher, F.M. (1927) *The Gang: A Study of 1,313 Gangs in Chicago*, Chicago: University of Chicago Press.

Tolson, A. (1990) 'Social Surveillance and Subjectification: The Emergence of "Subculture" in the Work of Henry Mayhew', *Cultural Studies*, 4(2): 113–127.

Ulusoy, E. and Fırat, F.A. (2018) 'Toward a Theory of Subcultural Mosaic: Fragmentation into and within Subcultures', *Journal of Consumer Culture*, 18(1): 21–42.

van den Hoonaard, W.C. (1997) *Working with Sensitizing Concepts: Analytical Field Research*, Thousand Oaks: SAGE.

Wheaton, B. (2000) '"Just Do It": Consumption, Commitment, and Identity in the Windsurfing Subculture', *Sociology of Sport Journal*, 17(3): 254–274.

Widdicombe, S. and Wooffitt, R. (1995) *The Language of Youth Subcultures: Social Identity in Action*, New York: Harvester Wheatsheaf.

Williams, J.P. (2006) 'Authentic Identities: Straightedge Subculture, Music, and the Internet', *Journal of Contemporary Ethnography*, 35(2): 173–200.

Williams, J.P. (2011) *Subcultural Theory: Traditions and Concepts*, Cambridge: Polity Press.

Williams, J.P. (2014) 'Subcultures and Deviance', in M. Dellwing, J.A., Kotarba and N.W. Pino (eds) *The Death and Resurrection of Deviance*, Cham: Springer, pp 108–123.

Williams, J.P. (2019) 'Subculture's Not Dead! Checking the Pulse of Subculture Studies through a Review of "Subcultures, Popular Music and Political Change" and "Youth Cultures and Subcultures: Australian Perspectives"', *Young*, 27(1): 89–105.

Williams, J.P. (2020) 'Myth and Authenticity in Subculture Studies', in B. van der Steen and T.P.F. Verburgh (eds) *Researching Subcultures, Myth and Memory*, London: Springer, pp 35–53.

Williams, J.P. (forthcoming) 'Subcultural Theory: More than Just Crime and Deviance', in K.D. Haggerty and L. Presser (eds) *The Oxford Handbook of Critical and Cultural Criminological Theory*, Oxford: University of Oxford Press.

Williams, J.P. and Kamaludeen, M.N. (2017) 'Muslim Girl Culture and Social Control in Southeast Asia: Exploring the Hijabista and Hijabster Phenomena', *Crime, Media, Culture*, 13(2): 199–216.

Williams, J.P. and Schwarz, K.C. (2021) *Studies on the Social Construction of Identity and Authenticity*, New York: Routledge.

Wilson, B. (2002) 'The Canadian Rave Scene and Five Theses on Youth Resistance', *Canadian Journal of Sociology/Cahiers canadiens de sociologie*, 27(3): 373–412.

Xiao, J. (2016) 'Striving for Authenticity: Punk in China', *Punk & Post-Punk*, 5(1): 5–19.

Xiao, J., Davis, M. and Fan, Y. (2022) 'De-Westernizing Punk: Chinese Punk Lyrics and the Translocal Politics of Resistance', *Young*, 31(1): 57–72. doi:11033088221112191.

Yinger, J.M. (1960) 'Contraculture and Subculture', *American Sociological Review*, 25(5): 625–635.

Yinger, J.M. (1984) *Countercultures*, New York: Simon & Schuster.

2

Subculture, Scene, Lifestyle, or Movement? Conceptualizing Straight Edge from Insider and Academic Perspectives

Ross Haenfler

On the straightedgeinterviews Instagram page, users continually debate the meaning(s) and significance of straight edge, a clean-living subculture often associated with hardcore punk music. Run by a New Zealander straight edger, the Instagram page boasts over 14,000 followers and features brief interviews of approximately 2,500 (and growing) self-identified straight edgers from all over the world, with new entries posted almost daily. In the comments under participants' profiles, users argue about who can legitimately claim the identity, whether straight edge *must* be connected somehow to punk, and whether medicinal cannabis products count as illicit drugs. Some bluntly disagree with interview subjects' interpretation of straight edge while others come to their defense. Participants challenge each other over whether straight edge is strictly a personal choice or is a collective challenge to a culture that from their point of view puts alcohol at the center of social life. They question whether straight edge should be a one-chance opportunity or if adherents can 'break edge' and later claim edge again. While most comments stay civil, discussions can get heated, suggesting that something vital is at stake. In the process of these exchanges, participants variously refer to straight edge as a subculture, scene, lifestyle, and, occasionally, movement, usually without making explicit what they mean by any of these terms. As they negotiate their interpretations of straight edge, their specific priorities often reflect broader understandings of the identity that correspond to these four concepts.

    Academics also routinely argue about how to interpret and conceptualize social phenomena. But how do such discussions reflect the lived experiences of the human beings involved? In this chapter, I reflect on my long-term study of straight edge to demonstrate connections and disjunctions between participants' perspectives and sociological concepts used to understand them. Straight edgers variously interpret their refusal of alcohol, tobacco, and illegal drugs as an individual/personal commitment and as a collective challenge/ social movement. Some view their abstinence as part of recovery from substance use disorders, others as part of a radical political project. Straight edgers routinely discuss their collective identity in terms of subculture, scene, lifestyle, and movement. Each of these parallels an academic concept with a long history, meant to illuminate patterns of social phenomena. After explaining these concepts, I show how each provides tools useful to the sociological analysis of straight edge. I argue that while concepts guide and emerge from both the research process and the interpretation of data, more important is the emergent meaning-making that transcends conceptual boundaries. Rather than make a strong case for the *best* concept, I argue that the complexity of straight edgers' lived experiences warrants multiple conceptualizations, including the concept of lifestyle movement. Finally, I show how an ethnographic, inductive research process, incorporating a variety of data sources and sites, helps develop sociological concepts but also reveals their limitations.

Studying straight edge

Straight edge emerged in the early 1980s US punk scene as a clean-living strand of hardcore punk (Haenfler, 2006; Wood, 2006; Stewart, 2017). Ian MacKaye, vocalist for Washington, DC band Minor Threat, popularized the term with the song 'Straight Edge', in which he questions the prevalent drug and alcohol use in the punk scene and claims to have an edge over those who use substances. Another of the band's songs, 'Out of Step', provided a basic credo with the lines '(I) Don't smoke, (I) Don't drink, (I) Don't Fuck, At least I can fucking think'. These ideas quickly resonated with many young US punks who adopted the identity in defiance of other punks, conventional peers, and their perceived 'mainstream' society (Rettman, 2017). Since then, straight edge has spread worldwide, becoming a symbolic resource for generations of adherents. Many display the group's symbol, an X, on clothing, in tattoos, or drawn on their hands with black felt pen. While often still associated with the hardcore music scene, the identity transcended such boundaries long ago and has for some become nearly synonymous with sobriety. Participants' common understanding seems deceptively simple: to claim the straight edge identity, one must abstain, completely, from alcohol, drugs, tobacco, and 'casual' or 'conquest' sex. Most frame straight edge as a lifetime commitment and insist that even one slip up means forfeiting their claim. However, straight edgers continually negotiate the meanings of straight edge, often in heated arguments via social media as illustrated here (see Williams and Copes, 2005). As straight edge has gained increasing attention and attracted greater interest, interpretive conflicts rage, making for fascinating, but complicated, research opportunities and a chance to develop and (re)consider concepts.

I have studied straight edge for nearly 25 years through a combination of in-depth interviews, participant observation, content analysis, social media observation, and survey data (Haenfler, 2006; 2012; 2018). While my own straight edge identity facilitated my transition from participant to participant-researcher, my research interests led me to study the culture. Though I trained broadly in interpretive sociology, my primary subdiscipline was Collective Behavior and Social Movements. I wanted to understand how individuals incorporated efforts at social change into their everyday lives, rather than as part of organized, collective movements and organizations publicly targeting the state and demanding policy change. I wondered: How do people try to live their lives in ways that facilitate social change? How do people unwilling or unable to participate in direct action seek to make change? And how do these efforts connect to electoral and contentious politics? These questions led to my desire to test and stretch the dominant paradigms explaining social movements and change. Straight edge seemed to me a 'messy' grouping that did not fit neatly into any existing conceptual category, and I quickly observed that insiders also struggled to coherently describe their collective identity and practices. Part lifestyle, part subculture, part music genre, and, I would eventually argue, part movement, straight edge provided an opportunity to explore the intersections of multiple concepts related to my research questions.

Employing an inductive, grounded theory approach centered on participant observation and in-depth interviews allowed me to theorize from my data rather than testing hypotheses or working from preconceived notions about the setting (Charmaz, 2014). I have logged hundreds of hours at hardcore shows and recorded and transcribed interviews with over 75 straight edgers. However, as social media has become increasingly interwoven into social experience, including subcultural experience, I have gathered data across a variety of digital platforms.[1] Observing, screenshotting, and analyzing interaction on the publicly shared straightedgeinterviews Instagram page—both interview responses and subsequent comments—provided access to perspectives previously understudied using more conventional approaches (Laestadius, 2016). Likewise, monitoring posts in a straight edge Facebook group enabled me to anonymously witness real-time discussion, especially of contentious issues. These digital (rather than co-present, embodied) interactions are likely the primary mode of interaction between many straight edgers the world over, efficiently connecting more, and more diverse, subculturists than ever (see Manovich, 2009). This 'naturalistic observation'

(Lincoln and Guba, 1985) provides data unaffected by my presence, emerging organically between participants rather than in response to my questioning. These various sources and methods enabled me to cross-check claims and develop new lines of inquiry.

Academic perspectives: subculture, scene, lifestyle, movement

Theory explains, but also guides research questions, methods, and the interpretation of results. Conversely, following a grounded theory approach, empirical observation generates theory. In tandem, we develop theoretical concepts to describe and think critically about patterns of human interaction, even if those concepts serve only as abstract, interpretive 'ideal types' rather than objects or objectively observable 'realities' (Weber, 1968). Concepts serve as a point of reference to which we can compare empirical (but always interpreted) observations. Before engaging insiders' perspectives, I briefly review several academic concepts, each of which offers some sociological understanding of straight edge.

Subculture has a long history, replete with competing paradigms and associated concepts (see Williams, 2011). The term gained particular prominence when the University of Birmingham's Centre for Contemporary Cultural Studies used subculture to describe primarily working-class youth engaged in symbolic resistance (semiotic warfare) to a hegemonic, dominant society via their style (Hall and Jefferson, 1976; Hebdige, 1979). Subcultures offered young people, including mods, rockers, skinheads, and punks, an opportunity to win some cultural space, but ultimately did little to change participants' class subordination, and even *reinforced* or ensured class inequality. Avoiding an overemphasis on spectacular style, social class, and youth, I suggest a somewhat broader conceptualization focused on '*shared identity*, *distinctive meanings* around certain ideas, practices, and objects, and a sense of *marginalization* from or *resistance* to a perceived "conventional" society' (Haenfler, 2023, p 19). In foregrounding distinction, marginalization, and resistance, this definition suggests that subculture does not describe simply any subcategory or 'piece' of a larger society, or people who happen to share certain interests, and is also not confined to a certain age or social position. Coming from the punk scene, straight edge brings together people critical of a perceived status quo who often use music and style to distinguish themselves. Many report feeling marginalized due to their abstinence and other aspects of their identities at some point in their lives. The group's ubiquitous symbol, the X, conveys a shared identity and its 40-year musical history provides not only a soundtrack but also a reference point for old and new participants alike.

Highlighting the shortcomings of the University of Birmingham's Centre for Contemporary Cultural Studies' approach, post-subculture scholars proposed *scene* and *neo-tribe* as alternatives (Bennett, 1999). In contrast to subculture, scene describes fluid, temporary, leisure- and consumerist-oriented groupings as having little stylistic or ideological coherence. Rave and electronic dance music, as well as large music festivals, bring a diversity of people together temporarily, and primarily to have a good time. They are defined by neither social class nor shared politics. The notion of scene seems useful to understanding contemporary straight edge. Although some share common styles, many straight edgers are virtually indistinguishable from their more conventional peers. And while some explicitly connect straight edge to radical politics, others clearly *separate* their straight edge identity from any sort of politics, framing it as a personal lifestyle choice. Further, hardcore shows and festivals temporarily bring straight edgers together, but some adherents have little consistent contact with other straight edge people.

Straight edgers' everyday practices may also be conceptualized as *lifestyles*, patterns of action that differentiate people, including consumption habits, leisure activities, personal tastes, and the various ways people express their sense of self (Sobel, 1981; Chaney, 1996). Lifestyle has class-based connotations, for scholars and laypersons alike, with upper classes distinguishing themselves through consumer goods and embodied ways of being (Bourdieu, 1984). It also implies considerable agency, suggesting that people can adopt certain modes of being from an array of choices, for example taking on a 'healthy lifestyle' by building exercise into their routines, eating organic foods, and wearing 'sporty' clothes. As a significant dietary choice that frames much of participants' lives, straight edge has much in common with other activities often described as lifestyles such as vegetarianism, yoga, and 'green living'.

Like subcultural studies, *social movement* studies include a variety of complementary and competing paradigms, including collective grievance, political opportunity, resource mobilization, and new social movements (see McAdam et al, 2001). Social movements are organized, collective, public challenges to authorities, often facilitated by professional or semi-professional organizers via social movement organizations. Strategic actors gather resources, issue claims, and push for policy change or political realignment. Many march in the streets, commit civil disobedience, and use a variety of tactics to pressure public officials. With no formal organization, membership, reflexive strategy, or public political program, straight edge does not fit the mold of the social movement that organizational scholars typically study. New social movements theory (see Melucci, 1980; Laraña et al, 1994), emphasizing collective identity, symbolic action in the cultural sphere, and 'post-materialist' values, comes closer. Still, in some ways straight edge differs significantly from the feminist, civil rights, peace, and environmentalist groups new social movement theorists tend to describe.

Finally, to bridge the gaps among these concepts, my colleagues and I proposed the notion of *lifestyle movements* as 'loosely bound collectivities in which participants advocate lifestyle change as a primary means to social change, politicizing daily life while pursuing morally coherent "authentic" identities' (Haenfler et al, 2012, p 14). In contrast to protest movements, they emphasize relatively individual, private action, encouraging participants to make changes in their ongoing lives in the hopes that such efforts will collectively produce larger cultural change. For many participants, personal identity work—living a moral life in line with one's values—is equally (and in some cases more) important than measurable social change (Haenfler, 2019). Common examples include locovores and slow food advocates, abstinence pledgers and anarchists, and some vegans and vegetarians. Straight edge, I will argue, falls into this conceptually 'in between' space.

As academic concepts, subculture, scene, lifestyle, social movement, and lifestyle movement each address relationships between leisure and politics, coherence and difference, authenticity and consumerism, and individual and collective orientations. Each, as I note, offers useful understandings of straight edge. But how do these perspectives relate to *insider* (emic) perspectives? In the following section, I demonstrate in greater detail how individuals interpret their commitment to straight edge, relative to each of these ideas. Other concepts, not deployed by insiders and beyond the scope of this chapter, may also be useful in examining subcultural groupings, for example fandoms (Hills, 2002); alternativity (Spracklen and Spracklen, 2018); deviant leisure (Williams, 2009); counterculture (Yinger, 1982); and implicit religion (Stewart, 2017).

Insider interpretations: the many meanings of straight edge

While academic discourse often veers wildly away from participants' lived and felt experiences, individuals *do* talk about straight edge as a subculture, a scene, a lifestyle, and, less frequently, a movement, often while articulating how best to characterize what they believe, feel, and do. Each term implies interpretive understandings of straight edge. Those who use *subculture* cherish straight edge's historical connection to hardcore punk, valorize its perceived outsider or countercultural status, and attempt to maintain some sort of boundaries around the identity. *Lifestyle*, on the other hand, connotes more individualistic meanings centered on the personal fulfillment and empowerment they feel as they abstain from drugs, alcohol, and tobacco. In this case, straight edge is primarily a dietary choice, one expression of self that may be more, or less, significant than others. Those who understand straight edge as a *movement* place an even greater emphasis on collective cultural challenge and often connect other activist concerns with sobriety. Anti-racism, antifascism, environmentalism, gender and sexual justice, animal liberation, indigenous rights, and other causes become part of a more 'radical sobriety' (see Kuhn, 2019). Importantly, even if specific individuals gravitate toward one understanding more than others, they may use each of these terms, depending on the context or the sense of straight edge they wish to convey in the moment. Insiders' ambiguity offers an important insight to researchers: multiple perspectives may inform our theorizing, some directly connected to insiders' accounts and vernacular, others less so.

Straight edge as subculture and scene

Straight edgers commonly refer to themselves as a subculture. Yet their use of the term differs somewhat from early academic definitions cited earlier, typically linking it to punk and hardcore and focusing little, if at all, on social class. Straight edgers claim to be part of a subculture primarily to highlight their differences from a perceived 'mainstream' and to emphasize their shared identity (Copes and Williams, 2007). Jordan,[2] a married, middle-aged father of two who continued to play in straight edge hardcore bands, relished the sense that straight edge set him apart, even as he led in many ways a conventional, middle-class life:

> 'Being that I came from the punk scene the rebellious part of it is what many of us liked, we liked being different from other people and finding straight edge just enhanced that feeling tenfold because anyone can stick on combat boots and have a mohawk. That's very external. But finding something internal like being able to say no to drugs and alcohol in a society that seems to relish those things really turned me on.' (Interview 2020)

As Jordan suggests, some straight edgers see it as a subculture within punk; they identify with punk's broad anti-establishment ethos and practice, while pushing back on what they see as punk's excesses. Participants may or may not refer to the marginalization or resistance included in my definition of subculture—though many *do* report feeling marginalized and in opposition to society, even beyond their abstinence.

While certainly subcultural in many respects, straight edge—at least as a term—long ago transcended its connection with hardcore as people increasingly adopted the expression as a synonym for sobriety. In fact, some report that others apply the term to them, at least initially. People in recovery, some of whom report little or no history in punk or hardcore whatsoever, now find support in straight edge Facebook and Instagram groups, much to the consternation of certain long-term adherents. Some relative newcomers claim to have been straight edge 'all my life', a notion that makes little sense to scene veterans because it equates straight edge simplistically with abstinence rather than a carefully considered subcultural commitment. Jordan often argued on social media against equating straight edge with sobriety, leading others to accuse him of 'gatekeeping':

> 'So nowadays when you see people who have absolutely no idea what straight edge is or where it came from now calling themselves straight edge simply because they're sober, it drives me up the wall. ... I think it's fantastic they are sober and I would obviously never knock them for that but to simply be okay with everyone under the sun calling themselves straight [edge] as just simply because they don't drink really waters [it] down.' (Interview 2020)

Jordan and others like him, often (but not always) middle-aged, see straight edge as undermined by people who claim the identity as a descriptor but not as a subcultural commitment. Explicitly invoking subculture, Garrett, a fitness coach and grappling competitor, said in an Instagram exchange: 'There's a difference between being drug free and straight edge and the misuse for straight edge to mean "currently sober" undermines the commitment and the subculture of straight edge.' These comments exemplify the shared sense of 'outsider' status and particular meanings prevalent in academic understandings of subculture.

When they say *scene*, adherents describe common practices and shared meanings, but also people gathering in shared spaces, especially at hardcore shows but also online (see Williams, 2006). Their usage is vague; scene might refer to their local, embodied interactions at shows, the global straight edge community, or their social connections facilitated by social media. Veronika, 37, a professional photographer and vocalist for a hardcore band, described the scene in terms of a more abstract imagined community:

> 'Social media plays such a huge role now in how the scene is connected. Like, there's so much more cohesiveness in the scene, just through the internet, and through social media. Like I grew up experiencing that through message boards, and, you know, kind of the nascent stages of social media. But now it's just like, half the friends that I've made in the scene and can stay connected to are all through Instagram. And, like, I can feel a sense of closeness and belonging to these people even though they live in an entirely different state.' (Interview 2019)

Participants also use scene to compare and contrast different styles and music genres, for example the 'metal', 'hardcore', 'crust', and 'art punk' scenes. Alejandro, a Mexican-American death metal musician with roots in hardcore and straight edge, embodies the fluidity and porousness of boundaries (for example, long hair, metal band shirts). Describing changes in his local scene, he illustrated the transitory nature of music communities:

'[T]his scene is flourishing now, and in two years the space most of those kids are going to move on and go to college, or they're going to move away or they're going to get into different kinds of music and they're going to disappear into a different scene. This scene is eventually going to perish, you have to enjoy it while you have it ... cause it's going to disappear, especially in hardcore. Anything is short-lived [in] hardcore.' (Interview 2017)

Alejandro and others also associated scenes with particular venues—an art space, basement, club, and so on that, like the historic New York venue CBGB, which hosted a variety of genres and served as a number of versatile subcultural hubs. Those spaces, too, were often transitory, as some venues closed and others opened.

Scene, widely used by insiders, accurately captures straight edge's stylistic diversity, relative lack of class consciousness, and the fluidity of hardcore music events. However, straight edgers often *do* see themselves in opposition to a perceived mainstream, engaging directly in lifestyle politics, and the longevity, shared identity, and shared sense of community remain more consistent and deeply experienced than the scene concept implies.

Straight edge as lifestyle

Straight edgers also regularly call their practices a lifestyle, particularly when they focus on their everyday choices. In these cases, participants foreground personal benefits and focus less on straight edge's potential collective resistance. Pépe, a 38-year-old biodiesel logistics technician from Rio de Janeiro, upon learning about straight edge, said on Instagram, 'I realized that straight edge is not a movement but a lifestyle'. This interpretation highlighted the perceived personal health benefits of abstaining from drinking and smoking. Mickey, a New Zealander who runs men's mental health groups, said:

[Straight edge] is a personal thing for me. It's being the best and most authentic version of myself. I didn't like who I was when I was drinking [and using]. I like who I am now a whole lot more ... claiming edge has been an important part of my journey to getting healthy and staying that way. It's helped me deal with childhood traumas and sort a lot of my mental health issues that were doing an incredible amount of damage to me and those around me. Kia Kaha ['Stay strong' in Māori]! (Instagram 2022)

As Mickey exemplifies, many straight edgers highlight both authenticity—suggesting substance use created a false or inauthentic self—and that sobriety helps them confront unhealthy habits or personal traumas.

While lifestyle resonates with many straight edgers, some avoid linking their identity to a lifestyle. For Ian MacKaye, whom adherents credit with having created the term straight edge, the 'lifestyle' label further codified substance use as normative and, ironically, clean-living as somehow deviant:

> Anytime someone says to me, 'So do you live the straight edge lifestyle?' I think, it's not a fuckin' lifestyle. Like, partying? *That's* a fuckin' lifestyle. Getting high? *That's* a lifestyle. Being involved with religion? *That's* a lifestyle. But *not* engaging in substances to change your way of thinking? That's just *life*. (Pierschel and Kirchner, 2010, 38:19)

What's more, the notion of lifestyle does not capture the depth of connection and commitment many feel, giving, for some, an impression that adopting or shedding the identity was as easy and about as meaningful as switching up a clothing style or ordering a new dish at a restaurant. Lifestyle, while deployed as shorthand to describe the personal choice to be drug-free, did not always reflect the intense, immersive, embodied, connecting cultural experience of straight edge. Similar to the arguments revealed previously, Tammy posted on Instagram:

> There is a different [sic] between being straight edge and being sober. You get one shot and that's it. This isn't AA where there's a rotating door and you can come and go when it's convenient. This behavior is disrespectful to the countless ones of us who have made a lifetime commitment. This is spitting on that. You got sober? Awesome I'm honestly happy for you. As an alcoholic with bi-polar disorder, anxiety, ptsd, and bbd, I personally know the struggle of obtaining your sobriety and maintaining it. I'm not some 19-year-old kid who's got a chip on their shoulder. I'm a 39-year-old woman who had to claw there [sic] way through 21 years of misogynistic bullshit and abuse in the sxe scene to be taken seriously and I will not be qui[e]t when some fucking kid comes in and makes that look like a passing faze [sic] and a joke. You wanna use sxe as a crutch when it's convenient? Then there's the fucking door. (Instagram)

Framed by many as a lifetime commitment, lifestyle, at least on its own, seems an inadequate label for straight edge to many participants. Nevertheless, as the label and identity continued to spread beyond hardcore, describing straight edge as a lifestyle may continue to make sense to some.

Straight edge as social movement

Of the terms I reviewed thus far, straight edgers are least likely to describe themselves as a social movement. This is unsurprising, given that both scholarly and colloquial understandings center around organized, public protest by strategic claims-makers demanding change of (usually) a corporate or governmental entity. Yet the movement concept does help make sense of straight edge, especially contemporary scholarship that theorizes the micro-foundations of cultural challenges and protests (for example, Jasper, 2014). Straight edge intersects with a variety of causes including antifascism, anti-racism, anti-capitalism, and, especially, animal liberation (see Kuhn, 2019). Some adherents report that their sobriety informs their activism and, unburdened by intoxication and distraction, makes them more effective activists. Josh, the drummer for a well-known vegan straight edge band, said:

> 'For me [straight edge has] evolved into taking that clarity I have from not being inebriated to doing something positive for myself and the world. It seems to me to be kind of a natural extension of having a clear mind. Participating in social issues and struggles—anti-racist, anti-sexist, anti-homophobic kind[s] of struggles. Becoming vegan. Straight edge for me became less of just a personal choice and more of a personal choice that helped me be active politically in a positive way.' (Interview 2011)

For Josh and many others, music became a vehicle to educate and motivate their peers to take action, whether in their daily lives, the streets, or both. Indeed, some straight edgers form connections to activist organizations; Animal Liberation Front activists and vegan straight edgers Walter Bond and Peter Daniel Young both served prison time for liberating animals from fur farms and other acts of sabotage. Young said:

> Straight edge kids had a *profound* impact on the animal liberation movement in the '90s, and frankly to the current day. You'd show up at demos, um, in the mid-'90s, '95, '96, and they'd look like hardcore shows. Every single person was wearing the, you know, [hardcore band] One King Down hoodie, the Earth Crisis sweatshirt or what have you. So, um, straight edge *was* activism. (Pierschel and Kirchner, 2010, 47:08)

Some viewed drugs and alcohol as tools of domination employed, or at least encouraged, by the state. Colombian musician Rico, who lives in New York City and plays in several hardcore bands, said: 'For me straightedge is a political position mainly of resistance towards the self-destruction that has been normalized through the years and the indoctrination by the state which uses illegal and legal drugs as a means to dominate us' (Instagram). Criticizing and rejecting tobacco and pharmaceutical companies who knowingly minimized the harms caused by their products (for example, cigarettes and opioids) made straight edge feel like a movement for some participants.

Yet the whole notion of straight edge as a movement made others nervous, prompting objections going back many years. Many straight edgers soured on the notion of movement since 'Hardline', a relatively rigid and conservative strand of straight edge, emerged in the 1990s with bands such as Vegan Reich, Statement, and Raid. Insiders frequently call this aspect of straight edge a movement because of its more outspoken and uncompromising stances against drugs, alcohol, and harm to animals, as well as its intimations against non-procreative sex, same-sex relationships, and abortion (Wood, 2006). Hardline, along with the youth crew and early vegan straight edge scenes (discussed later in this chapter), left a negative impression that resonates with some participants today. More recently, right-wing groups such as the mixed martial arts Rise Above Movement have sometimes co-opted straight edge for their own purposes (Miller-Idriss, 2020).

For some, 'movement' held connotations of judgment, exclusion, conformity, narrow-mindedness, and 'militancy'. In the liner notes of the 1995 compilation record *XXX—Some Ideas are Poisonous*, Kent McClard of Ebullition Records wrote:

> We are all autonomous people. We are not a cult or a following or a movement. My anarchist perspective has always been a big part of my straight edge ideals, and I will never give up my identity or individuality to be a part of some movement. Yes, I am straight edge, just as the people that play in these bands are straight edge, but we all have our own ways of expressing that concept, and our own ways of living it. (*XXX—Some Ideas are Poisonous*, 1995, liner notes)

Concerned with the more militant strands of straight edge prominent in the 1990s and 2000s, Ian MacKaye reiterated his view of straight edge as primarily an individual choice:

> I don't accept it as a movement. That doesn't mean that people who do I think are dumb or wrong or anything, it just means that I don't ... I just see people as people. It was always in my mind a celebration of an individual's right to choose his or her life, like way of living. The problem with movements is that movements start to lose quite often sight of humanity, of human beings, individuals. (Pierschel and Kirchner, 2010, 58:50)

Others echo this perspective, insisting they are straight edge for themselves rather than any sort of collective challenge.

In any case, dominant organizational and political theories of movements do not neatly fit with straight edge given its lack of formal organization and more cultural challenge. Even more so than many movements, straight edge integrates lifestyle choices meant for self-growth with a collective challenge directed towards drinking culture and the alcohol and tobacco industries. Building on new social movement theory, I have suggested that straight edge exemplified the 'newest' form of movement, that is, less formal, focused on cultural change, and more individualized than dominant conceptions of social movements might allow (Haenfler, 2006). At best, social movement, like subculture, was a partial and incomplete 'fit' for straight edge, signaling the need for a different framework.

Straight edge as lifestyle movement

The interpretive tensions expressed by participants—between subculture and scene, lifestyle and movement—have deeply informed my own conceptual thinking about straight edge. As I have shown, my empirical observations reflected each concept in some ways. Yet none of these frameworks helped me fully theorize my observations of straight edge, hinting that another approach may be necessary, especially to account for the conceptual space between subculture and social movement. After all, social movements scholars had been questioning the limitations of the dominant political process paradigm, suggesting that a variety of change-oriented (or resistant) groupings fall outside of organizational, protest-oriented, state-centered models (for example, Snow, 2004; Jasper, 2014). Likewise, subculture scholars continually debated the nature of subcultural leisure and resistance (for example, Paris and Ault, 2004; Blackman, 2014; Williams and Hannerz, 2014).

As mentioned, straight edgers refer to themselves as both lifestyle and movement; lifestyle movement is not in their vernacular. Yet in certain respects, this concept better accounts for the ways that straight edge, like other lifestyle movements, interweaves self-actualization and social transformation. Adherents engage in seemingly individualized action (abstention, wearing clothes with straight edge messages, getting straight edge tattoos) as part of a collective identity. Many claim that straight edge has profoundly impacted their personal lives, helping them to break unhealthy patterns and confront life's challenges with a 'clear mind'. Yet as much as some claim to be straight edge 'just for myself', they consistently position their abstinence in opposition to 'drinking culture', 'alcohol culture', and 'drug culture'. Few straight edgers advocate for policy changes regarding drugs, tobacco, and alcohol. (In fact, if anything, most advocate for an end to punitive/criminalizing approaches to drugs and support for expanded treatment options.) Rather, they offer their personal abstention—practiced alongside others making similar choices and claiming the identity—as a cultural challenge and a form of 'lifestyle activism' (Portwood-Stacer, 2013). On the *xsisterhoodx* e-zine, Veronika wrote:

> For me personally, being straight edge isn't just simply being drug-free, but being actively against toxic drug and alcohol culture. ... I advocate for a cultural shift where 'It's OK Not to Drink' isn't just a slogan on a T-shirt, but an actual mindset, and where turning 21 isn't synonymous with getting shit-faced. (kellysisterhood 2021)

At diyconspiracy.net, Chris, singer for vegan straight edge band Wake of Humanity, alludes to this cultural resistance as well:

> The society in which we live in really has normalized addiction. It's become such a part of so many people's lives from so many different walks of life. ... Socializing in general for most people lends itself to engaging in what's become the 'bar culture' that perpetuates this behavior. I think [Washington D.C. straight edge band] Coke Bust said it best, 'Fuck Bar Culture!'. (Mittens XVX 2018)

Straight edgers suggest a subjective understanding that their individual actions—taken in concert with many others doing the same thing—could change social expectations around drinking, smoking, and eating/using animal products. Yet in interviews, many insisted, at least initially, that straight edge was, first and foremost, a 'personal choice'. Upon further questioning, many acknowledged that they intended their personal abstinence as an act of refusal and resistance, as well as for their own well-being. Turkish straight edger Ahmet demonstrates the connection between lifestyle and community, inward and outward focus:

> It's all about a clean mind. First for yourself then for society. If you ignore and exclude yourself, your problems will of course not benefit society and yourself. ... For me this lifestyle is a system that allows people to listen to themselves, face their problems and find themself [sic] as a result. (Instagram 2020)

Some adherents' insistence on framing straight edge in individualistic terms reflects a late-capitalist glorification of the individual and straight edge's punk roots that emphasize individuality and resistance to conformity. Additionally, the 'youth crew' (late 1980s, early 1990s) and early vegan straight edge (mid-1990s) scenes too often gave a judgmental, arrogant impression, exemplified by the tongue-in-cheek t-shirt slogan 'Straight edge means I'm better than you', also adopted by famous professional wrestler C.M. Punk in his role as a heel (villain). Indeed, straight edge attracted some men who used the ideology as a vehicle for violence (Purchla, 2011). As a result, many contemporary straight edgers continue to position themselves against the specter of intolerant, hypermasculine 'tough guys', which for some means consistently performing open-mindedness.

Perhaps regardless of straight edgers' intentions, their collective refusal prefigures the world they claim to desire, a world where it is 'OK not to drink', where people feel completely comfortable in their abstinence. In the tradition of socialists, anarchists, feminists, queer communities, and black feminists, they engage in 'the deliberate experimental implementation of desired future social relations and practices in the here-and-now' (Raekstad and Gradin, 2020, p 10). Yet even prefiguration implies a more 'deliberate' and reflexive approach than the subculture-ness of straight edge. Coming full circle, at first glance straight edge resistance seems compatible with contemporary subcultural theory, and yes, straight edge has much in common with punk, goth, and other groupings we commonly label subcultural. Current understandings of subculture that highlight meaning-making (informed by symbolic interactionist and, to some extent, post-subcultural perspectives)—decentering stable identities, consistent communities, youth, and social class—provide a helpful framework for theorizing straight edge. However, straight edge is also comparable to locovores, abstinence/virginity pledgers, simple living advocates, ethical vegetarians and vegans, craftivists, and others that issue a cultural challenge primarily through individual action understood as collectively important. Like these lifestyle movements, straight edge shows the importance of identity work and identity as a site of social change; the diffuse structure and importance of (sub)cultural entrepreneurs; and the potential links between lifestyle change and contentious politics.

Conclusion

If I were to adopt straight edgers' vernacular, I would have to variously describe straight edge as subculture, scene, lifestyle, and movement. As I have shown, each of these words carries multiple emic meanings that only partially correspond to their conceptual (etic) use by scholars. Subculture is useful in analyzing straight edgers' more spectacular, stylistic elements, their focus on authenticity, their shared meanings and practices, and their subjective understandings of resistance. Scene and lifestyle speak to the diverse expressions of and diffuse communities within straight edge. Social movement seems less useful, but still offers insights into the more outward-facing connections between straight edge, activism, and various causes. Given the (at least partial) applicability of each of these ideas, straight edge demonstrates the potential danger of approaching the research process through one conceptual lens and the benefits of an inductive, emergent, grounded theory approach to observing 'subcultural' groupings in all their complexity. Beyond straight edge, many such groupings actually straddle a variety of concepts. Is breaking (breakdancing, b-boying, b-girling)—an event scheduled for the 2024 Olympics—a subculture, lifestyle, or sport (Maese, 2021)? We could ask the same of skateboarding, electronic/video gaming, parkour, and roller derby (see Dupont and Beal, 2021). Do we best explain fan fiction communities, comic book collectors, cosplayers, and tabletop gamers as subcultures, fandoms, or pop culture trends? How do we best theorize body modification as tattoos and less-conventional piercings become increasingly common in many cultures? Is QAnon a political movement, a conspiracy theory, a subculture, a massively multiplayer online game, or something else entirely?

I suggest that inductive studies of these and other 'messy' groupings may yield new insights relative to established concepts and, as is the case here with lifestyle movement, provoke newer concepts capturing the conceptual in-betweens. Putting concepts into conversation with one another, informed by the emergent, interpretative analysis of participants' experiences, is likely to produce more robust and relevant theories. I say conversation, not competition, because I am not suggesting that one must win over others. Rather, that creative collision may force us to reconsider their explanatory benefits and limitations. Trying to squeeze social groupings exclusively into one or another conceptual framework may promote oversimplifications; again, the complexity of straight edgers' lived experience warrants multiple conceptualizations. However, while there may not be a *best* concept, there are surely some that are *better* at helping understand specific phenomena. Using my background in subcultural studies helped me engage with movement scholars' critiques of their subfield. Likewise, studying social movements helped me rethink the ongoing conversation about subcultural resistance. These intersections led me to the concept of lifestyle movement, but not every comparison of concepts necessitates something new.

Just because I advocate considering multiple conceptualizations of alternative cultural and social patterns does not mean I uncritically accept conceptual ambiguity. Clear concepts help researchers make comparisons to similar social phenomena across settings and at different times, facilitating a productive scholarly conversation by ensuring that researchers share some common (if disputed and incomplete) understandings. They help us ask and answer questions, reflect on findings, and connect abstract theory to empirical observations (Williams, 2011), 'sensitizing' us to our social worlds by giving 'the user a general sense of reference and guidance in approaching empirical instances' (Blumer, 1954, p 7). If subculture (or any of the concepts discussed here) describes everything, then it really describes nothing. Clarity without rigidity is my goal.

I have also demonstrated how relying upon a mix of research methods and data across a variety of intersecting sites helped me navigate the complexity of insiders' meanings and practices. As I sought to compare and develop new concepts, digital domains proved especially useful; most subcultural interaction arguably occurs via these platforms (rather than at hardcore shows, for example) and these 'natural' interactions, emerging without any researcher prompt, offered rich data. The back and forth between digital and other sites pushed me into new areas of inquiry. For example, observations of Instagram interactions informed later interview questions, and interview data sensitized my online observations. As with any research setting, the form of digital platforms carried opportunities and constraints. Webzine writers might focus primarily on reviewing records and concerts rather than other issues of concern. Most Instagram users keep their posts relatively short, offering an imperfect window into their meaning, and people who post may represent only a fraction of adherents. But observed over time, these data, often involving interactions between multiple people across vast geographies, provided insights unavailable to me via other means.

Finally, I hope to model here how we might honor and share insiders' interpretations without holding them responsible for our theorizing. Previous generations of subcultural theorists often overlooked or undervalued participants' subjective experiences. For at least the past 20 years, a plethora of scholars with subcultural roots have conducted ethnographic and historical research as critical insiders (for example, Hodkinson, 2002; Feldman-Barrett, 2009; Bakrania, 2013; Worley, 2017; Lohman, 2017; Lane, 2020). Part of testing our interpretive framework relies upon participants' reactions; when they read our work, do they recognize some sense of themselves in our analyses, even when critical, and perhaps, even see themselves and their practices in a new light?

Notes

[1] In addition to the Instagram and Facebook data referenced in this chapter, some primary examples include Sunny Singh's YouTube channel Hate5Six which documents hardcore shows; digital 'zines such as NoEcho.net, diyconspiracy.net, xsisterhoodx.com, and uniteasia.org, which feature interviews with straight edge people; and the *This is Hardcore* and *Turned Out a Punk* podcasts.

[2] With the rare exception of public figures, all names are pseudonyms, including those of Instagram and Facebook users. Regarding public social media posts, I included no potentially compromising information.

References

Bakrania, F. (2013) *Bhangra and Asian Underground: South Asian Music and the Politics of Belonging in Britain*, Durham, NC: Duke University Press.

Bennett, A. (1999) 'Subcultures or Neo-Tribes? Rethinking the Relationship Between Youth, Style, and Musical Taste', *Sociology*, 33(3): 599–617.

Blackman, S. (2014) 'Subculture Theory: An Historical and Contemporary Assessment of the Concept for Understanding Deviance', *Deviant Behavior*, 35(6): 496–512.

Blumer, H. (1954) 'What is Wrong with Social Theory?', *American Sociological Review*, 18: 3–10.

Bourdieu, P. (1984) *Distinction: A Social Critique of the Judgement of Taste*, New York: Routledge.

Chaney, D. (1996) *Lifestyles*, London: Routledge.

Charmaz, K. (2014) *Constructing Grounded Theory* (2nd edn), Thousand Oaks: SAGE.

Copes, H. and Williams, J.P. (2007) 'Techniques of Affirmation: Deviant Behavior, Moral Commitment, and Subcultural Identity', *Deviant Behavior*, 28(3): 247–272.

Dupont, T. and Beal, B. (eds) (2021) *Lifestyle Sports and Identities: Subcultural Careers Through the Life Course*, New York: Routledge.

Feldman-Barrett, C. (2009) *We are the Mods: A Transnational History of a Youth Subculture*, Bern: Peter Lang.

Haenfler, R. (2006) *Straight Edge: Clean Living Youth, Hardcore Punk, and Social Change*, New Brunswick: Rutgers University Press.

Haenfler, R. (2012) '"More than the X's on My Hands": Older Straight Edgers and the Meaning of Style', in A. Bennett and P. Hodkinson (eds) *Ageing and Youth Cultures: Music, Style and Identity*, Oxford: Berg, pp 9–23.

Haenfler, R. (2018) 'The Entrepreneurial (Straight) Edge: How Participation in DIY Music Cultures Translates to Work and Careers', *Cultural Sociology*, 12(2): 174–192.

Haenfler, R. (2019) 'Changing the World One Virgin at a Time: Lifestyle Movements, Abstinence Pledgers, and Social Change', *Social Movement Studies*, 18(4): 425–443.

Haenfler, R. (2023) *Subcultures: The Basics*, 2nd edition. New York and London: Routledge.

Haenfler, R., Johnson, B. and Jones, E. (2012) 'Lifestyle Movements: Exploring the Intersection of Lifestyle and Social Movements', *Social Movement Studies*, 11(1): 1–20.

Hall, S. and T. Jefferson (eds) (1976) *Resistance Through Rituals: Youth Subcultures in Post-war Britain*. London: Hutchinson.

Hebdige, D. (1979) *Subculture: The Meaning of Style*. London: Methuen.

Hills, M. (2002) *Fan Cultures*, New York and London: Routledge.

Hodkinson, P. (2002) *Goth: Identity, Style and Subculture*, Oxford: Berg.

Jasper, J.M. (2014) *Protest: A Cultural Introduction to Social Movements*, Malden, MA: Polity Press.

kellysisterhood (2021) 'Straight Edge Interview Project- Veronika R. (she/her), age 35, Orange County, California.' https://www.xsisterhoodx.com/straight-edge-interview-project-veronika-r-she-her-age-35-orange-county-california/

Kuhn, G. (2019) *X: Straight Edge and Radical Sobriety*, Oakland: PM Press.

Laestadius, L. (2016) 'Instagram', in L. Sloan and A. Quan-Haase (eds) *The SAGE Handbook of Social Media Research Methods*, London: SAGE, pp 573–592.

Lane, D. (2020) *The Other End of the Needle: Continuity and Change Among Tattoo Workers*, Brunswick: Rutgers University Press.

Laraña, E., Johnston, H. and Gudfield, J.R. (eds) (1994) *New Social Movements: From Ideology to Identity*, Philadelphia: Temple University Press.

Lincoln, Y.S. and Guba, E.G. (1985) *Naturalistic Inquiry*, Beverly Hills: SAGE.

Lohman, K. (2017) *The Connected Lives of Dutch Punks: Contesting Subcultural Boundaries*, Cham: Palgrave Macmillan.

Maese, R. (2021) 'How Break Dancing Made the Leap From '80s Pop Culture to the Olympic Stage', *Washington Post*, February 9, https://www.washingtonpost.com/sports/2021/02/09/break-dancing-olympic-sport-paris-2024/

Manovich, L. (2009) 'How to Follow Global Digital Cultures, or Cultural Analytics for Beginners', in F. Stalder and K. Becker (eds) *Deep Search: The Politics of Search Beyond Google*, Wien: Studien Verlag/Transaction Publishers, pp 198–211, http://manovich.net/index.php/projects/how-to-follow-global-digital-cultures

McAdam, D., Tarrow, S. and Tilly, C. (2001) *Dynamics of Contention*, Cambridge: Cambridge University Press.

Melucci, A. (1980) 'The New Social Movements: A Theoretical Approach', *Social Science Information*, 19(2): 199–226.

Miller-Idriss, C. (2020) *Hate in the Homeland: The New Global Far Right*, Princeton: Princeton University Press.

Mittens XVX (2018) 'Wake of Humanity: We're Not the Cool Kids. We Want to Change the World.' DIY Conspiracy.net, https://diyconspiracy.net/wake-of-humanity-interview/

Paris, J. and Ault, M. (2004) 'Subcultures and Political Resistance', *Peace Review*, 16(4): 403–407.

Pierschel, M. and Kirchner, M. (2010) *Edge: Perspectives on a Drug Free Culture*. DVD. Compassion Media.

Portwood-Stacer, L. (2013) *Lifestyle Politics and Radical Activism*, New York and London: Bloomsbury.

Purchla, J. (2011) 'The Powers That Be: Processes of Control in "Crew Scene Hardcore"', *Ethnography*, 12(2): 198–223.

Raekstad, P. and Gradin, S.S. (2020) *Prefigurative Politics: Building Tomorrow Today*, Cambridge: Polity Press.

Rettman, T. (2017) *Straight Edge: A Clear-Headed Punk History*, Brooklyn: Bazillion Points Publishing.

Snow, D. (2004) 'Social Movements as Challenges to Authority: Resistance to an Emerging Conceptual Hegemony', *Research in Social Movements, Conflicts and Change*, 25: 3–25.

Sobel, M.E. (1981) *Lifestyle and Social Structure: Concepts, Definitions, Analyses*, New York: Academic Press.

Spracklen, K. and Spracklen, B. (2018) 'Constructing a New Theory of Alternativity', in K. Spracklen and B. Spracklen (eds) *The Evolution of Goth Culture: The Origins and Deeds of the New Goths*, Bingley: Emerald Publishing, pp 27–35

Stewart, F. (2017) *Punk Rock is My Religion: Straight Edge Punk and 'Religious' Identity*, London: Routledge.

Weber, M. (1968) *Economy and Society: An Outline of Interpretive Sociology*, New York: Bedminster Press.

Williams, D.J. (2009) 'Deviant Leisure: Rethinking "The Good, The Bad, and the Ugly"', *Leisure Sciences*, 31(2): 207–213.

Williams, J.P. (2006) 'Authentic Identities: Straightedge Subculture, Music, and the Internet', *Journal of Contemporary Ethnography*, 35(2): 173–200.

Williams, J.P. (2011) *Subcultural Theory: Traditions and Concepts*, Malden, MA: Polity Press.

Williams, J.P. and Copes, H. (2005) '"How Edge Are You?" Constructing Authentic Identities and Subcultural Boundaries in a Straightedge Internet Forum', *Symbolic Interaction*, 28(1): 67–89.

Williams, J.P. and Hannerz, E. (2014) 'Articulating the "Counter" in Subcultural Studies', *M/C Journal*, 17(6). https://doi.org/10.5204/mcj.912.

Wood, R.T. (2006) *Straightedge Youth: Complexity and Contradictions of a Subculture*, Syracuse: Syracuse University Press.

Worley, M. (2017) *No Future: Punk, Politics and British Youth Culture, 1976–1984*, Cambridge: Cambridge University Press.

Yinger, J.M. (1982) *Countercultures: The Promise and Peril of a World Turned Upside Down*, New York: Free Press.

3

Ghosts in the Machine: (Post)subculture and the 'Problem' of Contemporary Youth

Andy Bennett and Daniel Bennett

I have been involved in the sociological study of youth culture since the early 1990s. I commenced this work during the era of transition between analog and digital media. The academic world which I entered was still dominated by hard copy material, most of which was accessed via university libraries. At the time I began my academic career, the work of the Birmingham Centre for Contemporary Cultural Studies (CCCS) was collectively celebrating its 30th anniversary. Even at that time, many people in youth research who I spoke to suggested that the work was dated, while colleagues from other countries whom I met largely at conferences at that time suggested that the work was very Anglo-centric and made no sense in national contexts where socioeconomic histories were qualitatively different from those of Britain. Mike Brake (1985) argued that even the climate could have a significant effect on everyday manifestations of youth culture in different local contexts. Despite such critical observations, however, there was little in the way of a counter-discourse of conceptual theory. Steve Redhead's (1993) edited collection *Rave Off: Politics and Deviance in Contemporary Youth* had tentatively set the stage for what would later be termed post-subcultural studies. But beyond that, there was little in the way of work that contested the dominance of subculture as a meta concept in the cultural study of youth. Towards the end of the 1990s, I published an article that, along with work by other sociologists, namely David Muggleton and Steven Miles, would begin to flesh out the conceptual territory of post-subcultural studies. Influenced by the work of French sociologist Michel Mafessoli (1996), my article 'Subcultures or Neo-Tribes? Rethinking the Relationship Between Popular Music and

Youth Culture' (Bennett, 1999) used Mafessoli's concept of *tribus* to take subculture by its conceptual horns, proclaim what I considered to be its overly deterministic, class-based interpretation of youth cultures and argue instead for a more reflexive, fluid, and cross-class interpretation of youth culture. This paper continues to be my most highly cited article and also the most contentious piece I have published, sparking at one stage an academic debate that largely took place in the academic journal *Journal of Youth Studies* (see Bennett, 2005; Blackman, 2005; Hesmondhalgh, 2005; Shildrick and MacDonald, 2006). By the time I was invited to write a chapter for the current book, everyday culture—including youth cultures—had become largely digital, there was a new generation of youth culture scholars, and I also had a teenage son who had his own experiences and stories to tell about what it means to be young. What follows is born of a series of reflections on my own career as a youth culture researcher and an ongoing series of conversations with my son in which the then and now of youth cultures is invariably a topic of discussion. I claim no universal truths in this account. It is instead an opportunity to reassess what myself and others have suggested about the nature of youths and their cultures and to ponder all of this in the context of an era where youth culture is as much a historical terminology as something that bespeaks a contemporary status quo for young people.

The 'golden age' of subculture

I grew up during the 1970s in what could be seen as the tail end of a 'golden age' of youth culture (at least in an Anglo-American context). I went to a comprehensive school in the north of England. The first time I read Paul Willis' (1977) account of working-class 'lads' disrupting the classroom environment and creating their own counter-school culture, I recognized this as my own comprehensive school experience, generally on the receiving end of the lads' pranks. The photo on the cover of Hall and Jefferson's (1976) *Resistance Through Rituals* could easily have been taken in the playground of my own school. The more 'daring' of my school peers would arrive in the classroom with feather cuts, flared trousers, and 'bovver boots' or platform soles. Before I had grown out of my teens, glam had been replaced by punk which in turn had been replaced by new wave. I thus had a firsthand experience of at least part of what Hebdige (1979) would later term the sartorial history of British youth culture. For these reasons, among others, it is easy for me to see how the concept of subculture, despite its subsequent global resonance as a meta-concept for understanding style-based youth, is rooted in a particular time and place, specifically postwar Britain. None of my school peers used the term 'subculture' and, as Hebdige was later to claim, would not have recognized themselves in the scholarly works of the CCCS and those many scholars who would take inspiration from this body of work.

In fact, it would be reasonable to suggest that the CCCS's interpretation of British 'working class youth' which, as my own case suggests, also included a fair number of lower-middle-class youth, was in many ways a romanticized account born of an intellectual desire to map onto the practices of youths (which in the case of the CCCS were typically viewed from afar) a cultural Marxist agenda (Frith, 1984). The centrally defining premise of the CCCS subcultural theory, as meticulously set out in 'Subcultures, Conflict and Class', Hall et al's (1976) opening essay in *Resistance Through Rituals*, was that items of fashion and other commodities acquired by a newly affluent postwar British working class youth were used to frame sensibilities of resistance to class oppression as part of a new chapter in a theater of struggle that had raged for the past 150 years. It would later be argued that the CCCS's 'from afar' methodology of observing the everyday practices of youths was inherently problematic, not least of all because of the grandiose claims made about sartorial youth culture representing the then latest chapter in the working-class resistance to oppression. This criticism was exemplified in Stan Cohen's (1987) now famous observation that in the CCCS accounts of youth cultures, the young people themselves merely flitted across the screen. But even in the case of those few youth cultural researchers from the CCCS who, to coin a favorite expression of ethnographic researchers, got their hands dirty by getting out into the field, the class-bias appears to remain in how the hard-earned data were eventually interpreted. Although Willis' (1977) argument that the working-class counter-school culture simply served to ensure that working-class males left school without any qualifications and thus ended up in the manual jobs they had always been destined for, my own experience was that many of my lower-middle-class peers also engaged in the tussles and buffoonery of the counter-school culture as well. In fact, I clearly remember the school physics teacher gently herding one such group of middle-class counter-school participants into a corner of the room and inquiring in hushed tones "Why are you carrying on like this when you are all clearly very intelligent people?" From memory all but one of those who were chastised by the physics teacher on that day eventually went on to university.

Such impressions of my comprehensive school years remained with me and were still very much in my mind when I began to formulate my own academic criticisms of the CCCS during the mid-1990s. As noted earlier, the fruits of that particular labor formed part of a post-subcultural literature through which I and, as it turned out, several other British academics, who had all come of age in the 1970s and experienced similar things to me in school and post-school, hoped to set the theoretical record straight. Although my own neo-tribal take on youth cultures (Bennett, 1999) differed from the work of David Muggleton (2000), who adopted a Weberian perspective in his explanation of individualized trends in youth consumption, and Steven

Miles (2000), who substituted subculture for lifestyle in a critique of the homological and semiological accounts of youth style presented by Willis (1978) and Hebdige (1979) respectively, this new body of work had as its common core a significant departure from the structuralist accounts of the original CCCS work. The emergence of post-subcultural theory sparked significant debate, with a number of scholars arguing that, in emphasizing the importance of consumption, post-subcultural theorists were essentially abandoning *any* consideration of structural inequalities (including how such inequalities may bar actual access to consumption) (for example, Shildrick and MacDonald, 2006). Similarly, Blackman (2005) argued that in emphasizing what he identified as a postmodern consumerist definition of youth culture, post-subcultural theorists overlooked a rich legacy of political protest associated with youth subcultures between the mid and late 20th century. As I noted in my critical review of the subculture–post-subculture debate (Bennett, 2011) a number of these criticisms are fair but others misinterpret the post-subcultural studies agenda. Indeed, in that essay I suggested that a productive way forward might be to look at ways of bringing the two opposing debates in the study of youth cultures closer together. Significantly, however, what appears to have happened since the publication of that piece is the further bifurcation of subcultural and post-subcultural theory into increasingly distinct camps. In relation to subcultural studies, this has also acquired a new historical resonance, as seen for example in much of the work published by the British-based Subcultures Network, an initiative that was initially funded by the UK's Arts and Humanities Research Council. While such developments are in many ways positive, not least of all as signs of an acknowledgment that youth cultures are now regarded as a bona fide aspect of cultural history, it is equally fair to say that many of the more pointed questions posed during the subculture–post-subculture debate remain unanswered. Particularly the question of what defines a 'subculture' and where the parameters between sub- and dominant (or mainstream) culture are located. Twenty years ago, Bennett (1999) and Muggleton (2000) argued that such a distinction was problematic given the increasingly pluralistic and fragmented (Chaney, 2004) nature of contemporary society. Twenty years on this issue has undoubtedly intensified, rendering the definition of 'subculture', or at least its relatively uncritical acceptance, problematic.

This problem is further intensified by the colonization of subcultural studies by what could termed 'ageing subculturalists'. At the initial point of subcultural theory's inception in the early 1970s, many of those researching subcultural youth were not members of youth cultures themselves. In the current era, youth researchers without some prior, or ongoing, involvement in a subcultural setting are rather in the minority. One could of course argue that such a development is inevitable and also that in many well-documented cases the ability to use insider knowledge (Bennett, 2002) to generate and interpret data collected on youth subcultures is a highly valuable asset (for example, Hodkinson, 2005). At the same time, however, one could argue that this has resulted in a situation which is the obverse of what happened with the CCCS in the early 1970s but is no less problematic in overall terms. With the CCCS, it was a case of the imposition of subculture on youth came from without—as part of a requirement to fulfill the execution of a cultural Marxist interpretive agenda. What we are now witnessing could be regarded as the imposition of subculture from within by ageing 'subculturalists', whose time served in moshpits, at festival sites, in gig vans, or behind mixing desks, and so on, provides a legitimation for their continued use of subculture and its ascription to others in an essentially uncritical way. Although in this new paradigm of subcultural research the term subculture appears to have distanced from its original cultural Marxist agenda, something which has in turn adhered it to a global community of researchers who feel confident using the term without needing to rehearse its original UK-centric baggage, other problems arguably begin to emerge. The world is very different now, even to how it appeared in the early 2000s. Hebdige's (1979) reflections on the dangers of mainstream appropriation of subcultural style is now inseparable from the consumption of style. Branding is such a central part of youth culture that it has become an accepted part of the way in which young people interpret the significance of the styles they consume. Questions of 'authenticity' versus 'inauthenticity' are seemingly considered passé as a new post-ironic stance dominates social media platforms. This list of features in a changed world could go on, but even a cursory glance at such changes prompts a salient question. How does the continued pursuance of a subcultural model of investigation, nuanced by a historical understanding of what this approach entails, serve to eclipse a fuller understanding of youths and their youth cultural practices today?

Who am I?

At the time of writing, I am Professor of Cultural Sociology at Griffith University in Australia. With the move to Australia, in 2007, came my introduction to a new set of youth cultural terminologies, including larrikins (Rickard, 1998), bodgies and widgies (Stratton, 1984), and surfies (Pearson, 1982). The cultural terrain of everyday life in Australia has also proved instructive in terms of my perspective on the CCCS subcultural theory and its UK-centric qualities. Although a strong working-class ethic underpins much of Australian society and culture, many of those who subscribe to this enjoy levels of affluence that afford middle-class lifestyles. Being the father of a teenage son has also introduced me to a new world of youth cultural practices and involved me in some insightful conversations regarding who and what youth cultures are today. How these conversations do, or do not, in my view map onto current youth culture debates in the academy has also been a source of interest to me in recent years. In the 20-odd years since the publication of the early post-subcultural studies, the unravelling of the threads of semiotic logic that first piqued the interest of scholars such as myself, David Muggleton, and Steven Miles has continued apace. This is not to say that the 'classic' youth styles of old do not remain in circulation. Indeed, a cursory review of contemporary scholarship quickly reveals that much of this continues to trade in an established currency of sartorial terms such as punk, metal, hip hop, hardcore, and so on (for example, Nilsson, 2016; Lewin, 2020). These styles continue as youth styles but are increasingly read as minority texts of style in the broader cultural landscapes of youth. Some have questioned whether the term 'youth culture' is even of relevance at all now, alleging that the major milestones of youth culture are located in the past while the youths of today seem little concerned with this legacy (Young, 1985). Others suggest that what was once a clearly defined youth culture is now a multigenerational culture with hippies, punks, rappers, and ravers spanning much of the life course from pre-teen to third age (Bennett and Hodkinson, 2012). In tandem with this, it is frequently claimed that what were once strong demarcations of youth and youth sensibilities also appear to carry less gravitas today. I have talked at length on this topic with my son. His response to the question of youth cultures frequently relates to how current perceptions of youth culture seemed plagued by accounts from the past. A particularly salient example of this, he suggests, is the apparent need to categorize youth cultural styles in particular ways. Also, while terms such as the internationally recognized emo or more locally specific eshay (slang for an Australian urban youth culture) are familiar to him, his suggestion is rather that most youth (including among his own peer group) will assume a more middle ground stance towards style, for example, adopting a hip hop or goth aesthetic without buying completely into these styles. Such a sensibility aligns closely with the observations of Miles (2000) who suggested that more rigidly defined youth subcultural styles have given way to an emphasis on stylized youth identities based around more individualized lifestyle aesthetics.

Another significant topic of conversation between the two of us has been music. Much has been written in the past about the significance of music as a critical bone of contention between youth and the parent generation to the extent that the authorities even saw fit to ban some popular artists from performing and censor others (for example, Street, 1992). In the pre-digital era, when music was largely consumed via mainstream media and through retail, the musics of young people were more audible to the parent culture and thus more apt to raise moral panics and attempts to suppress or remove such music from public soundscapes. As my son has reinforced in conversations, the ways in which young people now consume music is such that, while some lyrical and also video content remain contentious, its lack of presence in mainstream soundscapes means that much less attention is paid to it. The fact that music artists have, in the past, been taken to court on the grounds that their music have incited acts such as youth suicide (Carlson et al, 1989) appear incongruous to my son and his peers. A further point that is often made by him is that while artists and genres were frequently categorized into particular types of music whose perceived impacts on young listeners ranged from negligible to serious/pathological, a salient impact of the age of digital music distribution is that the field of artists and (sub)genres available for streaming and download is such that it has become increasingly difficult to navigate this field and pinpoint specific artists and genres as being of concern. This in itself is significant as, while the ability of the parent culture to censor artists and music judged to be a threat young people has significantly decreased, the negative impacts of music on youths does not appear to have increased. A further point that has frequently been raised by my son is that practices of access to and consumption of music also function to reduce friction between parents and youths. Digital downloads/streaming and the use of earbuds or headphones has signaled an end, or at least a drastic reduction of, the kinds of conflict that used to arise when families argued over whether or not to let their teenage children watch a music program on the family television set, or when loud music playing from a teenage bedroom disturbed the rest of the family and/or was considered by parents to distract from the task of doing homework or revising for exams.

Another point of discussion between myself and my son has been about the place of music within youth cultures and if and how this has been impacted by access to digital technology. A point he frequently makes in relation to this is that although new music continues to be made and new pop icons continually appear (and often quickly fade again), for young people today music is frequently a mode of entertainment consumed within a broad nexus of other media and entertainment options including video games, YouTube, texting, and tweeting (see Nowak and Bennett, 2020). The ease with which the current generation of youth adapts to developments in digital technology has given rise to the term 'digital natives', the latter having been disputed given its assumption of equal access to digital technology by all young people in all places around the world (see Facer and Furlong, 2001). There can be little doubt, however, that in instances where access to digital technology is available to youth, this has facilitated a new sphere of cultural competence among young people. Frequently, this is interpreted in terms of contemporary youth's propensity for using digital media to engage in negative and antisocial forms of behavior (Subrahmanyam and Šmahel, 2011). Clearly, the presence and scale of this problem must be acknowledged, but equally it needs to be acknowledged that the presence and problematic nature of such behavior among youths were also to be found in the pre-digital age (for example, Oswell, 1998). The scale and aptitude of the current youth generation's ability to use digital media has been most recently illustrated by the COVID-19 pandemic. For example, during periods of 'hard lockdown' young people continued to make and discuss music using online platforms (for example, Howard et al, 2021).

Strangers in a strange land

As this chapter has previously established, contemporary youth exist in a world already informed by ideas about what youth and youth culture should be, and, of equal significance in the context of the current discussion, what it shouldn't be. Unlike the initial decades of the postwar era, when such impressions of youth were formed and propagated primarily by moral guardians from pre-war and wartime generations whose opposition to youth was managed by an 'othering' of youth born out of fears and concerns for the fate of young people in the face of what they considered a corrupting popular culture, today concerns about youth are more complex in nature. Thus, while concerns about youth continue among institutions of authority and other moral guardians, signature concerns are also expressed by those who were once youths, in a postwar sense, themselves, and consider the time of their own youth to have constituted a more 'authentic' era of youth culture while lambasting current youth for their fickle and effete nature. While, on the one hand, youth are blamed for various 'wicked problems', such as violence, binge drinking, vandalism, and so forth, equally they are stigmatized for things such as lack of engagement with politics tied in with a more general attitude of apathy that is underpinned by tendencies toward narcissism, escapism, and retreatism.

Significantly, the accusations in this latter category frequently seem impervious to the importance of socioeconomic context and how this has radically altered over the last 50 years. Thus, if the hippie 'counter-culture' was a reaction to a technocratic arrogance that rode on the wave of a strong postwar economy (Roszak, 1969), and punk was in turn a reaction to the perceived arrogance of the counter-culture's 'drop-out' and 'drop-in' again sensibility, as the economy slowed and the social fabric became more stymied, the youth cultures that followed faced an increasingly more complex and uncertain array of socioeconomic circumstances. It is perhaps this post-1970s youth cultural legacy, rather than the 'glory days' of the 1950s through to the 1970s, that bear most relevance when attempting to make sense of where contemporary youth sit in terms of both their understanding of the world and their attempts to formulate a youth cultural identity of their own. Indeed, my son's own accounts of his and his peers' experiences reflect on this at some level. Thus, while listening with keen interest to my stories of seeing what are now considered 'classic' rock and pop acts live at venues and festivals around the UK, for my son this is part of a bygone era. Consumption choices in style and music, as noted earlier, are now considered more individual and in many ways more discrete. A preference for a music artist is frequently considered to relate to a few songs rather than a whole album (if such a product even exists for a given artist) or a desire to see them live. The wearing of tour t-shirts and such is considered the purview of a small hardcore of youth music followers, who are frequently perceived as trying 'too hard' to be 'authentic' music fans according to a historical code of what this entails. As noted earlier in this chapter, David Muggleton's (2000) cornerstone text *Inside Subculture: The Postmodern Meaning of Style* suggested the end of an era, as young individuals pursued their own sense of fashion and style unfettered by historical stylistic conventions. For Muggleton, this observed phenomenon demarcated the end of the age of youth subcultures—and the beginning of a new era—post-subculture. At some 20 years remove from the publication of Muggleton's study, it is difficult to see the direct relevance of either of these terms for understanding how young people today articulate their identities. Certainly, fashion and style continue to matter for youth but the range of clothing and related accessories available to create stylized identities are increasingly broad and increasingly plural in terms of the meanings that young people inscribe in them. While some media pundits continue to mourn the loss of 'authentic subcultures' and others continue to locate and demonize 'subcultures' as the root of an endless list of social ills and dysfunctionalities in the world, contemporary youth itself often feels—and is—alienated from both sides of this debate. According to my son, the 'digital' press cuttings of great rocker, hippie, and punk moments to be found on YouTube bear interesting reminders of a world that existed in a pre-digital state, or provide a useful source of reference for songs and albums that have been recycled through more recent mediums such as Spotify or on computer video games such as 'Far Cry'. According to my son and his peers, while many young people are respectful of the youth cultural past they consider its critical relevance as something more likely to filter through the memories of the parent culture than having an immediate currency for the here and now, and for the meaning of their own lives.

Contemporary youth exist in a world that is characterized by new, or at least more readily acknowledged aspects of risk (Beck, 1992) relating to economic, environmental, and, more recently, pandemic issues. Moreover, such risks are understood and individually managed by young people largely on the basis of information available via digital media platforms (Vickery, 2017). Each of these characteristics is accepted on their own terms and considered to be a part of the normal, everyday experience of being young. In the 1970s subcultural theorists enjoyed the luxury of waxing lyrical about the lives of young people without demonstrating any obvious understanding of what those young people actually did in their everyday lives apart from being members of 'subcultures'. In response, McRobbie offered the critical observation that 'few writers seemed interested in what happened when a mod went home after a weekend on speed. Only what happened out there on the streets mattered' (1990, pp 68–69). This was, and remains, a crucially pertinent observation, but stood in a relatively isolated position as an objection to the conceptual bias that pervaded in a field of research seemingly obsessed with uncovering and defining pure 'subcultural beings' (Bennett, 2015). Today, such a false separation of the spectacular from the mundane, if always unjustifiable, seems both an impossible and also unnecessary task. The 'culture' of youth is in every sense uncovered only through understanding the fuller experience of youth. Youth can no longer be hermetically sealed by the researcher into the rocker's jukebox bar or the hippie's bedsit (Willis, 1978). To extrapolate from my son's own account, in the 2020s a conversation between two friends on Discord, or the sharing of images and texts on Instagram, says as much about the cultural worlds of young people as their choice of music or fashion. When researchers initially began to ponder the effects of digital media on youth this was frequently accompanied by an expressed anxiety that communication through digital media would replace face-to-face contact and add to feelings of isolation and alienation among youth (for example, Twenge, 2019). As other research has revealed, however, in many cases young people's communication with each other through digital media devices frequently complements rather than replaces face-to-face communication (Robards and Bennett, 2011). It is also something that happens in more characteristically youth spaces (Lincoln, 2012). Prior to the pre-digital age, young people's non-face-to-face communication was typically via the telephone in the domestic family household, something that in and of itself could lead to tension between parents and their children due to, for example, parental anxiety over mounting telephone charges or loud conversations going on when the rest of the family were trying to watch television or sleep. Communication via digital media is more readily available, cheaper, and can be conducted from designated youth spaces, such as a bedroom or games room/study and so on, or even—and commonly—in spaces removed from the family home altogether. From listening to my son it seems that such digital facility and the freedom that it affords to create new spaces of cultural expression and exchange has to a fair degree replaced a tendency toward the need to create youth spaces through spectacular forms of stylized difference. As noted earlier, the emergence and rapid escalation of the COVID-19 pandemic in early 2020 provided a critical insight into the importance of digital media in young people's lives. While most obviously demonstrated by the ease though which schools and colleges around the world were able to switch from classroom to home-based schooling, the prevalence of digital technology in the life world of youth meant that the cultural practices of young people could also adapt to and/or remain unaffected by the new demands of the COVID-19-world (Kligler-Vilenchik and Literat, 2020) than would have been the case in the pre-digital age.

Indeed, in many ways, the threat to the stability of everyday life presented by the rapid escalation of the COVID-19 pandemic points to the resilience of a youth generation for whom the crisis adheres with the contours of a risk landscape that already frames their understanding of the world. As my son has opined, living through a time where the transition from youth to adulthood is becoming increasingly complex and fragmented (Blatterer, 2007), young people are now accepting of the fact that the concept of 'future' is contingent upon a range of factors, many of which are irresolvable through any form of short-term political strategy. While this isn't to suggest that all youth are conversant with the contemporary political landscape (in a local, national, or global context), there is a growing sense of disillusionment with mainstream politics, one salient example of this being Fridays for Future, the global climate strike movement initiated by a 15-year-old school student, Greta Thunberg, in 2018 (von Zabern and Tulloch, 2021). If youth feel alienated from a political arena that seems to possess no clear objectives for addressing longer-term issues such as climate change, a problem that the current youth generation will need to deal with irrespective of whether there is a current political will to engage with the matter or not, they feel equally alienated from a world that seeks to push them into preparing for an uncertain future. In my son's view, for his generation there is a feeling that while previous generations of youth have been privileged with a time and space in which to enjoy being young, the pressure on youth today to plan for the future is such that the time of their youth is a time that is being spent elsewhere. Music, in as much as it serves as a commentary on the dissatisfaction of youth, tends not to focus on the macro-political but on the personal feelings of insecurity experienced by the individual. This transition does not cohere with the 'subcultural' text of youth as there is no overarching agenda here, but rather an engagement with song at the level of individual attachment and pathos.

Contemporary youth is frequently criticized for its perceived complacency. Often, we are told, young people seem as unconcerned with political issues as they are with current affairs in an overall sense, a criticism also made of youth by politicians themselves (Henn et al, 2002). Aligned with this is a moral panic concerning youth's apparent disinterest in newspapers and TV and radio newscasts and their preference instead for other 'news' outlets such as Facebook, blogs, and YouTube (Marchi, 2012). Such 'accusations', however, typically fail to acknowledge the broader socioeconomic and technological contexts in which contemporary youth finds itself. Just as dominant notions of youth culture today 'seem particularly plagued by memories of the [past]' (Lipsitz, 1994, p 17), so the rhetoric of apathy and disconnectedness that pervades discussions of contemporary youth fail to grasp how radically altered life opportunities coupled with the radical expansion of media information and communication have produced different ways for young people to engage with and evaluate the world around them. While my son does not claim to be a spokesperson for an entire generation, his feeling, supported by conversations with peers, is that young people today are generally more aware of global issues than they are typically given credit for and that their knowledge comes from the multifarious channels through which information is now gathered. It would be disingenuous to suggest that those channels through which young people do gather information about the world are somehow hermetically sealed off from 'official' channels of news media information and other current affairs digests. As a cursory look at YouTube content reveals, much of the content posted there is harvested from terrestrial news channels. What does, perhaps, appear more evident in the domain of YouTube, Facebook, TikTok and so forth is an avenue for critical takes on world issues. For example, homemade videos produced by young people and posted online to their peers often present satiric but well substantiated commentaries on world affairs (see, for example, Willett, 2008); this might range from searing commentary on the one-sided and bigoted views of political leaders of so-called democratic nations (Penney, 2020) to criticism of how supposedly 'green' and 'energy saving' products are frequently produced at enormous cost to the environment and in a way that is guided by the same economic principles of profit and loss that govern the most environmentally unfriendly modes of industrial production (Bosworth, 2021).

Subculture to post-subculture to … culture

To some readers, the foregoing account of discussions between a youth researcher and his son may appear to have strayed some way from a discussion of how we interpret subcultures or post-subcultures in a contemporary age. In engaging in those conversations, however, I was reminded of the fact that neither subcultural or post-subcultural researchers, myself included, have invested much time in trying to uncover what was going on in young people's lives beyond those elements that related directly to stylistic and musical preferences. Our interpretations of these young people, thus, began with a concept and worked backwards from there to uncover things that would fit a neat picture of the kind of youth—subcultural or post-subcultural—that we wished to find. I have frequently claimed that crude essentialization was the work of the subcultural researcher, whereas post-subcultural researchers were engaged in a search to uncover the more individual motivations of youths for engaging with style and music. I am no longer convinced by the soundness of that argument. There are clearly things that bond young people and make them want to be together, whether in physical or digital space—but these may have less to do with common stylistic and musical preferences. Subculture and post-subculture have not gone away as concepts but now sit side by side, each arguing for a particular set of interpretations of youths. But this debate seems to be edging into a vacuum, its focus increasingly on exceptions rather than on the majority of young people. The majority of young people instead exist as ghosts in a conceptual machine that refuses to acknowledge them. One reads about these young people in transitions studies, health and education research, and so forth. But in those fields of research young people are rarely presented as having cultural lives. Rather they are objects of un- and underemployment, well-being, or educational (non)achievement. Just as subcultural and post-subcultural studies did little to acknowledge what most young people do most of the time in building cultural lives for themselves, so these other fields of youth research also do little to fill in those knowledge gaps. Rather than reifying youths as subcultural or post-subcultural, it may ultimately be more productive to speak in terms of cultures of young people and begin to map from there how and why the cultural practices that young people engage in matter to them and how they draw on the vast array of cultural resources, material and digital, available to them to negotiate and make sense of the myriad everyday situations in which they find themselves.

References

Beck, U. (1992) *The Risk Society: Towards a New Modernity*, trans. M. Ritter. London: Sage.

Bennett, A. (1999) 'Subcultures or Neo-Tribes? Rethinking the Relationship between Youth, Style and Musical Taste', *Sociology*, 33(3): 599–617.

Bennett, A. (2002) 'Researching Youth Culture and Popular Music: A Methodological Critique', *British Journal of Sociology*, 53(3): 451–466.

Bennett, A. (2005) 'In Defence of Neo-Tribes: A Response to Blackman and Hesmondhalgh', *Journal of Youth Studies*, 8(2): 255–259.

Bennett, A. (2011) 'The Post-Subcultural Turn: Some Reflections Ten Years On', *Journal of Youth Studies*, 14(5): 493–506.

Bennett, A. (2015) ' "Speaking of Youth Culture": A Critical Analysis of (Post)Youth Culture in the New Century', in D. Woodman and A. Bennett (eds) *Youth Cultures, Transitions and Generations: Bridging the Gap in Youth Research*, Basingstoke: Palgrave Macmillan, pp 42–56.

Bennett, A. and Hodkinson, P. (eds) (2012) *Ageing and Youth Cultures: Music, Style and Identity*, Oxford: Berg.

Blackman, S. (2005) 'Youth Subcultural Theory: A Critical Engagement with the Concept, its Origins and Politics, from the Chicago School to Postmodernism', *Journal of Youth Studies*, 8(1): 1–20.

Blatterer, H. (2007) *Coming of Age in Times of Uncertainty*, New York: Berghahn Books.

Bosworth, K. (2021) 'The Bad Environmentalism of "Nature is Healing" Memes", *Cultural Geographies*, 29(3): 353–374.

Brake, M. (1985) *Comparative Youth Culture: The Sociology of Youth Cultures and Youth Subcultures in America, Britain and Canada*, London: Routledge and Kegan Paul.

Carlson, S., Luce, G., O'Sullivan, G., Masche, A.A. and Frew, D.H. (1989) *Satanism in America: How the Devil Got More Than His Due*, El Cerrito: Gaia Press.

Chaney, D. (2004) 'Fragmented Culture and Subcultures', in A. Bennett and K. Kahn-Harris (eds) *After Subculture: Critical Studies in Contemporary Youth Culture*, Basingstoke: Palgrave Macmillan, pp 36–48.

Cohen, S. (1987) *Folk Devils and Moral Panics: The Creation of the Mods and Rockers* (3rd edn), Oxford: Basil Blackwell.

Facer, K. and Furlong, R. (2001) 'Beyond the Myth of the "Cyberkid": Young People at the Margins of the Information Revolution', *Journal of Youth Studies*, 4(4): 451–469.

Frith, S. (1984) *The Sociology of Youth*, Ormskirk: Causeway Press.

Hall, S. and Jefferson, T. (eds) (1976) *Resistance Through Rituals: Youth Subcultures in Post-War Britain*, London: Hutchinson.

Hebdige, D. (1979) *Subculture: The Meaning of Style*, London: Routledge.

Henn, M., Weistein, M. and Wring, D. (2002) 'A Generation Apart? Youth and Political Participation in Britain', *The British Journal of Politics and International Relations*, 4(2): 167–192.

Hesmondhalgh, D. (2005) 'Subcultures, Scenes or Tribes? None of the Above', *Journal of Youth Studies*, 8(1): 21–40.

Hodkinson, P. (2005) '"Insider Research" in the Study of Youth Cultures', *Journal of Youth Studies*, 8(2): 131–149.

Howard, F., Bennett, A., Green, B., Guerra, P., Sousa, S. and Sofija, E. (2021) '"It's Turned Me from a Professional to a 'Bedroom DJ' Once Again": COVID-19 and New Forms of Inequality for Young Music-Makers', *YOUNG: Nordic Journal of Youth Research*, 29(4): 417–432. doi: 10.1177/1103308821998542.

Kligler-Vilenchik. N. and Literat, I. (2020) 'Youth Digital Participation: Now More than Ever', *Media and Communication*, 8(2): 171–174. https://doi.org/10.17645/mac.v8i2.3180.

Lewin, P.G. (2020) ' "Don't Call Me White" (or Middle Class): Constructing an Authentic Identity in Punk Subculture', in J.P Williams and K.C. Schwartz (eds) *Studies on the Social Construction of Identity and Authenticity*, London: Routledge, pp 89–106.

Lincoln, S. (2012) *Youth Culture and Private Space*, Basingstoke: Palgrave Macmillan.

Lipsitz, G. (1994) 'We Know What Time It Is: Race, Class and Youth Culture in the Nineties', in A. Ross and T. Rose (eds) *Microphone Fiends: Youth Music and Youth Culture*, London: Routledge, pp 17–28.

Maffesoli, M. (1996) *The Time of the Tribes: The Decline of Individualism in Mass Society* (trans D. Smith), London: SAGE.

Marchi, R. (2012) 'With FaceBook, Blogs, and Fake News, Teens Reject Journalistic "Objectivity"', *Journal of Communication Inquiry*, 36(3): 246–262.

McRobbie, A. (1990 [1980]) 'Settling Accounts with Subcultures: A Feminist Critique', in S. Frith and A. Goodwin (eds) *On Record: Rock Pop and the Written Word*, London: Routledge, pp 66–80.

Miles, S. (2000) *Youth Lifestyles in a Changing World*, Buckingham: Open University Press.

Muggleton, D. (2000) *Inside Subculture: The Postmodern Meaning of Style*, Oxford: Berg.

Nilsson, M. (2016) 'No Class? Class and Class Politics in British Heavy Metal', in G. Bayer (eds) *Heavy Metal Music in Britain*, London: Routledge, pp 161–180.

Nowak, R. and Bennett, A. (2020) 'Music Consumption and Technological Eclecticism: Investigating Generation Y's Adoption and Uses of Music Technologies', *YOUNG: Nordic Journal of Youth Research*, 28(4): 347–362. doi: 10.1177/1103308819896173.

Oswell, D. (1998) 'A Question of Belonging: Television, Youth and the Domestic', in T. Skelton and G. Valentine (eds) *Cool Places: Geographies of Youth Cultures*, London: Routledge, pp 35–49.

Pearson, K. (1982) 'Surfies and Clubbies in Australia and New Zealand', *Journal of Sociology*, 18(1): 5–15.

Penney, J. (2020) '"It's So Hard Not to be Funny in This Situation": Memes and Humor in U.S. Youth Online Political Expression', *Television & New Media*, 21(8): 791–806.

Redhead, S. (ed) (1993) *Rave Off: Politics and Deviance in Contemporary Youth Culture*, Aldershot: Avebury.

Rickard, J. (1998) 'Lovable Larrikins and Awful Ockers', *Journal of Australian Studies*, 22(56): 78–85.

Robards, B. and Bennett, A. (2011) 'My Tribe: Postsubcultural Manifestations of Belonging on Social Network Sites', *Sociology*, 45(2): 303–317.

Roszak, T. (1969) *The Making of a Counter Culture: Reflections on the Technocratic Society and its Youthful Opposition*, London: Faber & Faber.

Shildrick, T. and MacDonald, R. (2006) 'In Defence of Subculture: Young People, Leisure and Social Divisions', *Journal of Youth Studies*, 9(2): 125–140.

Stratton, J. (1984) 'Bodgies and Widgies – Youth Cultures in the 1950s', *Journal of Australian Studies*, 8(15): 10–24.

Street, J. (1992) 'Shock Waves: The Authoritative Response to Popular Music', in D. Strinati and S. Wagg (eds) *Come on Down?: Popular Media Culture in Post-War Britain*, London: Routledge, pp 302–324.

Subrahmanyam, K. and Šmahel, D. (2011) *Digital Youth: Advancing Responsible Adolescent Development*, New York: Springer.

Twenge, J.M. (2019) 'More Time on Technology, Less Happiness? Associations Between Digital-Media Use and Psychological Well-Being', *Current Directions in Psychological Science*, 28(4): 372–379.

Vickery, J.R. (2017) *Worried About the Wrong Things: Youth, Risk and Opportunity in the Digital World*, Cambridge, MA: MIT Press.

von Zabern, L. and Tulloch, C.D. (2021) 'Rebel with a Cause: The Framing of Climate Change and Intergenerational Justice in the German Press Treatment of Fridays for Future Protests', *Media, Culture & Society*, 43(1): 23–47.

Willett, R. (2008) 'Consumption, Production and Online Identities: Amateur Spoofs on YouTube', in R. Willett, M. Robinson and J. Marsh (eds) *Play, Creativity and Digital Cultures*, New York: Routledge, pp 54–70.

Willis, P. (1977) *Learning to Labour: How Working Class Kids Get Working Class Jobs*, Farnborough: Saxon House.

Willis, P. (1978) *Profane Culture*, London: Routledge and Kegan Paul.

Young, T. (1985) 'The Shock of the Old', *New Society*, February 14, p 246.

PART II

Contextualizing Interpretive Practice

4

No More Heroes: Portuguese Punk and the Notion of Subculture in the Global South

Paula Guerra

Based on a long study of Portuguese punk over the past 40 years,[1] this chapter explores the reconceptualization of the concept of subculture through the internet in a non-Anglo-Saxon context. The methodology is based on 217 in-depth interviews with key actors in the Portuguese punk scene. These interviews are a substantial part of a collection intended for public use and represent an interpretivist approach to Portuguese punk that avoids situating it in a simplistic dichotomy between co-optation and counterculture. We are interested in how punk is crossed by tensions and contradictions as it uses various means to manage a counter-hegemonic orientation. Punk's informal and decentralized social networks, including the internet, social media and live shows, allow the flow of records, fanzines, bands, ideas, and styles. At the same time, the impact of a Do-It-Yourself (DIY) ethic enables the recording and releasing music and organizing concerts and fanzines, independent of state or corporate interests. These different media and practices make possible a distinct global dialogue, through which we can see the dialectics between identity and differentiation, and globalism and territoriality. Studying them interpretively make visible the imbalances present in the global pattern of punk, namely between centre and periphery, as is the case in Portugal (Wallerstein, 2004).

In this chapter, we first analyse the concept of subculture and its main critics before explaining the historical trajectory of Portuguese punk. Then we analyze empirical material regarding the internet's role in establishing various forms of activism/resistance in Portuguese punk. The internet has compressed the world, and this shift has been accompanied by a fear of the atomization of social actors, a return to bedroom culture, and the dangers of fake news and post-truth (McIntyre, 2018). It is therefore a significant contemporary area of research into social practices and representations. We then frame our findings in terms of subcultural perspectives to better describe the Portuguese case.

Take me to your special party

Studies of subcultures are anchored in two sociological traditions: the Chicago School and the work of the Centre for Contemporary Cultural Studies (CCCS). The former, based on studies carried out in the 1920s and 1930s, was concerned with how immigration to and changes occurring in large urban centers in the United States affected the socialization of young 'ethnic' populations. The CCCS, from around 1960, traversed various fields of study (Guerra 2020a; 2020b; 2021). Hebdige (1979) notes that in the postwar period, due to structural factors such as the media and the emergence of a consumer society, a fragmentation occurred in how social classes were understood. The CCCS sought to understand how youth subcultures responded to problems affecting working-class youth (Guerra, 2014). For the CCCS, subcultures were a paradigm of resistance through style, a way for young people to carry out collective resistance through a process of bricolage in which consumer goods were subverted from their original meanings and made subversive parodies. Yet this subversion ultimately failed to change power relations, and structural problems such as social inequality and low wages remained unchanged. Hebdige (1979) argued that symbolic and subversive creativity was a cycle: initially, a process of subcultural stylization was created, but when economic forces co-opted and began to sell this subcultural style to the masses, it lost its subversive character (Hesmondhalgh, 2005; Debies-Carl, 2013). This perspective of subcultures remained current until the late 1980s and early 1990s (Sandbrook, 2007; 2011).

In the mid-1990s, the post-subcultural approach emerged, shaped by the emergence of neoliberalism (Thornton, 1995; Muggleton, 2000; Bennett and Guerra, 2019). In this approach, young people's identities are seen as reflexive and transitory, no longer dependent on social factors such as class or local community, but rather variables such as taste, aesthetics, and affectivity (Bennett, 1999; 2011). Diversity and fluidity meant it was difficult for young people to commit to well-defined and delimited subcultures as barriers between subcultures became insignificant due to the recycling of new musical styles and genres (Sweetman, 2013). Issues such as authenticity and rebellion lost their meaning, resulting in a 'supermarket of style' (Polhemus, 1994), in which youths' decisions became individualistic and fragmented (Debies-Carl, 2013).

A new media studies approach argued that digital media served as a reinforcement for trends of identity fragmentation, with online relationships characterized by weak commitments (Turkle, 1995; Castells, 2001; Hall and du Gay, 2011). The concept of neo-tribes, based on the work of Maffesoli (1996) and Bauman (2001) and triggered by Bennett (1999), considered the fluid and unstable fragmentation and individualization in the tastes of young people. Another widely used concept was scene(s), which articulates the local and global dimensions of contemporary dynamics, indicating specific clusters of sociocultural activities that are aggregated by their location (a neighborhood, city, or urban area) and/or type of cultural production (a style of music). The conjugation between music and taste/identity have allowed the exploration of the idea of translocalism, whereby geographically dispersed groups of musical agents engage in collective cultural practices that transcend physical barriers (Xiao and Guerra, 2018). The post-subcultural approach had its heyday in the early 21st century, but there has since been a reaction against it (Blackman and Kempson, 2016; Williams, 2019). Hodkinson (2007) states that subculture is still a relevant concept, and it is necessary to distinguish ephemeral groups from those requiring commitment and continuity. Structural factors continue to be fundamental for the identities, lives, and social practices of young people, as some face limited cultural choices (Withers, 2021).

Connect to the world: the genesis of punk in a Southern European context

To make sense of the subcultural reality of punk in Portugal, we must take into account the particular specificities of the country. Given that most subcultural studies have been conducted in Northern countries, particularly the United States and United Kingdom, we see Wallerstein's (2004) world-system theory, in which the Global South has several specificities, as an important interpretive frame for this task. Wallerstein (2004) defines Portugal as a 'semi-peripheral' country, closer to the nations of the Global South than to the North. The realities of the South imply new epistemologies to analyse the social phenomena of these countries (Santos, 2014; Guerra, 2018; Guerra and Xiao, 2018), with quantitative and qualitative differences in the constitution of youth cultures. Wallerstein (2004) sought to understand the capitalist world-system based on an international division of labor, based on four categories: core, semi-periphery, periphery, and external. The core regions, such as the United States and Northern Europe, gained most from the world capitalist system, with free trade and the various changes that have occurred in the world economies (industrialization, digitalization). The peripheral zones, which correspond to the Global South, historically exported raw materials to the core regions and were expropriated of their capital surplus through unfavorable trade relations with the Global North. The external areas maintained their own economic systems, so were situated outside the capitalist world-system.

Most important for this chapter is the semi-periphery, which presents an intermediate level of development between the core regions and the peripheral zones, often serving as a buffer between them. As Guerra (2020b) shows, this specific position in the world economy, associated with low wages and precariousness, influences the interpretative practices of young Portuguese, including two relating to Portuguese punks.

First, they seek cosmopolitanism, due to four decades of dictatorship, which led to a distancing from the cultural practices of Europe and the United States. Cosmopolitanism here means those who seek authentic experiences in other cultures, characterized by the confluence among global capitalist flows and the growth of cosmopolitan habits due to the internet and social media networks. There is an increasing demand for cultural difference and novelty (Friedman et al, 2015). For Regev (2013), rock music was associated with the idea of cultural modernization. In a semi-peripheral country such as Portugal, this association relates to youths—including punks'—incessant search for everything from abroad. English and American punk are viewed as ways of broadening horizons. Yet cosmopolitanism, like punk, cannot simply be copied. A confluence must occur between global punk scenes and that of Portugal. This cosmopolitanism is combined with local sensibilities in diverse ways, including the use of both local and international languages, lyrics with specific themes, and different production and distribution strategies.

Second, Portuguese punks are adopting DIY practices to respond to the absence of material cultural goods, from clothing to recordings. For Threadgold (2018), DIY cultures in the Global North may involve strategies of *choosing poverty*, where actors opt for marginal jobs that allow them more time and space for their creative passions, and a means of challenging neoliberal logic. DIY strategies in semi-peripheral countries of the South are qualitatively different (Greene, 2016; Guerra, 2018). There is a concern with resistance to capitalist logic, but it is mostly a way of responding to the absence of cultural supply in response to a cultural vacuum. The Portuguese semi-periphery is characterized by low wages and job insecurity. One way to deal with this reality is to adopt DIY strategies and careers.

We must interpret such punk and DIY strategies by recognizing Portugal's sociocultural reality, with its history of a dictatorship from 1933 to 1974 that was marked by censorship and the repression of democracy and liberties (Chilcote, 2010). Portugal's dictatorial regime with political police, the International and State Defense Police (PIDE), arrested and tortured anyone who resisted, even if that resistance was 'only subcultural'. Young people were either in the army, fighting in the Portuguese colonies in Africa, or in clandestine organizations such as the communists. Thus, until 1974 Portugal was not fertile ground for the emergence of youth cultures in the CCCS sense of the term. Even after the 25th of April Revolution that year,[2] the emergence of these cultures was slow. Yet, the revolution did allow greater freedom of cultural experimentation and new capacities to look abroad. It also brought young people into the public sphere, revealing the backwardness of Portugal cultural reality. A profound cultural revolution began, marked by confrontation between cosmopolitanism and social conservatism (Guerra, 2016; 2018; 2020a). Here lies the genesis of punk in Portugal. It was about young people's dissatisfaction with both the cultural orthodoxy and the path taken by the revolution (Abreu et al, 2017). More was needed and punk appeared as one expression of a radical desire for freedom at various levels and the desire to belong to an international movement.

Punk subculture emerged in the 1980s as massive social changes were taking place: entry to the European Economic Community; Portugal's greater openness to foreign countries; urbanization; and the emergence of spaces for youth sociability, such as Rock Rendez Vous[3] (Guerra, 2016; Guerra and Bennett, 2020). Since the 1990s, punk has expanded across the country, with the creation of strong local scenes, such as in Coimbra and Aveiro. The political concerns of Portuguese punks has also expanded. The current importance of punk as a movement, scene, and lifestyle is based on two issues: after the financial crisis of 2011–2016 punk as praxis, especially through DIY strategies, gained importance as a way to circumnavigate financial difficulties; political struggle remains central to punk (Guerra, 2014; 2018).

As a semi-peripheral country, Portugal has a relationship of both closeness to and distance from the core countries that have spawned music subcultures, the United Kingdom and the United States. One prominent aspect is the use of the English language in the names of bands, records, fanzines, and song lyrics. However, Portuguese has again started to dominate since 2008, perhaps showing the vigor of the Portuguese punk scene and its dissemination/ consolidation in local environments. It is important to examine how the actors look at the relationship of Portuguese punk with events on a global scale. We found two dominant positions in our research. The first is a perspective where national punk copied English or American punk, importing a punk sound and aesthetic. We found two sub-dimensions: one where imitation was not negative, since punk would be an "importer of other realities" (Frederico, 49 years, university graduate, translator, Porto) for young Portuguese people; and another that evaluates mimicry negatively— copying something from abroad becomes a small humiliation due to the state of Portuguese musical culture.

The second position looks at Portuguese punk as something different because of the balance between local and global dimensions. Portuguese punk is seen as what it has been able to reappropriate, a consequence of the resources and the social and political needs of each location. This is similar to Regev's (2013) view of the formation of aesthetic cosmopolitanism. This perspective has three sub-dimensions. The first is objectivist, seeing the Portuguese scene as unique because Portugal and England (for example) are different realities. There is a correlation between the small, poor country, with an informal economy and the constitution of a tiny, informal scene. The second sub-dimension considers that this view contains the potential for reinvention. The scarcity of resources serves as a stimulus for a DIY approach (McKay, 1998). The third sub-dimension involves the adaptation of messages and causes defending Portuguese reality. There are reports of the use of pamphlets and flyers from international organizations to disseminate their respective messages in Portugal.

New forms of resistance/activism

With this in mind, we must (re)conceptualize Portuguese punk in terms that move us away from an Anglo-Saxon focus (Guerra, 2014; 2016; 2020b). Drawing on diachronic and synchronic research, we have sought to understand the social, cultural, and symbolic meanings of punk. We focus on virtual sociabilities and their impacts on offline life, especially how they generate new forms of resistance/activism and how these link with the concept of subculture.

Since the 1990s, Portuguese punk, like youth cultures more generally, has been characterized by a liberal use of the internet and social media. The possibilities of accessing new ideas, sounds, and struggles; establishing contacts with groups, bands, or individuals; and establishing musical or historical archives have created new feelings of global belonging. This first became possible through contacts established with scenes outside Portugal, which created a confluence between the local and the global. However, as Portuguese punk becomes part of a global punk community, it remains anchored in a local context.

Of the interviewees, 90 percent had a Facebook account, which they used to get information about the Portuguese scene. There was recognition that social networks are here to stay. These new digital possibilities serve to keep the punk scene alive. Our database of bands active in Portugal between 1977 and 2016 shows that out of a total of 539, 43 percent have a Facebook account. However, 39 percent date back to the decades before 2000, when these services emerged. The virtual global framework thus does not negate the micro and meso scales of social relations. One possibility is the ability to engage in global struggles. Elsewhere (Guerra, 2020b; 2021; Guerra and Silva, 2021), we have analysed how the cultural ideals of May 1968 took a long time to penetrate Portuguese culture. Currently, Portuguese punks are involved with new global struggles (Bennett and Guerra, 2019). For some, these struggles are real, but potentially overwhelming:

'Currently, punk covers all kinds of causes ... punk also defends antifascism and anti-racism but I think it's starting to be an increasingly nihilistic attitude. ... People nowadays are starting to relinquish causes because they think there is nothing they can do and that the only possible solution is to throw it all down and start all over again because ... the world will end.' (Sofia, 23 years, university student, Porto)

For others, social media platforms enable subcultural groups to effectively communicate their struggles with like-minded people around the world:

'Nowadays, in musical terms, with a band, that is to spread a message or alert to a certain message for a certain type of struggle, and you with a computer can transmit a message to thousands of people in completely different places. You can be in Coimbra to spread your message, to communicate with people in Japan, South Africa, Brazil, in a matter of seconds. You can mobilize people to your cause ... or make your band known.' (Belmiro, 37 years, upper secondary education, warehouse manager, Coimbra/London)

In a country still marked by the memory of isolation, the ability to dialogue with and enjoy experiences and novelties from all over the world is highly valued in the Portuguese punk scene. The internet is important to promote bands, but it is also a space in which resistance and activism strategies occur on several fronts (Guerra, 2020b). This interdependence is not linear; not all global struggles (mostly originating in the North American reality) manage to arouse local interest. We can, however, see changes in local causes and struggles. For example, it was through the internet, and the growing visibility of hip hop, that anti-racist struggles became spaces of resistance.

Fishman and Cabral (2016) speak of a profound deficit of political mobilization in Portugal, but there is a shift in civic participation towards new forms of self-mobilization based on 'linking social capital' (Hawkins and Maurer, 2010). In Portugal, these new forms of participation generate associativism. There are no avoidance lifestyles or individualized resistance. In these forms of mobilization, we can see the growth of cosmopolitanism in struggles—for example, #MeToo and #BlackLivesMatter, which are simultaneously important to Portugese punk but extend far beyond it as well.

Music&Riots, an online music magazine/independent record shop has a DIY ethos and an extremely politicized stance. Through its social networks, always in English, we can see how anti-racism marks its daily life. On the other hand, Pedro, a central figure in the Portuguese punk movement, says that on issues like anti-racism or misogyny, punks must choose which side they want to fight on, and work every day to solve the problems:

'I think what happened with #MeToo, Black Lives Matter and so many other things, is that suddenly the lid blows off and people have to choose a side … it's either be part of the problem or part of the solution. … I believe you have to choose a side, and work for things to change. … Enough is enough! We stand in solidarity with Black Lives Matter and those protesting against brutality. The time for change is now and real change requires real action.' (Pedro, 54 years, university degree, musician, Coimbra)

These and other data highlight the reactive character of these global struggles in the contestatory repertoire of Portuguese punk. Portuguese punks rarely start a fight; they have several causes in their repertoire, but when they take these struggles to the 'street', it is generally reactively. Despite the new forms of political participation, Portuguese punks still have a low rate of political participation (Rodrigues, 2015).

Despite the influence of global struggles, we cannot ignore the importance of national or local struggles against issues that affect people's daily lives. Portuguese punk was associated with social mobilizations during the period of financial intervention (2011–2016): the Geração à Rasca movement and the Que se Lixe a Troika! protest. Even currently, in demonstrations against racism in Portugal, they assume a local character:

'It is against racism, against capitalism and against the precarization of work … a significant proportion of the people who were precarious and who secured a significant proportion of the work that kept society going during the quarantine are, in many cases, poor people. … We must be part of a solution to combat unemployment, exploitation and precariousness.' (Sophia, 27 years, university graduate, Lisbon)

The narrative of punk resistance, whether local or global, remains relevant, and resistance is based on individualized revolt against the system (Williams, 2006). Portugal's dictatorial regime reinforced the importance of DIY due to a lack of (sub)cultural production chains. The Portuguese punks of the 1970s and 1980s wanted to imitate the clothing of English and American punks, but had nowhere to buy it, so they made it.

DIY may aim to do something that nothing else does, or meet some material necessity, emerging to circumnavigate dominant logics and procedures. There is pressure to do something, to change things. In a logic of reappropriation of Portuguese punk in relation to the international, the differences were inevitable given the objective difference of the Portuguese cultural and musical situation in relation to the British case. The 'old' Portuguese capacity of 'figuring it out' emerged, forcing the actors to adapt and reinvent processes:

'Doing a lot with little: it was a bit reinvented and it was "do it yourself", with few means, with something to say. ... There was no support, there were no means and ... because of this most people were pushed or let themselves fall into the middle of the punk or hardcore philosophy.' (Luís, 39, secondary education, cameraman, Lisbon, involved in a punk band)

We should see DIY not only as know-how, but as an ethos at the heart of the punk movement to achieve authenticity and independence (Oliveira and Guerra, 2016; Guerra and Quintela, 2020; Guerra and Feixa, 2021). One of the particularities of Portuguese punk is the polyvalence of its members, who are guided by a plurality of assumed positions (Guerra, 2021). This refers both to the exiguity of the scene, which engages members in multiple tasks, especially outside urban centers, and the persistent scarcity of cultural production chains.

The internet has further boosted this DIY logic. New tools generated new possibilities to record music at home and release it globally. Musicians saw a chance to do everything autonomously, thus staying true to one of punk's first causes: the closeness between bands and fans. This new reality has served to accelerate the dynamism of the scene, while simultaneously making the boundary between the virtual and the local more porous (Bennett and Peterson, 2004).

'I think DIY is the best thing that punk gives to people. ... It not only makes people be better; it helps to build a sense of community, cooperation, availability.' (Humberto, 35 years, university degree, record shop owner, Lisbon)

'What is crucial to punk is the strength ... that it has to go beyond the issues. Even if you have no one to sell your records [or] schedule your concerts, you learn to do things yourself ... you realize you will not be forever dependent on others to live.' (Matias, 37 years, musician, bar owner, producer, road manager, Lisbon)

It is difficult not to associate the virtual DIY strategies of the Portuguese punks with the concept of resistance advanced by the CCCS perspective. Several interviewees felt their lives were guided through practices of active resistance toward the dominant society. For many, the idea of resistance is associated with DIY. It is a habitus present among Portuguese punks, a praxis that is literally internalized and externalized (Bourdieu, 2010):

'[You can't] expect an existing structure to help, from a financial point of view, whether to build a business, do an education programme, to be creative or artistic. You have to make your alternatives, spaces of association with other values.' (Arnaldo, 33 years, university degree, designer, Lisbon)

We are in the presence of what Holston (2008) calls 'insurgent citizenship', enhanced by new technologies, creating spheres of resistance and contestation that subvert the patterns of 'productive citizenship'. This is based on the ownership of private property. The DIY strategies of the Portuguese punk scene depart from this idea of citizenship, as their uses of private property break with this paradigm of capital accumulation at the expense of promoting a strong and lasting community (Eversley, 2014).

The mobilization of a DIY know-how and ethos is important for the emergence of DIY careers (Haenfler, 2017; Reitsamer and Prokop, 2018). With the advent of the culturalization of the economy, we see the reinterpretation of economic principles, with increasing importance given to autonomy, authenticity, and creativity, which are valorized by DIY. Many members manage to translate their subcultural capital into a professional trajectory (Hesmondhalgh and Baker, 2011). The forms of DIY resistance presented by our interviewees follow three dimensions: micro, meso, and macro (Haenfler, 2004). We can see the macro in Matias' words, where resistance is a struggle against hegemonic society and capitalism to achieve social change (Haenfler, 2019).

Regarding the meso dimension, visible in the words of Matias and Arnaldo, we have a more specifically DIY ethos—the ability to do things with a scarcity of resources. This counter-hegemonic logic is essential for the creation and perpetuation of the scenes. The main function of this dimension is to solidify the frame of reference of a subculture to frame macro moments of resistance (Moore and Roberts, 2009; Williams, 2009). The micro dimension, finally, refers us to the field of individual practices and the day-to-day lives of punk scene members.

Nobody left! The necessary redefinition of subcultural belonging

The internet has enabled a real democratization of access to information for Portuguese punks. Another advantage lies in the new dissemination possibilities for bands. Several musicians stated that they use the internet for this purpose. The third advantage deals with the conditions of creation and musical production. New resources and tools make it possible for practically anyone to play and even record from home, dramatically widening the horizons of possibility for agents of the underground scene.

Similarly, the relationship of Portuguese punk with international punk is a conflicted one, full of advances and retreats. If some interviewees look at Portuguese punk as an imitation (albeit a gateway to a new universe of the possible), others focus on the reappropriation of punk for the national and local context. This reality is characteristic of semi-peripheral countries and is further accentuated by the urgency of the internet. The punk way of being still seems exotic, and continues to disturb a society that, in punk eyes, is too conservative. For this reason, Portuguese punk identity implies a regular attachment to a wider, more cosmopolitan world.

Yet two factors are key to understanding the tension between Portugal and the global punk reality. The first is the search for cosmopolitanism via the English language. If you want to be publicized on social networks, you must use English. The importance of the internet for the Portuguese punk scene is also explained by the search for a cosmopolitanism denied until 1974 and difficult to access until the 1990s. In contemporary Portugal, we see the offer of a plurality of musical genres that corresponds to the existence of omnivorous cultural tastes (Guerra, 2020a). Therefore, one of the particularities of the Portuguese punk, cosmopolitanism, would not be possible without the extended and intense use of the internet and social networks.

Another characteristic of national punk is the existence of DIY strategies of a qualitatively different character to that of the Global North. Threadgold (2018) mentions poverty choice, which implies more than one possibility. Global cultural and musical fields are extensive and robust, but the situation is different in Portugal, where such a thing is still not consolidated, there are scarce resources, and no critical mass for the intensive development of an alternative music scene. The youngest also face obstacles such as low salaries and precariousness in accessing the labor market, and there are high rates of youth unemployment. This makes the DIY option appealing for those choosing a musical or cultural career. It is not a 'poverty choice', but rather an escape from the poverty faced by many Portuguese.

The internet has boosted these DIY strategies, so it is unsurprising that Portuguese actors have seized on the possibilities of the internet. Yet the actors don't use DIY to resist; it is an art of existence. Social networks are ubiquitous in the punk scene. This has led to a sense of belonging, allowing contact between members of the punk community to last beyond more active involvement. This is more important as individuals and musical forms age (Bennett, 2013), and was cited as a common advantage by respondents. Others valued the possibility of communication between geographically dispersed scenes because it facilitates the sense of community beyond time and distance. Thus, in line with Hodkinson's (2003) work, while we recognize the capacity of the internet to enable greater cultural fluidity, here it reinforces a punk sense of belonging. Basically, the internet serves to reinforce a sense of belonging, identity, and shared space (Williams, 2006; 2011).

Conclusion

So, should we speak of subcultures or post-subcultures? The Portuguese case indicates that we can go beyond these concepts. Cultural homogeneity does not apply to the Portuguese reality, marked by the appropriation of a cosmopolitan capital. Yet the idea of a simple symbolic struggle, in which nothing changes, does not take into account the profound resistance at the heart of the Portuguese scene, whether at the level of DIY practices or in the forms of political self-mobilization.

Political self-mobilization may be somewhat fragmented when based on the internet and social media networks compared to traditional ways of doing politics, but this does not negate more institutionalized forms of activism, such as the constitution of new associations. On the other hand, we have a scene marked by a strong cosmopolitanism, through the conjugation of very diverse styles and genres due to the possibilities afforded by the internet. Yet the vast majority of actors still clearly define themselves as punks. Despite all the fluidity and fragmentation, actors continue to look for anchors in their lives—in this case, punk—to deal with uncertainty.

The relationship between local and global, influenced by the ubiquitous penetration of new media technologies, is essential to the Portuguese reality. Punk appeals to a global community, but all punk communities can only be fully realized in the 'local'. The Portuguese scene illustrates this reality: it is a local scene, with multiple 'internal' scenes, but always looking at the global context. Our data show that punk's strength is its ability to adapt, enhanced by the internet. Portugal adapted to the reality of the 1970s and 1980s through a DIY logic and by seeking international novelty; it has now adapted to the era of the internet and social media networks. We saw the growth of participation in social and community movements (Miles, 2015), with local and global anchorages, from the fight for decent housing to the current struggles of #MeToo and #BlackLivesMatter. Finally, we found a confluence, whereby the physical and the virtual intersect and reinforce each other.

Notes

[1] The project 'Keep it simple, make it fast! Prolegomenons and punk scenes, a road to Portuguese contemporaneity (1977–2012) (PTDC/CS-SOC/118830/2010)' (KISMIF) is funded by FEDER (in English, European Regional Development Fund (ERDF)) through the COMPETE Operational Program from the Foundation for Science and Technology (FCT). Project details can be found at https://www.kismifcommunity.com. This publication was supported by the FCT within the scope of UIDB/00727/2020.

[2] Also known as the Carnation Revolution, this military *coup d'état*, followed by a social movement, overthrew the dictatorship and began the process of democratization.

[3] A well-known club in the 1980s and 1990s, and a major promoter of alternative rock in Portugal.

References

Abreu, P., Santos Silva, A., Guerra, P., Oliveira, A. and Moreira, T. (2017) 'The Social Place of Portuguese Punk Scene: An Itinerary of the Social Profiles of its Protagonists', *Volume!*, 1(14): 103–126.

Bauman, Z. (2001) *The Individualized Society*, Cambridge: Polity Press.

Bennett, A. (1999) 'Subcultures or Neo-Tribes? Rethinking the Relationship between Youth, Style and Musical Taste', *Sociology*, 33(3): 599–617.

Bennett, A. (2011) 'The Post-Subcultural Turn: Some Reflections 10 Years On', *Journal of Youth Studies*, 14(5): 493–506.

Bennett, A. (2013) *Music, Style, and Aging: Growing Old Disgracefully?*, Philadelphia: Temple University Press.

Bennett, A. and Peterson, R.A. (eds) (2004) *Music Scenes: Local, Translocal and Virtual*, Nashville: Vanderbilt University Press.

Bennett, A. and Guerra, P. (eds) (2019) *Underground Music Scenes and DIY Cultures*, Oxford: Routledge.

Blackman, S. and Kempson, M. (eds) (2016) *The Subcultural Imagination: Theory, Research, and Reflexivity in Contemporary Youth Cultures*, Oxford: Taylor & Francis.

Bourdieu, P. (2010) *Distinction*, London: Routledge.

Castells, M. (2001) *The Internet Galaxy*, Oxford: Oxford University Press.

Chilcote, R.H. (2010) *The Portuguese Revolution: State and Class in the Transition to Democracy*, Lanham: Rowman & Littlefield.

Debies-Carl, J.S. (2013) 'Are the Kids Alright? A Critique and Agenda for Taking Youth Cultures Seriously', *Social Science Information*, 52(1): 110–133.

Eversley, M. (2014) 'Space and Governance in the Baltimore DIY Punk Scene: An Exploration of the Postindustrial Imagination and the Persistence of Whiteness as Property', BA thesis, Wesleyan University.

Fishman, R. and Cabral, M.V. (2016) 'Socio-Historical Foundations of Citizenship Practice: After Social Revolution in Portugal', *Theory and Society*, 45(6): 531–553.

Friedman, S., Savage, M., Hanquinet, L. and Miles, A. (2015) 'Cultural Sociology and New Forms of Distinction', *Poetics*, 53: 1–8.

Greene, S. (2016) 'Peruvian Punk as a Global Means of Underground Production', *Popular Music and Society*, 39(3): 286–300.

Guerra, P. (2014) 'Punk, Expectations, Breaches and Metamorphoses: Portugal, 1977–2012', *Critical Arts*, 28(1): 111–122.

Guerra, P. (2016) 'Keep it Rocking: The Social Space of Portuguese Alternative Rock (1980–2010)', *Journal of Sociology*, 52(4): 615–630.

Guerra, P. (2018) 'Raw Power: Punk, DIY and Underground Cultures as Spaces of Resistance in Contemporary Portugal', *Cultural Sociology*, 12(2): 241–259.

Guerra, P. (2020a) 'Under-Connected: Youth Subcultures, Resistance and Sociability in the Internet Age', in K. Gildart, A. Gough-Yates, S. Lincoln, B. Osgerby, L. Robinson, J. Street, P. Webb and M. Worley (eds) *Hebdige and Subculture in the Twenty-First Century: Through the Subcultural Lens*, London: Palgrave Macmillan, pp 207–230.

Guerra, P. (2020b) 'Iberian Punk, Cultural Metamorphoses, and Artistic Differences in the Post-Salazar and Post-Franco Eras', in G. McKay and G. Arnold (eds) *The Oxford Handbook of Punk Rock*, Oxford: Oxford University Press, pp 1–19.

Guerra, P. (2021) 'So Close Yet So Far: DIY Cultures in Portugal and Brazil', *Cultural Trends*, 30(2): 122–138.

Guerra, P. and Xiao, J. (2018) 'A Comparison between Portuguese and Chinese Punks: A Genealogy, Style, and Space', in J. Xiao (ed) *Punk Culture in Contemporary China*, Singapore: Palgrave Macmillan, pp 177–200.

Guerra, P. and Bennett, A. (2020) 'Punk Portugal, 1977–2012: A Preliminary Genealogy', *Popular Music History*, 13(3): 215–234.

Guerra, P. and Quintela, P. (2020) 'Fast, Furious and Xerox: Punk, Fanzines and DIY Cultures in a Global World', in P. Guerra and P. Quintela (eds) *Punk, Fanzines and DIY Cultures in a Global World*, London: Palgrave Macmillan, pp 1–15.

Guerra, P. and Feixa, C. (2021) 'Not Just Holidays in the Sun: Mapping, Measuring and Analysing DIY Cultures Impact across Cities in the Global South', in R. Campos and J. Nofre (eds) *Exploring Ibero-American Youth Cultures in the 21st Century: Creativity, Resistance and Transgression in the City*, London: Palgrave Macmillan, pp 243–258.

Guerra, P. and Silva, E.A. (2021) 'Batalhas sem heróis: as metamorfoses do punk na sociedade brasileira contemporânea', *Revista Sapiência*, 10(5): 1–24.

Haenfler, R. (2004) 'Rethinking Subcultural Resistance: Core Values of the Straightedge Movement', *Journal of Contemporary Ethnography*, 33(4): 406–436.

Haenfler, R. (2017) 'The Entrepreneurial (Straight) Edge: How Participation in DIY Music Cultures Translates to Work and Careers', *Cultural Sociology*, 12(2): 174–192.

Haenfler, R. (2019) 'Changing the World One Virgin at a Time: Abstinence Pledgers, Lifestyle Movements, and Social Change', *Social Movement Studies*, 18(4): 425–443.

Hall, S. and du Gay, P. (eds) (2011) *Questions of Cultural Identity*, London: SAGE.

Hawkins, R.L. and Maurer, K. (2010) 'Bonding, Bridging and Linking: How Social Capital Operated in New Orleans Following Hurricane Katrina', *British Journal of Social Work*, 40(6): 1777–1793.

Hebdige, D. (1979) *Subculture: The Meaning of Style*, London: Methuen.

Hesmondhalgh, D. (2005) 'Subcultures, Scenes or Tribes? None of the Above', *Journal of Youth Studies*, 8(1): 21–40.

Hesmondhalgh, D. and Baker, S. (2011) *Creative Labour: Media Work in Three Cultural Industries*, London: Routledge.

Hodkinson, P. (2003) '"Net.Goth": Internet Communication and (Sub)cultural Boundaries', in D. Muggleton and R. Weinzierl (eds) *The Post-Subcultures Reader*, Oxford: Berg, pp 285–298.

Hodkinson, P. (2007) 'Youth Cultures: A Critical Outline of Key Debates', in P. Hodkinson and W. Deicke (eds) *Youth Cultures: Scenes, Subcultures and Tribes*, London: Routledge, pp 1–23.

Holston, J. (2008) *Insurgent Citizenship: Disjunctions of Democracy and Modernity in Brazil*, Princeton: Princeton University Press.

Maffesoli, M. (1996) *The Time of the Tribes: The Decline of Individualism in the Mass Society*, London: SAGE.

McIntyre, L. (2018) *Post-Truth*, Cambridge, MA: MIT Press.

McKay, G. (ed) (1998) *DIY Culture: Party and Protest in Nineties Britain*, London: Verso.

Miles, S. (2015) 'Young People, Consumer Citizenship and Protest: The Problem with Romanticizing the Relationship to Social Change', *Young*, 23(2): 101–115.

Moore, R. and Roberts, M. (2009) 'Do-it-Yourself Mobilization: Punk and Social Movements', *Mobilization*, 14(3): 273–291.

Muggleton, D. (2000) *Inside Subculture: The Postmodern Meaning of Style*, Oxford: Berg.

Oliveira, A. and Guerra, P. (2016) '"I Make the Product": Do-it-Yourself Ethics in the Construction of Musical Careers in the Portuguese Alternative Rock Scene', in P. Guerra and P. Costa (eds) *Redefining Art Worlds in the Late Modernity*, Porto: University of Porto, pp 135–148.

Polhemus, T. (1994) *Streetstyle: From Sidewalk to Catwalk*, London: Thames & Hudson.

Regev, M. (2013) *Pop-Rock Music: Aesthetic Cosmopolitanism in Late Modernity*, Cambridge: Polity Press.

Reitsamer, R. and Prokop, R. (2018) 'Keepin' it Real in Central Europe: The DIY Rap Music Careers of Male Hip Hop Artists in Austria', *Cultural Sociology*, 12(2): 193–207.

Rodrigues, C. (2015) 'Participation and the Quality of Democracy in Portugal', *Revista Crítica de Ciências Sociais*, 108: 75–94.

Sandbrook, D. (2007) *White Heat: A History of Britain in the Swinging Sixties*, London: Abacus.

Sandbrook, D. (2011) *State of Emergency: Britain, 1970–1974*, Harmondsworth: Penguin.

Santos, B.S. (2014) *Epistemologies of the South: Justice against Epistemicide*, Boulder: Paradigm Press.

Sweetman P. (2013) 'Structure, Agency, Subculture: The CCCS, Resistance through Rituals, and "Post-Subcultural" Studies', *Sociological Research Online*, 18(4): 227–236.

Thornton, S. (1995) *Club Cultures: Music, Media and Subcultural Capital*, Cambridge: Polity Press.

Threadgold, S. (2018) 'Creativity, Precarity and Illusio: DIY Cultures and "Choosing Poverty"', *Cultural Sociology*, 12(2): 156–173.

Turkle, S. (1995) *Life on the Screen: Identity in the Age of the Internet*, London: Phoenix.

Wallerstein, I. (2004) *World-Systems Analysis: An Introduction*, Durham, NC: Duke University Press.

Williams, J.P. (2006) 'Authentic Identities: Straightedge Subculture, Music, and the Internet', *Journal of Contemporary Ethnography*, 35(2): 173–200.

Williams, J.P. (2009) 'The Multidimensionality of Resistance in Youth-Subcultural Studies', *Resistance Studies Magazine*, 2(1): 20–33.

Williams, J.P. (2011) *Subcultural Theory: Traditions and Concepts*, London: Polity Press.

Williams, J.P. (2019) 'Subculture's Not Dead! Checking the Pulse of Subculture Studies through a Review of "Subcultures, Popular Music and Political Change" and "Youth Cultures and Subcultures—Australian Perspectives"', *Young*, 27(1): 89–105.

Withers, P. (2021) 'Ramallah Ravers and Haifa Hipsters: Gender, Class, and Nation in Palestinian Popular Culture', *British Journal of Middle Eastern Studies*, 48(1): 94–113.

Xiao, J. and Guerra, P. (2018) 'Introduction: Context, Method and Theoretical Framework', in J. Xiao (ed) *Punk Culture in Contemporary China*, Singapore: Palgrave Macmillan, pp 1–24.

5

Still Crazy After All Those Years: A Trajectory of Discourses on Youth Subcultures in Korea, from Exclusion to Recognition to Legitimization

Hyunjoon Shin

Subcultural activism: a connection that stopped?

The impetus behind this chapter was my desire to rethink the relevance of *subcultural activism*, a concept developed in my previous work on indie music and the subcultures associated with it in South Korea (hereafter 'Korea') and in East Asia (hereafter 'Asia') more broadly (Shin, 2018; 2019). But far less attention was paid to my subcultural research than to my research on so-called K-pop music and related mainstream pop culture (Shin, 2009; 2016). I had expected that the concept of subcultural activism would precisely capture the ideas and practices of a translocal network of young radical activists in Asia. My primary goal in this writing is to challenge the binary thinking on subculture and activism—that subcultures exist only as cultural phenomenon and have little to do with politics, whereas activism is purely political and has no relevance to culture. This argument, however, comes from an Asian scholar who has felt social, cultural, and psychological pressures to interpret music cultural phenomena using such a dichotomy. It may not ring true to other scholars in other contexts.

To my knowledge, there was no literature that used the concept of subcultural activism at the time my 2018 paper was published. Only afterward did I find it mentioned, albeit with lack of rigorous conceptualization, in another study (Chiavacci and Obinger, 2018). This may be due to assumptions that 'subcultural activism' is too marginal or insignificant to become a serious agent of social and political changes in the Korean context. The concept may even end up being a short-lived misnomer. Regardless, I still believe that the cases reported in my research are examples of 'subcultures', arguably misperceived as non-active, and of 'activism', seemingly misconstrued as non-cultural. To understand the lack of engagement with subcultural activism, I now believe that there is a need to take a broader view of different conceptualizations of subculture by multiple actors in different periods and places across Asia. Doing so will hopefully provide some tentative answers to questions that arise from the concept's lukewarm reception, namely: How has subculture been used as a concept to make sense of music-related Asian youth cultures; and why has subculture as a concept been dissociated with political activism in Asian contexts? To consider these questions within the Korean context, I will look at the debates on subcultures in different periods before moving on to the current issue. To that end, I will first examine how the subculture has been conceived, perceived, and contested in Asia and then will delve into details about the Korean cases.

Bringing on an inter-Asia frame

A lot of ink has been spilled about the evolution of the concepts and theories of youth subcultures in academia. Rather than repeating what's already been widely discussed, I will mention some well-known Western studies in this area of research that I have cited in my previous work, including Hall and Jefferson (1993 [1976]), Hebdige (1979), Bennett (1999; 2011), Thornton (1995), Maffesoli (1996), and Muggleton and Weinzierl (2003), as well as some recent studies that show diverging views that blurred or reconsidered the lines between subculture and post-subculture (Williams, 2011; 2019; Hodkinson, 2016). It is worth noting that the relations between these concepts have not been hotly debated in Asia and that concepts such as post-subculture, subcultural capital, neo-tribe, and so on are still rather alien in the region, or at least have not gone beyond academic attention.

Here, I want to briefly review the temporal trajectories, current terminologies, and generic characteristics of the subculture concept. I will focus on Japan and China, not only because they are the two best-known Asian countries to the world but also because they are often perceived as quite dissimilar in many aspects. Moreover, Japan and China had arguably forged their distinct subcultures before the concept of 'youth subcultures', as proposed by the Centre for Contemporary Cultural Studies (CCCS), was introduced, accommodated, or even recognized by academics in those countries. The most well-known examples of subcultures that took the path of so-called 'spontaneous evolution'[1] would be *otaku* in Japan and *liumang* in China.[2] Both were formed during the 1980s and almost became mainstream in the 1990s, before Western subcultural theories were commonly cited by Japanese or Chinese scholars.

It would not be fair to make national stereotypes of Japanese *otaku* and Chinese *liumang* since diverse types of subcultures have emerged (and disappeared) in the two countries. Yet, it cannot be denied that the dominant representations of the two have prevailed. The former is represented by an introspective and obsessive subject, while the latter by an extroverted and frivolous one. Genre-wise, manga and anime for *otaku* and literature and cinema for *liumang* had crucial importance for subcultural membership. Despite the differences, both had their own alluring powers to (mostly male) youths and constructed niche markets in the late 20th century, though neither remained fashionable after the millennium. These and other youth (sub) cultures in Asia have had their distinct trajectories and their own ecologies, economies, and, if one may say, politics. Although I do not deny the influences from 'outside' (that is, the West) in the formation of subcultures in Japan and China, influences alone cannot explain their complex evolution. The fact that the words *otaku* and *liumang* are not translatable into European languages would be one piece of evidence.

It is hard to say when or how subculture as a concept was imported or transmitted from the West (more precisely, the US and UK) to Asia. But it is worth comparing the translation of subculture, especially the prefix 'sub'. It has become *ya* (亞: secondary) in Chinese and *sabu* (サブ: sub) in Japanese. The difference, however, goes beyond the fact that the former is translated while the latter is transliterated. In China, it was in the 1990s that 'the word for subculture (*yawenhua* 亞文化) only began to be fitfully used by sociologists' (Clark, 2012, p 3). Clark traces the histories of *qingnian yawenhua* (青年亞文化) back to the practices among educated youth (知青) during the Chinese Cultural Revolution in the 1960s–1970s. Some might think that his interpretation of Chinese subculture is a far stretch, but his interpretation resists the dominant perception that subcultures in Asia were imported from or should be seen as influenced by the liberal West.

Before *yawenhua* began to be employed in China, Japan had already finished its transliteration and adjusted it to the Japanese phonetic system into *sabukaruchā* (サブカルチャー). However, the connotation of *sabukaruchā* as a Japanese word is not the same as that of subculture as an English word. According to some scholars (Ōtsuka and Ueno, 1998; Yoda, 2000), *sabukaruchā*, especially *otaku* culture, had been equated with postmodern culture in the West rather than with subculture as defined by scholarship from Birmingham's CCCS. In a similar vein, some research on youth cultures in China during the 2000s indicates that *yawenhua* in China had become like 'neo-tribe' or 'post-subculture' (Wang, 2005; Drissel, 2012).

I will not go deeper into the cases of Japan and China. What should be noted is that the subcultural turn in Asia was closely associated with the postmodern turn, although different countries were impacted differently due to unique different temporalities and spatialities. The Korean case has many differences from Japan and China, and one of them is its terminology. Koreans kept using the word *hawimunhwa* (하위문화/下位文化),³ literally meaning low-ranking culture. Despite the dark and inferior nuances that presuppose a conventional cultural hierarchy, it is still widely used in academic discourses in Korea.

I now turn to Korea beginning in the 1990s, during which cultural studies as an academic discipline and the concept of subculture attached to it were introduced. Hopefully, my discussion will implicitly continue the comparison with Japan and China because the subcultural turn as well as the postmodern turn took place, though unevenly, during a relatively short period across different parts of Asia. In Korea, it is during the introduction, appropriation, and transformation of cultural studies that *hawimunhwa* became the dominant or 'right' translation of subculture. Most of the written materials I will examine belong to subcultures' intellectual discourses. Yet, I will not pay too much attention to purely academic papers, which had limited impact on popular understandings. Due to the conditions of knowledge production in Korea, intellectuals have included professional journalists and independent critics as well as academic researchers. Therefore, I will take those journalistic discourses that had relative influence on common conceptions seriously. Quite a few sources that I draw from can be classified as not-too-academic but also not-too-journalistic.

A tough life of *hawimunhwa*: from exclusion to recognition

Korea's democracy began in 1987, one year before hosting the 24th Summer Olympic Games in Seoul. It should be noted that the sociopolitical conditions of Korea in the 1990s were quite different from those of Japan and China. The 1990s was the post-bubble period in Japan and the post-Tiananmen period in China. In contrast to those gloomy social atmospheres, Korea was in a relatively bright mood. In a way, it is understandable that Korean youths in the 1990s, precisely from 1988 to 1997, seemed to forget politics, histories, and everything else heavy and serious altogether. The cultural liberalization and economic affluence associated with political democratization were completely 'new' to Koreans. Likewise, youths cultivated a new culture for themselves and received a very generic name from mass media: 'New Generation'. It is this generation that was framed through the lens of subculture in the 1990s, but with much less severe criticisms than subcultures in the 1970s–1980s had received.

However, the New Generation was not the first case to be interpreted as a youth subculture, and it might be helpful to revisit the debates on 'youth culture', another generic concept for the cultural formation of Korea's equivalent of baby boomers in the 1970s. As I have written elsewhere (Shin, 2021), youth culture was hotly debated in the early to mid-1970s. On the one hand, liberal critics and journalists defended youth culture as 'anti-elitist, self-expressionist, anti-commercialist, a culture from below, a culture against standardization' (Kim, 1974a).[4] On the other hand, conservative cultural elites criticized youth culture as foreign, decadent, and un-national (see Kim and Shin, 2010). Neither of those publications explicitly used the word subculture.

Those who used the word subculture—*hawimunhwa*—were sociologists, for whom the meaning was largely negative and derogatory. For example, Yim Hŭi-sŏp argued that 'youth culture in Korea is closer to a subculture rather than a counterculture because there is no youth culture that directly challenges the core value of establishment culture or attempts to institutionalize new values'.[5] Another sociologist, Han Wan-sang, expressed disappointment with the evolution of Korean youth culture by saying that 'youth culture should be a wholesome counterculture', but that 'youth culture [in Korea] is being misguided into a low-ranking pop culture.'[6]

From these two US-educated sociologists, subculture was framed as 'merely' a pop culture phenomenon that lacked the 'challenging' or 'wholesome' values of a youth (counter)culture. I cannot and will not evaluate the concept of 'wholesome counterculture' as it appears self-contradictory or oxymoronic at best. However, it should be noted that the interpretation of subculture as low-grade pop culture shows the elitist view of progressive intellectuals at the time. Defining subculture as a 'misguided' form of youth culture, therefore, evaded serious attention, not least, theoretical articulation. As a result, subculture became excluded from the academic discussion on youth culture.

The debate forcibly stopped due to the tightening of the right-wing dictatorship after 1975 under the international political climate entangled with the 'Fall of Saigon'. Youth culture was too much of a romantic subject of public debate or intellectual discussion under the harsh, sometimes bloody, political repression. The political condition explains why 20 years passed before the discussion on youth (sub)culture was revived, during which time Korean society experienced significant changes. As a basic fact, the gross domestic product per capita was less than US$600 in 1974 while it skyrocketed to more than US$10,000 in the 1990s. It is worth noting that Korean baby boomers were too poor to become subcultural in the Western sense, let alone countercultural. Although they could form their own cultures in a vernacular way, they hardly were the children of affluence.

It was the 1990s when Korea began to witness the children of affluence, arguably for the first time in modern history. The vanguard of the New Generation, the children of the super-rich, was specifically dubbed as the 'orange tribe' or 'Apkujŏng clan'. Oranges, a very pricey imported fruit at that time, stood for luxury and Korean-American returnees, while Apkujŏng was and is the most affluent neighborhood in the Kangnam (aka Gangnam) area of Seoul. Hedonistic lifestyles combined with conspicuous consumption overrepresented the generation, and the mass media frequently exposed these as 'immoral' behaviors in the early 1990s.

It was in 1992 when associating or dissociating subculture with 'tribe' appeared in newspapers and magazines. One journalistic article stated, 'it is too early to say that the Apkujŏng clan has constructed its own authentic subculture' by quoting an interview with a young sociologist, who instead argued that 'a class culture [that is, high-class culture or bourgeois culture] is burgeoning'.[7] It is safe to say that the interviewee was one of the Marxist-influenced progressive sociologists, whatever the branch is, who dominated the critical, progressive, and left-leaning theoretical discourses that contributed to the anti-dictatorship social movement throughout the 1980s. Nevertheless, that view was challenged by a seminal book *New Generation, Do as You Want* (Mimesis, 1993), published in 1993. The book, written by an ex-student movement group, declared an alliance with the New Generation.

As its provocative rhetoric and visual image strategies had shocking effects on the 'old left' activists and intellectuals, it prompted debates around what New Generation meant. Among them, two publications are worth mentioning. One is the special issue of *Economy and Society* (no 21, spring 1994) and the other is a co-authored volume entitled *New Generation: Chaos and Order* (March 1994). They two take contrasting approaches in interpreting New Generation culture. The issue of *Economy and Society*, based on Marxist sociology, was critical of New Generation culture at both theoretical and practical levels, while the latter, based on popular cultural criticism, partly embraced the cultural identity of the New Generation.

In the former, none of the five contributing authors explicitly mentioned subculture. Rather, and like the previously mentioned interview, they framed New Generation culture not as youth subculture, but rather as a class-based consumer culture within Korea's then-new mode of capitalist accumulation. In the words of one author, New Generation culture was formed and reproduced by the 'exminfordsion strategy of capital by the intensification of consumption and the strategy of the commodification of culture' (Joo, 1994, p 90). Implicit in that argument were some shortcomings of old-school Marxism, such as the economic determinism of culture, the primacy of production over consumption, and so on.

In the latter, the framing of New Generation culture was more nuanced, and the concept of subculture—*hawimunhwa*—was explicitly used. While the authors were critical of equating New Generation culture with the orange tribe, they embraced the idea that it was 'a kind of subculture onto which conscious and unconscious desire resisting against the repressive education system and competitive value-regime are projected' (Hong, 1994, p 236). Further, they recognized 'that the subculture is differently located on the spectrum whose poles run from passive accommodation to explicit resistance' (Hong, 1994, p 236). Though Hong's argument was not so sophisticated, the quotes show a specific way of recognizing subculture in mid-1990s Korea. His focus is the possibility of resistance inside popular culture and subculture is the name of the possibility.

In the same year, Kim Chang-nam submitted his PhD thesis and published it as a monograph (Kim, 1994). At that time, a home-grown cultural studies school in the name of critical communication studies was its own kind of 'subculture' in media and communication studies circles. While Marxist sociology denounced New Generation culture as falling short of an 'authentic' subculture, critical communication studies interpreted New Generation and other relevant cultures at the time as youth subcultures, based on their readings of CCCS scholarship. Their mission was to recognize popular culture as the object of serious studies rather than criticizing its consumerist and capitalist characters. Popular culture criticism in *New Generation: Chaos and Order* was largely under the influence of critical communication studies.

These attempts to conceptualize New Generation culture as subculture were not without controversies inside media and communication studies. Some argued that New Generation culture was 'consumerist' (Kang, 1999) and that the view that supported the culture was 'populist' (Lee, 2000). However, to my knowledge, the criticism missed the point because those who employed the concept subculture did not uncritically celebrate consumerism and populism. Rather, there were other reasons to be reluctant to think of the New Generation culture through the concept of subculture. One of them is that the New Generation had become too successful to be called a subculture. At least after 1994, the cultural icons of New Generation culture were fully incorporated into the commercial mainstream and occupied television screens and radio airwaves. The most famous icon of New Generation culture is undoubtedly the dance pop or rap dance trio, Seo Taiji and Boys, who ambitiously fused the then-latest international genres of heavy metal, hip hop, and house/techno. Despite the lip-synch performances on TV shows, though with live dancing, the group constructed its own authenticity thanks to the messages and images that were perceived as rebellion or resistance against the establishment.[8] The subject of one chapter in *New Generation: Chaos and Order* (Hong, 1994) was none other than Seo Taiji and Boys.

Taking advantage of the passage of time, I would like to give answers to some issues raised by different interpretations of New Generation culture and youth subculture in the mid-1990s. Yet, I would like to point out that what I have written as subculture in this section is *hawimunhwa*, a translated word.

First, the adoption of *hawimunhwa*, literally translated as low-ranking culture and used as the Korean equivalent of subculture, was often unnecessarily misperceived as the antonym of high culture. Thus, subculture was under incessant criticism by the cultural conservatives, prestigious elites, and policy makers who still stubbornly thought that New Generation culture fell short of high culture. That is why the scholars and critics of critical communication studies adopted *hawimunhwa* for their struggles of recognizing popular culture in general despite the risk of being labeled as 'populist'. Those who benefited from these struggles were the New Generation culture's popular icons that employed the strategies of performing (that is, faking) subcultural resistance against the 'old and boring' high culture. It worked pretty effectively. The protest against cultural conservatism that had long suppressed free expression in popular culture was a sign of the times that was widespread in the 1990s.

Second, the celebration of *hawimunhwa* among the 'populists', however, was never homogeneous. Considering that popular culture in general and particularly subculture had been harshly criticized as commercial, capitalist, and consumerist by student activists and intellectuals during the 1970s–1980s, subcultures could not be celebrated without some reservations in the academia. In contrast, a group of independent critics and writers were much bolder at celebrating the New Generation culture in the name of *hawimunhwa*. Though theoretically poor and flimsy, they constructed the myth of rebellious, creative, and authentic popular culture. They made a loose alliance with some New Generation cultural icons and helped them be branded as rebellious artists. The artists hailed as the icons of New Generation skillfully performed anti-commercial gestures and displayed artistic autonomy. Seo Taiji and Boys was just the smartest case of them.

Third, it was believed, despite all the reservations, that New Generation culture challenged the myth of a homogeneous national Korean culture (*minjok munhwa*). As cultural nationalism had been shared both by the right-wing conservatives and the left-wing progressives for such a long time, *hawimunhwa* as a concept and a practice cut across overpoliticized and overideologized divisions held until the 1980s. By talking about subcultures in the plural sense, the idea that different cultures could co-exist was established as a consensus in the name of cultural diversity as well as openness, tolerance, inclusiveness, and so on. Regardless of whether using the word subculture explicitly or not, cultural diversity has become a norm in the official discussion of culture and arts since the late 1990s.

All these changes in recognizing popular culture, particularly youth subcultures, coincided with the moment when Korean independent music and arts made their collective voice publicly heard in the mid-1990s. While it was (mis)perceived as a continuation of New Generation culture in its earlier stage, 'indie culture'—*indimunhwa*—a generic title but with a specific meaning, quickly replaced the label New Generation and established itself as a darling term in public discourses. Based in Hongdae, a western part of metropolitan Seoul, the indie culture's artistic creativity, anti-commercialist attitude, and spontaneous characteristics went beyond all the reservations that had disqualified the New Generation culture in the specific sense as a subculture. Although the punk community was specially conceived as a subculture by academic researchers (Epstein, 2000; Epstein and Dunbar, 2007; Shin, 2011), diverse music genres as well as other diverse arts genres prospered in the area during a period of approximately ten years around the turn of the millennium.

By the language of cultural criticism and cultural studies in the West, Hongdae would have been described as a haven for bohemian subculture before hipsters and gentrifiers took over the area. In the late 1990s and the early 2000s, before musicians and artists recognized that they were, contrary to their will, inadvertently performing the role of urban pioneers, Hongdae had been perceived, conceived, and experienced as the pivotal place of Korean subcultures. Compared to the debate on New Generation culture in the early 1990s, indie culture was not subject to much criticism. It was because the main actors of indie culture looked uncompromisingly rebellious, alternative, and creative. Cultural critics and scholars widely supported the culture without much reservation. Put simply, it was the closest to the widely accepted definition of subculture (in the CCCS sense). The reservations toward New Generation culture in the early 1990s as a subculture, such as upper-class culture, commercial success, and artistic inauthenticity, did not apply to the indie culture, a broader term for subcultures based in Hongdae.

There emerged a radical branch of subculture in the early to mid-2000s. To illustrate this, let me quote one interview with a punk rocker in *Punk Anarchist* (2006), an amateur documentary: "[W]e play a role of the lowest-ranking culture even in youth subculture." His words can be interpreted to mean that he belongs to the underclass culture and the (under)class is "the most vulnerable one [class] inside the system". More i'mportantly, it shows that he was familiar with the word subculture. Moreover, I understand it as an orthodox or conventional understanding of subculture because the punk rocker associated the subculture to which he belonged with the class position in the society. He and his band members strongly identified themselves with the most radical branch of punk subculture, so-called crust punk. This interpretation of subculture by the punk rocker is radically different from the interpretation of the New Generation culture by critical communication studies in the mid-1990s. Nevertheless, when the punk rocker expressed his view of subculture, punk as a subculture was already marginalized in Hongdae area. What happened to subculture in the 2000s?

Hawimunhwa or *sŏbŭk'ŏlch'ŏ*

The Korean translation of *Subculture: The Meaning of Style*, by Dick Hebdige, was published in 1998. Since then, the term *hawimunhwa* has been actively appropriated by academics in sociology, pedagogy, media studies, fashion studies, and elsewhere. Over time, the stigmatization of 'decadent' or 'deviant' youths in the past finally disappeared after the millennium. Another critical moment occurred in 2009, when *hawimunhwa* was included in the high school textbook *Society and Culture*. It signified an official legitimization of *hawimunhwa* beyond popular recognition.

At this point, I have to mention that *sŏbŭk'ŏlch'ŏ* is the product of double transliteration: Roman script subculture into Korean script 서브컬처, followed by the McCune-Reischauer romanization of 서브컬처. Although romanization is neither official nor popular in Korea, it is widely employed in international Korean studies circles. Thus, I will use the esoteric spelling for the Western readership. If I may say in advance, a semantic gap between *hawimunhwa*, a translation of subculture, and *sŏbŭk'ŏlch'ŏ*, a transliteration of subculture, is never trivial.

As I said earlier in this section, what had been officially legitimized in the academia was *hawimunhwa*, although its meaning now varies according to the authors. But, in the popular usage, the translated term *hawimunhwa* based on Chinese ideograms gave way to a transliterated term *sŏbŭk'ŏlch'ŏ*. Although the two terms have co-existed and still are interchangeable, nuanced differences between them cannot be glossed over. At the time of writing this chapter, I even get a sense that *hawimunhwa* has almost been replaced with *sŏbŭk'ŏlch'ŏ*.

The switch from translation to transliteration in Korea seems to resemble the development of *sabukaruchā* in Japan during an earlier period. Yet, there was and is a decisive difference. In terms of media environments, the emergence of Korean *sŏbŭk'ŏlch'ŏ* coincides with the widespread availability and adoption of high-speed internet in the early 2000s. At that time, *sŏbŭk'ŏlch'ŏ* became nearly synonymous with 'internet culture', when millennials had unparalleled access to the internet and were seen as heavy digital users. A book edited by relatively young culture critics (Ch'oe and Humanities Co-op, 2016) described this interrelation between the switch from old media such as television to new media such as the internet. One contributor noted that 'subcultures today differentiate themselves from the mainstream of society by forming new networks using internet communities and social media services' (Song, 2016, p 174).

The dialectic between old media and new media is not the focus of this chapter, and it sounds outdated to say that internet culture itself is a subculture in the so-called post-digital age (Bell and Kennedy, 2000). The point I am trying to draw attention to in this chapter is that Korea experienced the most intense transformation of subculture during the 2000s before then-new media, such as the internet, became routinized alongside the extensive adoption of smartphones and the lessening of the digital divide. That means the discourses about youth identities were created, circulated, and discussed through internet before it was exposed to the wider public by old media (or legacy media).

It is symptomatic that publications since the mid-2010s choose *sŏbŭk'ŏlch'ŏ* rather than *hawimunhwa* (SEMA, 2015; Son, 2020; Kang, 2021). It cannot be said that the transition from *hawimunhwa* to *sŏbŭk'ŏlch'ŏ* would be just one of many examples of the magnetic power of English or other European languages in Asia. Rather, the change in terminology accompanied the change of meaning. Kang defines *sŏbŭk'ŏlch'ŏ* 'not as low-ranking (*hawi*) or protest (*chŏhang*) culture against mainstream culture but as taste communities in the periphery or diverse cultures in the society' (Kang, 2021, p 11). His definition may come as a surprise to those who are acquainted with the histories of subcultures. What might be more surprising though is the fact that this is the most widely perceived interpretation of subculture, exactly *sŏbŭk'ŏlch'ŏ*, in contemporary Korea at least since the early 2020s.

It might be tempting to conclude that Korean *sŏbŭk'ŏlch'ŏ* was heavily influenced by Japanese *sabukaruchā*, specifically *otaku* culture whose ethos is defined by object-oriented 'animalization' (Azuma, 2001; 2007). Although it is naïve to say that *sŏbŭk'ŏlch'ŏ* in Korea is a late imitation of *otaku* culture in Japan, the adoption of the transliterated word *sŏbŭk'ŏlch'ŏ* in Korea coincides with the establishment of a subcultural economy in the production and circulation of merchandise, so-called subcultural goods. Despite the rhetoric of non-mainstream and peripheral values, subculture has seldom resisted the 21st-century's consumerism, an important part of which is the so-called creative economy/industries. Subcultural goods have become the necessary, accessible, cheaper consumer goods under the economic conditions in which the youths without wealthy parents have quickly become the urban poor.

If I may stick to my concept of subcultural activism, it has waged a double-sided struggle. On the one hand, I have been uncomfortable with the uncritical legitimization of *hawimunhwa* in the official world of academia. On the other hand, I have been critical of the unconditional celebration of peripheral taste in the name of *sŏbŭk'ŏlch'ŏ*. However, does being against both just narrow down the place of those who think like me?

In the last phase of my research, I contacted Yoshitaka Mōri, my Japanese colleague who interpreted Japanese *otaku* culture as 'capitalist culture', even though he has been involved in cultural activism for a long time. To my question "Despite all those misperceptions about subculture, are you going to keep using the term *subculture* for your agenda?", he answered, "In English, yes. But in Japanese, no." His view does not mean that the English word subculture is intrinsically 'better' than the Japanese word *sabukaruchā*. Rather, it shows that talking about subculture is meaningful when it is connected with any kind of activism for the critical intellectuals in Asia. Probably, he and I share a view that so-called subcultures are rapidly commercialized by market forces and easily co-opted by government policies in Asia, including Japan and Korea. Thus, subculture has been and will be a conceptual tool for imagining alternative cultural activisms. I do not believe that it is just the imagination of a handful of intellectuals. A piece of evidence is documented in a journal special issue where activists as well as scholars wrote articles about subcultural activism (Pan and Shin, 2018). The scholars in those articles also constitute a kind of subculture in academia. And I think that all the subculturalists in Asia have been stigmatized as being crazy. They are still crazy.

Conclusion

To summarize the trajectory of discourses on youth subcultures in Korea is easy: it went through the process of exclusion in the 1970s, recognition in the 1990s, and legitimization in the 2010s. What was challenging was demonstrating that the process was uneven and its evolution involved sharp cultural struggles in each period. The recent contestation of terminology between *hawimunhwa* and *sŏbŭk'ŏlch'ŏ* shows that the struggles are hardly over. Last but not least is the subcultural activism betwixt and between the two poles. There have still been angry faces of subculture, although they are now less visible than before.

More broadly, in this chapter I have challenged two contesting interpretive views or biases on subcultures in historical and contemporary contexts. The first view is that subcultures in Korea have been merely imports, transplants, or imitations of what had already been formed in the West, especially in the UK and US. There is a wealth of literature on this that is easily accessible through a search in the database of Korean journal articles.[9] The adoption of Western theories and concepts are obvious in the bibliographies of articles found there. However, the practice of matching Western theories and Asian cases is becoming less relevant. For example, *hikikomori* (ひきこもり/引き篭も: severe social withdrawal) in Japan, Ingyŏ (잉여/剩餘: surplus or superfluous population) in Korea, and *tangping* (躺平: lying flat as a rejection of work) in China do not have exact equivalents in English and are hard to understand without considering the specific cultural contexts of those countries. It is highly probable that the variety of examples like these will only grow over time.

Another view or bias I challenge, as ironic as it may sound, is the opposite of the first. As mentioned earlier, some Asian subcultures are not easily translatable into any Western vocabulary. Yet, discourses on Asian subcultures in the narrow sense have tended to rely too much on culturalism or cultural essentialism that revoke 'Japan-specificity' or

'Chinese characteristics'. These claims largely come from Asian studies and not cultural studies. Although I am heavily against the overuse of the word Orientalism in a pejorative sense, too many studies have tended to be subject to national stereotyping even when it celebrates a subculture in Asia. From that point of view, we are dearly in need of more studies which view conceptualizations of different subcultures in different places from comparative or cross-cultural perspectives in regional Asian studies and which break away from national stereotyping.

That being said, my last remark is a question rather than a statement. Why do some studies on K-pop, the ultra-commercial pop music, and the culture and lifestyle associated with it, use the word subculture without clearly defining it? Inside Korea, K-pop appears to be very different from subculture, however loosely it may be defined. Yet, quite a few authors use the term subculture to refer to the fandom, overwhelmingly young and female, in the contexts of their societies. The cases run from *shamate* (杀马特) in China (Wang, 2014) to e-boys/e-girls in Europe and America. I am not entirely sure if that makes me an old guard of subculture or if it is young acafans being uncritical. I hope neither is true, as the emergence of subculture always emerges from the gaps betwixt and between binary divisions: elitism and populism, exclusion and legitimization, imitation and creation, English and non-English, and so on.

Note on the usage of Asian languages
This chapter uses the McCune-Reischauer romanization of Korean, Hepburn romanization of Japanese, and Hanyu Pinyin romanization of Mandarin Chinese. In terms of the order of the names, the surname is followed by the given name, observing the conventional East Asian order. Exceptions to systems are applied to names that have already been established internationally or those that have been chosen by the authors or the artists themselves.

Acknowledgments
This work was partly supported by the Korean government's National Research Foundation Grant Fund (NRF-2018S1A6A3A01080743). I appreciate Kim Chang-nam, Yoshitaka Mori, Jian Xiao, and Meicheng Sun for exchanging views about the issues in this writing.

Notes
[1] 'Spontaneous evolution' is borrowed from Japnese words *dokujishinka* 独自進化, literally independent or distinct evolution. It is argued by Japanese subculralists and cited in the Japanese version Wikipedia page: https://ja.wikipedia.org/wiki//サブカルチャー
[2] *Otaku* (おたく/お宅) denotes a person who is obsessed with certain things and *liumang* (流氓) is literally floating population and sometimes translated as 'hooligan'. There are lot of studies on two distinct subcultures both in the West and the East. My interpretation depends on the critical reading of Miyadai et al (1993), Ōtsuka and Ueno (1998), Yoda

(2000), Azuma (2001), Nanba (2007), Ueno and Mori (2002), Azuma (2007), Miyadai et al (2011), and Keliyan (2011) on *otaku* and other subcultures in Japan, and of Minford (1985), Yu (1992), Barmé (1992), Lu (1996), Barmé (1999), De Kloet (2005), Wang (2005), Zhu (2006), Clark (2012), Drissel (2012), Pan (2012), and Xiao (2018) on *liumang* and other subcultures in China.

3   In Japan, *kaibunka* was used in criminal sociology in Japan. It is based upon the Chinese ideograms 下位文化 which was shared by the Korean academy. The interrelation between Japan and Korea is obscure. At least in Korea, *hawimunhwa* has often been (mis)understood as low culture or low-grade culture as opposed to high culture in the popular vocabulary. As a contested term, *pubunmunhwa* (부분문화/部分文化), literally partial culture or part culture, had been used before the 1990s. A last comment is that *ciwenhua* (次文化), literally the next culture, is preferred to *yawenhua* in Taiwan.

4   Kim wrote that 'if you observed the Woodstock festival and the anti-war demonstrations in New York City and Washington DC, then the long hair and go-go dancing, the irresponsibility and deviance of [Korean] youth, would not be accused of being "decadent" so bluntly and inflexibly' (Kim, 1974b). Kim's conception of youth culture reminds me of contraculture or counterculture (Yinger, 1960; 1984). The translation of contra/counter varied and took the forms of *pan* (anti), *taehang* (opposition), *chŏhang* (protest). For relevant theory and debates, Yi (1974), Song (2005), and Joo (2006) are insightful.

5   The quote is originally from a symposium held 4 May 1974. It was reported in a newspaper article 'Youth Culture is Being Misled *(Ch'ŏngnyŏn munhwa ododoego itta)', Kyunhyang Sinmun*, 7 May 1974.

6   Ibid.

7   'Is "Class Culture" Budding? (Kyech'ŭng munhwa ssagi t'ŭnŭn'ga)', *Sisa Journal* 16 January 1992.

8   Seo Taiji, the leader of the trio, as rebel was well expressed in Jung (2007). To me, it shows both the merit and shortcoming of the writing by the so-called acafan.

9   See, for example, the database at https://www.kci.go.kr/kciportal/main.kci

References

Azuma, H. (2001) *Dōbutsu ka suru posuto modan: otaku kara mi ta nippon shakai* [Animalizing Postmodern: Japanese Society Seen from Otaku], Tokyo: Kō dansha.

Azuma, H. (2007) 'The Animalization of Otaku Culture', *Mechademia*, 2: 175–188.

Barmé, G. (1992) 'Wang Shuo and Liumang ("Hooligan") Culture', *The Australian Journal of Chinese Affairs*, 28: 23–64.

Barmé, G. (1999) *In the Red: On Contemporary Chinese Culture*, New York: Columbia University Press.

Bell, D. and Kennedy, B.M. (eds) (2000) *The Cybercultures Reader*, London: Routledge.

Bennett, A. (1999) 'Subcultures or Neo-Tribes? Rethinking the Relationship between Youth, Style and Musical Taste', *Sociology*, 33(3): 599–617.

Bennett, A. (2011) 'The Post-Subcultural Turn: Some Reflections 10 Years On', *Journal of Youth Studies*, 14(5): 493–506.

Chiavacci, D. and Obinger, J. (2018) 'Towards a New Protest Cycle in Contemporary Japan? The Resurgence of Social Movements and Confrontational Political Activism in Historical Perspective', in D. Chiavacci and J. Obinger (eds) *Social Movements and Political Activism in Contemporary Japan: Re-Emerging from Invisibility*, London and New York: Routledge, pp 1–23.

Ch'oe, S. and Humanities Co-op (2016) *Hŭlk'ŭk ch'ŏngch'un: Taehanmin'gug esŏ ch'ŏngnyŏn ŭro saranamgi* [Earthy, Earthy Youth: Surviving as a Youth in South Korea], Seoul: Sech'ang Media.

Clark, P. (2012) *Youth Culture in China: From Red Guards to Netizens*, Cambridge: Cambridge University Press.

De Kloet, J. (2005) 'Popular Music and Youth in Urban China: The *Dakou* Generation', *The China Quarterly*, 183: 609–626.

Drissel, D. (2012) 'Linglei, the Other Species: Hybridized Constructions of Alternative Youth Subcultures in China', in L. Lili Hernández (ed) *China and the West: Encounters with the Other in Culture, Arts, Politics and Everyday Life*, Newcastle upon Tyne: Cambridge Scholars Publishing, pp 155–174.

Epstein, S. (2000) 'Anarchy in the UK, Solidarity in the ROK: Punk Rock Comes to Korea', *Acta Koreana*, 3: 107–114.

Epstein, S. and Dunbar, J. (2007) 'Skinheads of Korea, Tigers of the East', in E. Jurriëns and J. de Kloet (eds) *Cosmopatriots: On Distant Belongings and Close Encounters*, Amsterdam: Rodopi, pp 155–175.

Hall, S. and Jefferson, T. (eds) (1993 [1976]) *Resistance through Rituals: Youth Subcultures in Post-War Britain*, London and New York: Routledge.

Hebdige, D. (1979) *Subculture: The Meaning of Style*, London: Methuen.

Hodkinson, P. (2016) 'Youth Cultures and the Rest of Life: Subcultures, Post-Subcultures and Beyond', *Journal of Youth Studies*, 19(5): 629–645.

Hong, C. (1994) 'Sŏt'aeji ron' [On Seo Taiji], in *Shinsedaeron: Hondon kwa chilsŏ* [New Generation: Chaos and Order], Seoul: Hyŏnshilmunhwayŏn'gu, pp 228–243.

Joo, C.Y. (2006) '1970nyŏndae ch'ŏngnyŏnmunhwa Sedae damnon ŭi chŏngch'ihak' [The Politics of Generation Discourses on the Youth Culture in the 1970s], *Ŏllon kwa sahoe* [Journalism and Society], 14(3): 73–105.

Joo, E. (1994) '90nyŏndae han'guk ŭi shinsedae wa sobimunhwa' [The New Generation and Consumer Culture in the 1990s South Korea], *Kyŏngje wa sahoe* [Economy and Society], 21: 70–91.

Jung, E. (2007) 'Articulating Korean Youth Culture through Global Popular Music Styles: Seo Taiji's Use of Rap and Metal', in K. Howard (ed) *Korean Pop Music: Riding the Wave*, Kent: Global Oriental, pp 109–122.

Kang, M.K. (1999) 'Postmodern Consumer Culture without Postmodernity: Copying the Crisis of Signification', *Cultural Studies*, 13(1): 18–33.

Kang, S. (2021) *Sŏbŭk'ŏlch'ŏ Pip'yŏng* [Subculture Criticism], Seoul: Communication Books.

Keliyan, M. (2011) 'Kogyaru and Otaku: Youth Subcultures Lifestyles in Postmodern Japan', *Asian Studies*, 15(3): 95–110.

Kim, C. (1994) 'Hawimunhwa chiptan ŭi taejungmunhwa shilch'ŏn e taehan il yŏn'gu: Taejungŭmak ŭl chungshimŭro' [A Study on the Popular Culture Practices of Subculture Groups: Focused on Popular Music], PhD dissertation, Seoul National University.

Kim, P. (1974a) 'Onŭllal ŭi chŏlmŭn usangdŭl' [Today's Young Icons], *Dong-A Ilbo*, March 29.

Kim, P. (1974b) 'Ch'ŏngnyŏnmunhwa wa maesŭk'ŏm' ['Youth Culture and Mass Communication], Seoul: Shinmun p'yŏngnon [Newspaper Review], p 57.

Kim, P.H. and Shin, H. (2010) 'The Birth of "Rok": Cultural Imperialism, Nationalism, and the Glocalization of Rock Music in South Korea, 1964–1975', *Positions*, 18(1): 199–230.

Lee, K. (2000) 'Detraditionalization of Society and the Rise of Cultural Studies in South Korea', *Inter-Asia Cultural Studies*, 1(3): 477–490.

Lu, S.H. (1996) 'Postmodernity, Popular Culture, and the Intellectual: A Report on Post-Tiananmen China', *Boundary 2*, 23(2): 139–169.

Maffesoli, M. (1996) *The Time of the Tribes: The Decline of Individualism in Mass Society*, London: SAGE.

Mimesis (1993) *Shinsedae, ne mŏttaero haera* [The New Generation, Do as You Want], Seoul: Hyŏnshilmunhwayŏn'gu.

Minford, J. (1985) 'Picking Up the Pieces', *Far Eastern Economic Review*, August 8.

Miyadai, S., Ishihara, H. and Ōtsuka, A. (1993) *Sabukaruchā shinwa kaitai: Shōjo, ongaku, manga, sei no sanjūnen to komyunikēshon no genzai* [Disassembling the Myth of Subculture: Thirty Years of Girls, Music, Comics, and Sexuality, and the Current Conditions of Communication], Tokyo: PARCO.

Miyadai, S., Kono, S. and Lamarre, T. (2011) 'Transformation of Semantics in the History of Japanese Subcultures since 1992', *Mechademia*, 6: 231–258.

Muggleton, D. and Weinzierl, R. (eds) (2003) *The Post-Subcultures Reader*, Oxford and New York: Berg.

Nanba, K. (2007) *Zoku no keifu gaku: Yūsu·sabukaruchāzu no sengo shi* [A Genealogy of Tribes: Histories of the Postwar Youth Culture], Tokyo: Seikyusha.

Ōtsuka, E. and Ueno, T. (1998) 'Sabukaru otaku wa naze hoshu to musubitsuitaka?' [Why Did Subcultural *Otaku* Make Alliance with Conservatives?], *Impaction*, 196: 6–21.

Pan, L. (2012) 'The Festival of Liumang: The Liumang Narrative in Contemporary China', https://www.harvard-yenching.org/research/festival-liumang-liumang-narrative-contemporary-china/

Pan, L. and Shin, H. (2018) 'Uncommon Commons: Rethinking Affects, Practices, and Spaces of Urban Activism in Asia', *Inter-Asia Cultural Studies*, 19(3): 355–358.

Punk Anarchist (2006) The Department of Anthropology, Seoul National University. https://youtu.be/S68XtbH7o4E

SEMA (Seoul Museum of Art) (2015) *Sŏbŭk'ŏlch'ŏ: Sŏngnan Chŏlmŭm* [Subculture: Angry Youth], Seoul: Seoul Ch'aekpang.

Shin, H. (2009) 'Have You Ever Seen the Rain? And Who'll Stop the Rain? The Globalizing Project of Korean Pop (K-pop)', *Inter-Asia Cultural Studies*, 10(4): 507–523.

Shin, H. (2011) 'The Success of Hopelessness: The Evolution of Korean Indie Music', *Perfect Beat*, 12(2): 147–165.

Shin, H. (2016) 'K-pop, the Sound of Subaltern Cosmopolitanism?', in K. Iwabuchi and E. Tsai (eds) *Routledge Handbook of East Asian Popular Culture*, London and New York: Routledge, pp 116–123.

Shin, H. (2018) 'Urban Commoning for *Jarip* (Self-Standing) and Survival: Subcultural Activism in "Seoul Inferno"', *Inter-Asia Cultural Studies*, 19(3): 386–403.

Shin, H. (2019) 'The Punk and the Post-Developing City: Subculture-Led Urban Regeneration in Seoul?', *City, Culture and Society*, 19. https://doi.org/10.1016/j.ccs.2019.100295.

Shin, H. (2021) 'Searching for Youth, the People (*Minjung*), and "Another" West while Living through Anti-Communist Cold War Politics: South Korean "Folk Song" in the 1970s', in M.K. Bourdaghs, P. Iovene and K. Mason (eds) *Sound Alignments: Popular Music in Asia's Cold Wars*, Durham, NC: Duke University Press, pp 131–152.

Son, C. (2020) *Sŏbŭk'ŏlch'ŏgye rŭl yŏhaenghanŭn hich'ihaik'ŏ rŭl wihan kaidŭ* [A Guide for Hitchhikers Who Travel the World of Subculture], Seoul: Worklife.

Song, C. (2016) 'Ch'ŏngch'un ŭi tŭrama" Segye ŭi chŏlmang, ch'ŏngch'un ŭi ŭngdap' [The Drama of Youth, the Despair of the World: The Response by Youth], in *Hŭlk'ŭk ch'ŏngch'un: Taehanmin'gug esŏ ch'ŏngnyŏn ŭro saranamgi* [Earthy, Earthy Youth: Surviving as a Youth in South Korea], Seoul: Sech'ang Media, pp 154–183.

Song, E. (2005) 'Taejung munhwa hyŏnsang ŭrosŏ ŭi Ch'oe In-ho sosŏl: 1970nyŏndae ch'ŏngnyŏn munhwa/munhak ŭi sŭt'ail kwa sobi p'ungsok' [Choi Inho's Novel as a Phenomenon of Mass Culture: The Style and Consumption of Youth Culture/Literature in 1970s Korea], *Sanghŏ hakpo (Sanghŏ Academic Journal)*, 15: 419–445.

Thornton, S. (1995) *Club Cultures: Music, Media, and Subcultural Capital*, Middletown: Wesleyan University Press.

Ueno, T. and Mōri, Y. (2002) *Jissen karuchuraru-sutadīzu* [Practicing Cultural Studies], Tokyo: Chikuma shobō .

Wang, J. (2005) 'Bourgeois Bohemians in China? Neo-Tribes and the Urban Imaginary', *The China Quarterly*, 183: 532–548.

Wang, W. (2014) 'Qingnian yawenhua zuowei balinghou he jiulinghou "wenxue shenghuo" de yanshen: cong xiaoqingxin yu shamate yawenhua tanqi' [Youth Subculture as an Extension of the 'Literary Life' of the Post-80s and Post-90s: Talking about Subcultures from *xiaoqingxin* and *shamate*], *Wenyi Zhengming* [Literary Debates], 6: 199–204.

Williams, J.P. (2011) *Subcultural Theory: Traditions and Concepts*, Malden: Polity Press.

Williams, J.P. (2019) 'Subculture's Not Dead! Checking the Pulse of Subculture Studies through a Review of "Subcultures, Popular Music and Political Change" and "Youth Cultures and Subcultures: Australian Perspectives"', *Young*, 27(1): 89–105.

Yi, C. (eds) (1974) *Ch'ŏngnyŏnmunhwaron* [Discourses on Youth Culture], Seoul: Hyŏnams.

Yinger, J.M. (1960) 'Contraculture and Subculture', *American Sociological Review*, 25: 625–635.

Yinger, J.M. (1984) *Countercultures: The Promises and Peril of a World Turned Upside Down*, London: The Free Press.

Yoda, T. (2000) 'A Roadmap to Millennial Japan', *South Atlantic Quarterly*, 99(4): 629–668.

Yu, B. (1992) 'Wang Shuo yawenhua ji qita' [Wang Shuo, Subculture etc], *Wenyi lilun yu piping* [Literary Theories and Criticisms], 6: 85–88.

Zhu, D. (2006) *Liumang de shengyan* [The Festival of Liumang], Beijing: New Star Press.

6

Interpreting Chinese Punk: From Doing Nothing to Hermit Lifestyle

Jian Xiao and Xinxin Dong

In China, a show called *The Big Band* invites old indie/punk bands to perform, which reshapes the subcultural phenomenon constructed for a limited audience into a popular form with a large fan base, and transforms a subcultural spectacle into a subdued, domesticated style. This is not surprising since the integration of commercialized popular culture with the state-directed apparatus of cultural industries leads to reduced space for experimentation, or more specifically, underground initiatives (Gu et al, 2021). The growth of indie music thus has become more commercial. While a lot of small clubs are closing and very large venues are opening, young bands cannot afford to play these and therefore search for what most people like and play that instead. Musicians even have to play in McDonald's because they are unable to book a mainstream livehouse.[1] As a consequence, although live-streaming services can expand an act's fan base, traditional live gig attendees regard virtual platforms and performances as 'inauthentic'. Young Chinese musicians, who lack economic and political support, are being pushed into more marginal positions in the platform era. This trend can also be seen in the punk phenomenon, where the avenues for live performances have closed and bands have suffered reduced income due to the failure of the singular business model, that is, gaining income only through selling tickets, exacerbated by the impact of the COVID-19 pandemic. Instead of giving up on the livehouses, punk musicians who have a bit of fame have turned to streaming platforms due to COVID-19 so that they can earn money to invest in traditional avenues for accruing punk rock capital. This action demonstrates one possibility regarding how the punk scene maintains its offline underground authenticity, paradoxically through online methods and commercial initiatives, that is, a resistant practice to new cultural trends through a seemingly compromised approach. It is thus particularly interesting to reflect on subcultural theories, especially those derived from a Western tradition, in interpreting long-term questions regarding what subcultural authenticity is, and how to understand it in the Chinese context.

We suggest that possibilities exist for applying other theoretical perspectives to understand subcultural phenomena in the Global South besides Western-inspired subcultural theories. More importantly, how to apply different theoretical frameworks to the punk phenomenon in China has become a key area of inquiry and needs to be carefully reflected upon and judged. This chapter will look at how the concepts of authenticity and resistance are developed in different sociocultural contexts and introduce a Chinese philosophical framework to give further interpretive power to local punk phenomena. The chapter looks at fieldwork cases of Chinese punks from 2013 to 2017 to interrogate these theoretical understandings. What we find from punk musicians is a direct response—not 'challenging'—to the political situation where the authorities have set certain expectations that are discerned by musicians who refuse to conform to them. Starting from this point, we demonstrate how notions of 'doing nothing' and the 'hermit lifestyle', developed from Chinese philosophy and society in comparison with concepts developed from Western contexts, are analytically applicable to understanding resistance and authenticity among Chinese punks.

Doing research on Chinese punk

While academic discussion is long absent in the case of Chinese punk, exceptions have included several ethnographic studies of punk musicians and some media reports. Examining Western punk is seen as an original point but there is also a need to enlarge the scope to include Eastern punk. To fill the gap of academic interpretations, the first author has researched Chinese punk since 2011 and maintained focus on it as a continuous project until the present day, while the first and the second authors together developed Chinese philosophical perspectives for this analysis. In this period, the research scope changed to stay aligned with global trends. Meanwhile, there were two questions to be answered across the whole process. First, are Western theories applicable to the Chinese punk phenomenon? This question was generated in the PhD research of the first author when first looking at the punk phenomenon. Second, questions that emerged from the fieldwork and interpretation process afterwards included whether Chinese punk practices could be regarded as resistant or if punk is still underground, a question very much related to authenticity as well. We believe that proposing these questions can help map the field of punk interpretation, which can continuously introduce new inquiries embedded in new cultural contexts, resulting in identifying problems or gaps in the interpretation process and introducing reinterpretations.

The discussion of resistance as a concept can be traced back to the doctoral supervision period of the first author, who completed her PhD at a British university. As punk resistance is a very well-known concept in the Western scenario, not only the actual practice but also the discursive practice became implicit in analyzing the Chinese context. While protests are forbidden in China, how to regard people's practices as being resistant becomes a crucial question and problem for interpretation. More importantly, this process directly influenced the fieldwork for the doctoral research since qualitative inquiry into practices became difficult both for the first author and the musicians. Thus, the first question regarding resistance required consideration about how to pose the question to musicians without making interpretive pre-assumptions. Discussing punks' relationships with authority figures became a strategy to get at the concept of resistance. The successful interpretation of punk practices then relied on careful interaction with punks when asking about their relationship with different authorities and mainstream culture. In this sense, 'resistance' does not serve as some signpost of discussion, but rather as a term for subsequent summarization and interpretation of punk practices. The application of authenticity, another concept related to punk culture and identity, was also problematic since the punk phenomenon was imported to China from the West and is thus deeply rooted in the nexus between the global and the local. To be specific, the local Chinese punk scene is shaped by particular Chinese social, cultural, and political contexts, but it is also part of the global punk community. The process of punk authentication in China thus cannot only be deemed a process of authenticating Western punk culture but it also has agency in establishing a Chinese style of punk culture, which is partially influenced by Chinese philosophies.

Resistance, authenticity, and doing nothing

In the Western tradition, punk research is very much related to subcultural research, framed by two core concepts: resistance and authenticity. The subcultural studies approach carried out at the Birmingham Centre for Contemporary Cultural Studies (CCCS) focused on addressing youth subcultures from the perspective of power. In theoretical terms, it employed the concept of cultural resistance. By directing their focus to some British youth subcultures (teddy boys, mods, rockers, hippies, punks, and so on), cultural studies scholars attempted to demonstrate how processes of resistance were activated against the dominant culture in a context of struggle, conflict, and oppression deeply anchored in their class positions. The CCCS researchers assigned great relevance to style, which Stanley Cohen (2002) described as subdivided on the basis of four central characteristics: clothing, music, rituals, and language. However, he noted also that style is not a quality inherent to subcultures, but something constructed. Hence, what creates a style is the stylization—the active organization of objects alongside activities and perspectives, which, in turn, produces an organized group with a coherent identity and distinctive way of 'being-in-the-world' (Guerra, 2010, p 416). In this context, style was understood as synonymous with resistance, a physical translation of symbolic guerrilla action against 'the system'—understood as an oppressive 'social order' that restricts labor opportunities and possibilities for social mobility among working-class youth. Hebdige (1979) famously discussed the cultural meanings of the punk phenomenon. He also used 'semiotic guerilla warfare' (Eco, 1972) to describe these subversive subcultural practices. While resistance clearly is a crucial concept for understanding subcultural practices, the general explanation cited here pertains to symbolic resistance.

Symbolic resistance is clearly not adequate in examining the punk phenomenon. The passivity in symbolic resistance lies in its 'magical' solution to class conflicts. In other words, symbolic resistance through consumptive appropriation is unable to achieve any substantial consequences and ultimately remains impotent. Williams (2011) points out that subcultural resistance can be understood on three dimensions: passive to active, micro to macro, and overt to covert. These various forms of resistance can also be seen in the practices of Chinese punk musicians (Xiao, 2018).

Chinese punk musicians treat the term resistance more as a musical inspiration or some term that they encounter in classical Western lyrics, rather than as a proper reflexive term or an actual practice. Chinese punk musicians' understanding of resistance comes from two aspects, one very similar to the Western model of resistance, in other words, radical politics, and the other from Chinese philosophy. In this sense, Chinese punks are not solely looking to Western ideologies for revolutionary prescriptions. As peak mobilizations subsided in the wake of the youth movement in Tiananmen Square in 1989, the energy for fighting for rights transformed into new forms of organization and sparked new political imaginations and cultures.

In an environment prohibiting any kind of protest, punk resistance is mostly covert, which leaves out the possibilities of applying other comparable concepts, such as *intervention*, *rebellion*, or *revolution*. It then becomes a question in terms of which circumstances are best for applying them. In Foucault's (1991) statement, resistance and domination occur simultaneously. Skott-Myhre (2009) points out that life force can be a simple assertion until the occurrence of domination, and the intervention against dominance can become resistance. In one case describing punk practices, the term *intervention* was chosen by a punk musician to interpret how they recorded policemen on

Tiananmen Square for their new album about criticizing Chinese authorities. They created a video about Chinese police and used the slogan A.C.A.B. ('All Cops Are Bastards'), popularized by the British Oi! punk band The 4-Skins in their 1980s song with the same title (see Xiao and Qu, 2019).

> 'We were filming in front of Tiananmen Square. At that time, a police officer said we would be allowed to shoot only if we had permission. I told him we didn't. We were then told we should go find People's Square. Then I said I was a citizen and that there was no sign saying "no photography". In the end, he confiscated my video camera. There was a big crowd at that moment.' (Punk musician Mr. L. (anonymous) interviewed by the first author in 2013)

We can notice that the elements of sound (the arguments), bodily performance (the gesture of filming and the bodily confrontation), interactions between the two oppositional actors (the punk musicians and the police), and between them and spectators (onlookers) constitute a process of intervention. The act of filming the police in Tiananmen Square is an interruption into the space with an implicit antagonistic attitude. Nevertheless, when the police started to respond and later confiscated the camera having had a fierce argument with the musicians, the antagonistic relationship became explicit, and the musicians' practices as a whole framed the intervention as punk resistance.

Rebellion may also be a relevant term and can be contextualized in two ways. In the West, rebellion is deemed something extraordinary and explosive that is embodied in protests or specific moments upsetting the order of daily life compared to resistance as daily acts of opposition to oppression (Diavolo, 2019). More importantly, it is seen as leading to revolution. Second, youth rebellion is, in Wolman's (1973) words, a period that seeks individual identity and independence from parental authorities. When looking at the career of Chinese punk musicians, most of them have experienced this type of adolescent rebellion. However, for Chinese punk musicians, this 'rebellion' goes on to last for their lifetime and becomes a series of daily responses to all forms of authority, thus linking back to resistance. Such resistance can occur in even the most mundane of practices. As one musician commented:

> 'This country regards people as idiotic with no feelings. You can have no expression; you can also have a sweet smile. But it will become a problem if you laugh out loud. If you laugh to an extreme extent, which makes them confused and worried, you will have a big problem.' (Interview)

Emotional 'acting out' in a collective form is interpreted by musicians as acting back against the 'people in charge', who are wary of music's revolutionary potential. The pogo dance, for instance, which is common at punk shows, was described as 'revolutionary' by one musician. This can also explain the severe controls on performances in China, to prevent performers from making political statements.

Noticeably, *doing nothing* is invested as a practice of resistance to the mainstream for some of the Chinese punk musicians. In describing the choice of living in a Shanghai suburb, one musician from Beijing believed that he chose a lifestyle of *doing nothing* to reject the dominant lifestyle practiced by the mainstream: competing for reputation, money or other material things. That said, the so-called lifestyle of doing nothing is not really about not acting or moving, rather, it is about choosing a slow pace and a mode of following individuals' own 'authentic' aspirations rather than social expectations. Interestingly, Chinese punk musicians often choose the term *doing nothing* when they describe a self-deemed deviant behavior from the mainstream, even if they run a restaurant or a bar. Thus, doing nothing in this scenario means rejecting and resisting the mainstream through self-actualization. This is also consistent with Lewin and Williams' (2009) analysis of punk ideology and subcultural authenticity, including the tenets of 'rejection' and 'self-actualization'.

When we look at the concept of authenticity in different sociocultural contexts, we can find that typically in the West, authenticity is often traced back to ancient Greek philosophy, discerning the nature of reality as 'authored' by gods (Schwarz and Williams, 2020). The European Enlightenment witnessed new conceptualizations of authenticity as an essential aspect of the human condition. In Fordahl's (2018) words explaining the shifting meanings of authenticity, 'whereas Plato's authenticity had been external, and Rousseau's individual, the authenticity of the twentieth century would be personal' (p 305). In summary, authenticity in the West has been framed in two distinct ways. The first is that authenticity is antagonistic to society (see Lewin and Williams, 2009). The second is that authenticity is tied to group membership or social identity (Schwarz and Williams, 2020). The notion of authenticity in different philosophies indicates a route of actualizing self, either in the individual or collective manner. In comparison, authenticity is often discussed in Confucianism in the context of Eastern philosophy. Chen (2015) points out that Confucian thinkers take the concept of self for granted, referring to a person's experience as a whole, differing from how Descartes or Kant ask the question, 'What is the self?'. Indicating if a self can be authentic or not depends on whether someone has the four predicates: *bo* (博, to be well-learned), *da* (大, ability to embrace the world), *jing* (精, to be the best), and *shen* (深, to be profound). Similar to 20th-century Western philosophers such as Heidegger or Sartre, Confucian thinkers declare that an authentic self should author their existence by following a grand vision (in Chinese terms, *zhi xiang* 志向) and constant re-innovation and creativity.

More importantly, authenticity is not only substantial in its ontological claim on selfhood but also in claiming substantial meaning of a self in the world. In both traditions, thinkers believe the ontological self and the social self are compatible. However, using either interpretive frame will affect how subcultural experiences and selves are understood.

The idea of doing nothing (*wu wei*, 无为) also exists in the Chinese context and serves as a political concept. It was Confucius who first explicitly put forward the term 'rule by doing nothing' (Han, 2021), and Taoism, represented by Laozi and Zhuangzi, that greatly developed and enriched the concept of 'governing by non-interference'. Taoism advocates this natural law and Laozi often requires people to 'do nothing'. This does not mean that ordinary people should not do anything, but rather should limit their activities to what is necessary and natural. From another perspective, this political stance not only suggests a natural and harmonious relationship between the ruler and the governed, but also implies a passive attitude from the governed. The term 'doing without contention' (*wei er bu zheng*, 为而不争) also encourages people to focus on process rather than result. Being deeply influenced by this philosophical political concept, Chinese hermits (*yin shi*, 隐士) have lately emerged as a phenomenon in China, referring to those educated people who hide and live in suburbs because they are not interested in or are tired of politics. This begins to shift doing nothing to a resistant subcultural practice as conceptualized by Corrigan (1976), where doing nothing is full of meaning.

In a similar sense, the Chinese hermit is also a social identity whose core value is the rejection of official careers. This includes not only the unwillingness to go along with secular officialdom, but also the disappointment and dissatisfaction with the real ruling class. Chinese hermit culture experienced an absolute opposition between being in the government and escaping to nature before the Sui and Tang dynasties, to the transformation between seclusion and officialdom in the late Ming dynasty. The formation of the 'deviant' hermit identity in Chinese society thus arose from the Taoist concept of 'outsider', that is, separation from the forces of law and tradition. For hermits (very similarly to subculturalists), keeping one's independence is a way of being authentic; an alternative way to actualize oneself, and more importantly, it is a form of subcultural, bottom-up, micro-level resistance.

Interpreting doing nothing as resistant and authentic living

When punk musicians talk about the question of authenticity, most of them believe that since overt activism is not allowed in China, doing nothing as a Chinese philosophy serves as a point of reference for some musicians to authenticate themselves as 'real' punks. For instance, some Chinese musicians use 'doing nothing' to explain their behaviors of showing indifference to politics and this becomes passive resistance to the politics. Besides the process of self-identifying as punk, musicians have also built communities in several different forms for managing and organizing their lifestyle as an authentic mode of living, and this process of authentication is through group-identification. Three cases in particular demonstrate this aspiration. In an interview, one musician who lived in the Beijing suburbs said:

> 'My friends and I formed a band—we were friends at the time. We went to a place far away from the city centre where all of the shops were closed. Our guitarist bought a house at that time. It was very cheap there. So we lived together and rehearsed there. We continued this lifestyle for a whole summer. We had a utopia even before this. At that time, we had 14 punks together. We lived in a one-bedroom flat. Some slept in the bed while some slept on the floor. We insisted on playing music. At that time, Sanlitun [an area near the centre of Beijing] was especially good and free. There were not too many extra things. It was very pure and cheap. We didn't go inside anywhere; we only drank by the roadside. We continued doing this kind of thing for nearly one year.' (Interview)

From the musician's description, at the core of the ideal punk lifestyle is sharing the same kind of life with people of similar interests. More importantly, doing nothing such as hanging out, drinking, and living together is a way to gain freedom and construct a utopia.

Another example is a space called 'Our Home', based in Wuhan and established by a Wuhan punk musician. The musicians, artists, and professionals who stayed in Our Home practiced Chinese-style squatting (renting a low-maintenance space rather than occupying a deserted space), which they managed in a Do-It-Yourself (DIY) and fair way. The whole community was based on rules of self-government; anybody could live there as long as there was an empty room.

> 'We decided to rent a house. If you want complete control over a place, the only choice is to rent. Fortunately, we were able to find a secluded house outside the city that had basically been abandoned. The rent was next to nothing. Although the house was a bit old, the surrounding scenery had a natural beauty we found invigorating. ... On a pillar along the outer wall, we mounted a red and black five-pointed star, and we gave the house a name: 'Our Home' Autonomous Youth Centre. ... The village where Our Home is located had been plagued by a garbage problem for four years, and no one had done anything

about it. This location is in a suburb of Wuhan. More specifically, it is in a village that is far from the city centre and has been nearly abandoned.' (Interview)

Only the government can own homes in China, and squatting is not recognized or protected by law. However, renting a cheap place in China functions in almost the same way as squatting in the West, in that a nearly abandoned place is regarded as being tucked away out of view but at the same time big enough to accommodate a community of like-minded people. One interviewee's experience of staying at Our Home was that it was completely free for those who want to stay there for a few days or even longer, with payment totally voluntary. Another key element is that they could communicate with other residents in the space. The place welcomed people of different kinds to join hands in creating dialogue and to put the idea of an autonomous style community into practice. From the very beginning, the musician and his followers asserted that:

> '[W]e must find a place within our own lives, a space to serve as a meeting ground and mediation space, to circulate information, to discuss the "symbols" of action we have encountered, to share the connectedness of our plights, to interpret it, and to attempt to take action to the best of our ability. It is apparent that discussion is the most noticeable activity in this space.' (Interview)

Our Home's blog has advertised themed workshops on topics such as women's rights, gay rights, and social movements. In addition, events such as film screenings and music performances were frequently held there. The discussions not only took place among the residents of Our Home but also extended to other countries. In a letter to a squat in Switzerland published via the Our Home blog, questions were asked regarding residents' activities and their influence on their neighbors. The activities at the Swiss squat were similar to those at Our Home: performances, discussions, film screenings, and the growing of vegetables. However, the Swiss squat could be seen as more radical in nature, on account of other activities such as the organization of protests, a feature totally absent from the Chinese scene. In the view of one Our Home community member, 'daily revolutionary' activities such as finding food in supermarket bins or growing vegetables without earning money are more characteristic of Chinese-style 'squatting'.

In another difference, conflict with the government over the right to squat has flared up in Switzerland, which has not been a problem for Our Home. Also, publicly demonstrating for women's rights or immigrants' rights does not really feature in the Chinese experience as compared to Swiss squatters'. What these differences between the Swiss squat and Our Home demonstrate most clearly is that politically related activity at Our Home is strongly discussion-oriented, rather than involving direct action such as taking part in social movements or speaking out for one's rights by resisting the government overtly. The manner in which life at Our Home is arranged has been described as 'trying to organize daily life in an anarchistic manner in order to form a life recognized by everyone'. The political aspirations of these practices can be explained as more covert than overt resistance (Williams, 2011), occurring in private subcultural rather than public spaces.

The third and final example is a gathering in a Shanghai suburb, organized by a Beijing punk musician. The musician claimed that his friends were similar to him in terms of their desire to escape the mainstream. Although not all of his friends identified as punks, he considered them to be living a punk lifestyle, which he described as individualistic and free, involving the rejection of mainstream values and supporting the idea of keeping to themselves:

'If people know that living is a natural thing [in] itself and enjoy it, politics will disappear. The housing market will go away. We don't need so many houses and cars. When people feel they are happy and wealthy because of living, nothing else is really needed. Now people just try to take everything.' (Interview)

In essence, the musician emphasized the importance of living without doing things according to society's rules. In interpreting this attitude, we attempt to further look into both globally transmitted punk philosophy and Chinese philosophy for an interpretation. Doing nothing thus becomes a form of 'escape', a rather spatial activity practiced by a comparable group of people, the hermit class in the ancient Chinese social context.

The hermit is regarded as a social identity in both Western and Eastern contexts. A Chinese hermit lifestyle includes symbols and practices such as living away from populated urban areas, drinking alcohol regularly, and wearing untidy clothes (clothes were important signs of rank and status in ancient Chinese society). Apart from that, hermits surrounded themselves with plants such plum, orchid, bamboo, and chrysanthemum (*mei lan zhu ju*, 梅兰竹菊), which symbolized the noble personality of ancient Chinese intellectuals as well as expressed attitudes of non-cooperation and authentic being. Here we need to recognize that hermits in China rely on some interaction with each other to support and maintain a network of knowledge and practices. In fact, many hermits do not reject social networks and can have close personal relationships with each other. Yet, hermit culture in China also refers to an unofficial seclusion. Some Western natural literature writers were also hermits, such as Henry David Thoreau and Mary Austin, who discussed issues of ecological environment in-depth within their literary works. Asian and Western hermits are similar in that most of them are highly educated with extraordinary cultural attainments but are fed up with the bustling world and aspire to a simple life. Yet one difference can be seen: Chinese hermits are a political concept while Western hermits are conceived along religious lines (Zhang, 2018). The Chinese hermit, whether active or forced, risks the 'defeatism' of life outside mainstream judgment. Similarly, the punk or punk spirit-driven communities encourage a collective lifestyle combining cultural symbols such as particular punk clothes, alcohol, punk zines, hangouts, and live shows, which become a form of protection for musicians who are politically disappointed. That said, through these seemingly doing nothing practices, punk musicians complete a process of self-actualization while rejecting the mainstream.

Comparing punk music with hermit music

To gain a deeper understanding of punk lifestyle, especially when punks escape to live on the margins of contemporary urban society, we need to further explore hermit music through a comparison with punk music. Hermit music, as a part of hermit culture, expresses a willingness or desire to hide in the mountains via music. It not only refers to the music itself, but also a set of songs, poems, dances, accompaniments, and other integrated elements of a performance system.

In terms of performance style, punk music can be regarded as the contemporary expression of hermit music. Hermit music was often performed in mountains, bamboo forests or by riversides, welcomed by people who have mutual interests. Chinese punk is also often away from the urban spotlight. Both forms have been loved and collected by people who sincerely love the meanings they convey. More importantly, punk musicians who sport Mohawks, skulls or leather jackets with patches and reject mainstream clothing and values can be comparable to hermits who dressed in leather and natural fabric, demonstrating their determination to escape from the formality of everyday life. As hermit music and punk music both advocate mental and physical freedom, alcohol and the practice of performing and drinking have become important symbols in both forms of culture. A famous hermit, Ruanji, had a song called 'Bacchanalia', created during the Three Kingdoms period (220–280 AD). It is said that the government of that time was fatuous and dark, and scholar-bureaucrat Ruanji was deeply at odds with it. To avoid trouble, he lived in seclusion in the mountains and forests, playing the *guqin* (古琴),[2] reciting poems, enjoying wine, and forgetting his worries. Through the expression of a chaotic and hazy mood, he vented his pent-up feelings arising from injustice. 'Bacchanalia' has tones that reflect the pressure of the main characters gradually growing frustrated (Yang and Cai, 2016).

In terms of expression, the artistic creation of the music of the Wei and Jin dynasties (220–420 AD) is characterized by pursuing a form of music independent of politics (Hourong, 2013). This is similar to the way punk musicians create music not for the purpose of adding positive values to Chinese governance. The anti-political meanings can often be found in the song lyrics. For instance, 'wall' as a symbolic representation of authoritarian control has constantly appeared in songs such as Discord's 'Keep Yourself' with its line 'Break the wall on the way', and in Hell City's 'Dead End', with the line 'Keep fire, keep power, ready to fight, knock down the wall'. Similarities in the attitude against mainstream values through doing things merely to survive are also visible in both hermit music and punk music. In one case, 'The Song of Playing the Clay Shoe' (Tr. Zhao Yanchun), the lyrics are:

> When the sun gets up, I get up;
> When the sun retreats, I retreat.
> I dig a well where from I drink;
> I do farming so that I can eat.
> What other force can Earth exert on me?

The ballad implies an ancient Chinese natural and cozy lifestyle set against social control, which is also in line with the DIY spirit advocated by punk artists. It reflects the natural and carefree lives of Chinese ancestors. A similar attitude of 'doing nothing' can be also seen in punk lyrics. The lyrics of the song 'Old Punk' (*lao peng ke*, 老朋克) from punk band Space Drift (*tai kong piao yi*, 太空飘移) for instance, state:

> Look around at the people who are there every day desperately busy
> Their every moment is filled with complaints in their ears
> You lost your way and didn't know what to do
> No need to complain, no need to ramble
> Just want to live a simple life every day
> Drinking beer and singing in the evening
> This is how you live the rest of your life
> Be a good old punk.

These lyrics show how punk musicians reject additional pressure from Chinese society. Through an attitude of rejection, they have also chosen to become an 'outsider' in mainstream society, living in harmony while doing nothing in the sense of productive labor for society. From the connotation of lyrics to the way of singing, from the spirit of DIY to the space and place of performance, punk culture can be regarded as a contemporary expression of hermit philosophy.

Conclusion

The punk phenomenon has developed for more than 40 years. As a typical subculture in the West, punk has been interacting with mainstream society politically, economically, and culturally throughout its development. Generally speaking, the CCCS tradition of subcultural studies ignored the complicated personal experience of subculture participants, while research on post-subcultural studies overemphasized individual experience, failing to link it to social and economic structures. Chinese punks embrace the 'global punk' network but are also acutely conscious of its contours. This research on punk in China presents a decolonizing intervention into 'global punk'. Indeed, applying concepts based on Western subcultural practices in a different context requires modification. But more importantly, this process becomes a moment for critical reflection on both concepts and interpretations.

In this chapter, we reviewed the concepts of 'resistance' and 'authenticity' and proposed Chinese philosophy as a new interpretive frame to understand Chinese punk musicians. Both the terms 'doing nothing' and 'hermit lifestyle' better describe musicians' mentality of 'resisting' in the Chinese social context. As for 'authenticity', it enjoys a deeper discussion in the system of Chinese classical philosophy and has been discussed and developed by major philosophical schools such as Confucianism and Taoism. We need continuous reflection on the concepts we applied and on the changing social contexts that can influence existing phenomena.

Notes

[1] In 2018, a Chengdu punk band called Jie Wa occupied a McDonald's and performed there. For more details, see: https://mp.weixin.qq.com/s/AUNYgRTg0zQxKRBe6DRg_w

[2] '古琴', a traditional Chinese plucked instrument, favored by hermits and scholars.

References

Chen, X.W. (2015) 'The Value of Authenticity: Another Dimension of Confucian Ethics', *Asian Philosophy*, 25(2): 172–187.

Cohen, S. (ed) (2002) *Folk Devils and Moral Panics*, London: Routledge.

Corrigan, P. (1976) 'Doing Nothing', in S. Hall and T. Jefferson (eds) *Resistance Through Rituals*, London: Routledge, pp 84–87.

Diavolo, L. (2019) Resistance, Rebellion, Revolution: What They Are and How They Intersect, available from https://www.teenvogue.com/story/resistance-rebellion-revolution-explainer-interviews accessed in 12th 2021.

Eco, U. (1972) *Towards a Semiotic Enquiry into the Television Message Working Papers in Cultural Studies*, Birmingham: University of Birmingham.

Fordahl, C. (2018) 'Authenticity: The Sociological Dimensions of a Politically Consequential Concept', *American Sociologist*, 49(2): 299–311.

Foucault, M. (ed) (1991) *Discipline and Punish: The Birth of the Prison*, London: Penguin.

Gu, X., Nevin, D. and O'Connor, J. (2021) 'The Next Normal: Chinese Indie Music in a Post-COVID China', *Cultural Trends*, 30(1): 63–74.

Guerra, P. (2010) 'A instável leveza do rock. Génese, dinâmica e consolidação do rock alternativo em Portugal (1980–2010)' [The Unstable Lightness of Rock. The Genesis, Dynamics, and Consolidation of Alternative Rock in Portugal (1980–2010)], PhD dissertation, University of Porto.

Han, X.C. (2021) 'From Inaction Theory to Systematic Governance: Construction of State Governance Order', *Journal of Hunan Administration Institute*, 3: 48–60.

Hebdige, D. (1979) *The Meaning of Style*, London: Routledge.

Hourong, Y.X. (2013) 'Analyzing the Reason for the Establishment of Weijin Literati Music's Characteristics', MA dissertation, Art Academy of the University of Lanzhou, China.

Lewin, P. and Williams, J.P. (eds) (2009) 'The Ideology and Practice of Authenticity in Punk Subculture', in J.P. Williams and P. Vannini (eds) *Authenticity in Culture, Self and Society*, London: Routledge, pp 65–83.

Schwarz, K.C. and Williams, J.P. (2020) 'The Social Construction of Identity and Authenticity', in J.P. Williams and K.C. Schwarz (eds) *Studies on the Social Construction of Identity and Authenticity*, London: Routledge, pp 1–24.

Skott-Myhre, K.S. (2009) 'Of Families, Mothers, Gardens and Alchemy: Re-thinking Relations Between Women in Youth Work', *Relational Child and Youth Care Practice*, 22(2): 5–19.

Williams, J.P. (2011) *Subcultural Theory: Traditions and Concepts*, Cambridge: Polity Press.

Wolman, B.B. (1973) 'The Rebellion of Youth', *The International Journal of Social Psychiatry*, 18(4): 254–259.

Xiao, J. (2018) *Punk Culture in Contemporary China*, Singapore: Palgrave Macmillan.

Xiao, J. and Qu, S.W. (2019) 'Performance as Intervention: Understanding the Cultural Practices of Chinese Punk Musicians', *Journal of Popular Music Studies*, 31(2): 107–126.

Yang, Y.Y. and Cai, F. (2016) 'Study on the Relationship between Reclusive Tide and Music in Wei and Jin Dynasties', *Music Time and Space*, 7: 13–14.

Zhang, W. (2018) 'A Comparison of Chinese and Foreign Hermit Cultures', *The Farmers Consultant*, 16: 234.

7

The Dynamic Meaning of Subculture among DIY Indonesian Musicians

Oki Rahadianto Sutopo

Subcultural studies endures in a minor position in the Indonesian academic arena. In the latter half of the 20th century, Indonesia's New Order developmentalist regime (1966–1998) prioritized scientific studies that supported economic progress and national stability (Samuel, 1999). Only in the era of reformation (starting in 1998), which was accompanied by an atmosphere of democracy and freedom of expression, did subcultural studies prosper in a relatively more open manner. Since then, studies about popular music have been conducted by scholars from both within and outside Indonesia in various disciplines ranging from ethnomusicology to sociology (Baulch, 2002; Wallach, 2005; Richter, 2012). However, research that might draw upon the literature on music-based subculture is rare (for exceptions, see Baulch, 2003; 2004; Luvaas, 2009; Martin-Iverson, 2012). Meanwhile, and in contrast, debates regarding concepts such as subculture and post-subculture are alive and well in English-speaking countries (Blackman, 2005; Bennett, 2011) and expanding into many new territories (see Bennett, 2013; Bennett and Robards, 2014). In this chapter, I continue to critically contextualize the subculture versus post-subculture debate using my long-term study of Do-It-Yourself (DIY) Indonesian musicians by investigating the dynamic meaning of music subculture across different career stages and interlinkages within the changing socio-historical and cultural context. As I will suggest, the meaning of 'subculture' in the everyday lives of Indonesian musicians does not rigorously conform to the Centre for Contemporary Cultural Studies' (CCCS) thesis of resistance and class (Clarke et al, 1976), nor to the fluidity of identity thesis as proposed by post-subcultural scholars (Muggleton and Weinzierl, 2003). Using a biographical approach (Plummer, 2001), I highlight how DIY Indonesian musicians reflexively interpret and reinterpret the practical and symbolic meanings of their participation in music subcultures based on the temporal and spatial situatedness of their lived experiences. Thus, the DIY Indonesian musicians' subjectivity in their mundane practices becomes the center of analysis.

Life biographies as perspective and method

International literature on subcultures and post-subcultures is now extensive. Over the past three decades, ongoing debates regarding the use of subcultures and post-subcultures, especially in the British context (see Malbon, 1999; Weinzerl and Muggleton, 2003; Bennett and Kahn-Harris, 2004; Hodkinson and Deicke, 2007), have been relatively productive in understanding youth cultural practice in the context of rapid social change. Historically, the subculture approach as formulated by the CCCS in Birmingham was a response against the social deviance approach in the Chicago School tradition.[1] The CCCS oriented toward a neo-Marxist approach that drew on Gramsci and Althusser; thus, structural determinism and collective fixity were considered important factors in interpreting the meaning of resistance among working-class youth (Clarke et al, 1976; Hebdige, 1979; Blackman, 2005). However, many scholars challenged deterministic assumption, such as Clarke et al's (1976) argument that youth subcultures only 'solved' material problems in an imaginary manner.

In contrast, 'post-subcultural' theorists who assembled influence throughout the 2000s accentuated the cultural practices of contemporary youth in regard to agency, fluidity, and individualization (see Bennett, 1999; Muggleton, 2000; Stahl, 2003), concepts that highlighted individuals' reactions to societal shifts from modernity through to late modernity and the postmodern era (see Lyotard, 1979; Giddens, 1991; Beck, 1992; Maffesoli, 1996; Baudrillard, 1998). However, Shildrick and Macdonald (2005) argued that post-subcultural studies neglect social divisions and inequalities as pivotal aspects of the complexities of youth cultures. Indeed, these debates regarding how to make sense of youth and music cultures were not only intense in the 2000s (see Bennett, 2005; Blackman, 2005; Hesmondhalgh, 2005) but remain significant (Williams, 2018). Moreover, some scholars have moved beyond these debates by proposing alternative conceptualizations of youth cultural practices, such as appraising a global youth culture (Greener and Hollands, 2006), merging the intersections between class, gender, and ethnicity using a Bourdieusian approach (Jensen, 2018), synthesizing the domains 'culture' and 'transition' using a social generational perspective (Furlong et al, 2011; Woodman and Bennett, 2015), contextualization within the digital era

(Robards and Bennett, 2011; Bennett and Robards, 2014), and the rise of DIY careers (Bennett, 2018; Bennett and Guerra, 2018).

My research differs in various ways to many of these studies mentioned. First, I make use of a biographical approach,[2] which plays a part in subcultural studies by emphasizing DIY Indonesian musicians' trajectories as individuals in connection with the wider contexts in which they live. The experiences of the individual cannot be separated from the social, collective, cultural, and historical moment (Plummer, 2001, p 7). Using a biographical approach to study DIY Indonesian musicians has assisted me in exploring not only 'inside' their subcultural practices but also the representations of multiple intersections with family, community, and professional life as significant others. Hodkinson (2016) has argued that the importance of life biographies can go beyond the contextualization of youth cultural participation across time to create a dynamic emphasis on the connections of the present with both past and future. In this way, current practices can be understood as a part of 'whole lives' (Hodkinson, 2016, p 439). Second, I highlight the pivotal role of historical context and its interrelation with the dynamic meaning of subcultural participation at an individual level. In this biographical approach, a focus on historical change, moving between the changing biographical history of the person and the social history of their lifespan, is important (Plummer, 2001, p 39). Thus, in this chapter, participants' reflexive interpretations are shaped by 'generalized others' (see Holdsworth and Morgan, 2007), as well as by the shift toward the post-Reform era in Indonesia, which is characterized by total neoliberalization in many aspects of everyday life (Springer et al, 2016).

The analysis in this chapter draws on two extensive field studies conducted from 2013 to 2014 and in 2019, respectively. I applied qualitative methods of data collection and analysis in both studies. The earlier fieldwork was in Yogyakarta, Jakarta, and Bali, and that data represent Indonesian jazz musicians' career progression trajectories. The second project was carried out in Yogyakarta, Jakarta, and Bandung, and focused on the translocal imagination of metal music communities in Indonesia. Elsewhere, I have explained the distinctive characteristic of these cities and music scenes during the post-Reformation era in Indonesia (see Sutopo et al, 2017a; 2017b; 2020).

These studies followed a shift toward empirical work (see Bennett, 2003; Hodkinson, 2012), rather than relying heavily on the polished theoretical discussions as suggested by the CCCS. In this research, I acquired primary data using embedded participant observations I called *nongkrong*, which include the assemblage of hanging out together, having long informal conversations and 'doing nothing' (see Chapter 6, this volume). Having been a flexible and critical insider in various music communities for many years, I applied my own familiarity with the setting as a way to gain direct access to my informants and assist with the process of data verification and interpretation (Hodkinson, 2005; Heath et al, 2009). Elsewhere, I have described the distinct qualities of *nongkrong* with the aim to study music communities (see Sutopo and Nilan, 2018; Sutopo et al, 2020). During the process of *nongkrong*, I aimed to build a commensurate and mutual relationship as well as carve out trust with my informants so that they could share their subjective experiences openly. The result is that the voices of young DIY musicians have been central to this research. This aligns with an emic approach to interpretive practice, where research participants are studied in their own right and with emphasis on their own points of view (Jones, 2009).

In this chapter, in order to understand how DIY Indonesian musicians construct and reconstruct the dynamic meanings of subcultures, I focus on the narratives of four informants—Ableh, Warboy, Jungkat, and Yudha[3]—who started participating in subcultural groups in Yogyakarta and later moved to different cities. The four informants mentioned have been continuously committed to their subcultural lifestyles, not only in terms of 'musicking' (Small, 1998) but also in regards to developing music careers throughout their life biographies. Following Plummer (2001), this study can be characterized by researched life stories in which the phenomena I report do not naturalistically occur in everyday life. Rather, I had to approach and coax participants; I interrogated their experiences, often in special settings, using special implements. The role of researcher is clearly important to this activity (Plummer, 2001, p 28).

Setting the arena: from New Order to post-Reform era in Indonesia

The 1950s to 1960s can be argued as the decade of emergence of youth cultures in Southeast Asia (Barendregt et al, 2017), including Indonesia. In terms of music, rock 'n' roll was one of the most popular forms of musical and lifestyle expression for middle- and upper-class youth. Arguably, young people in Indonesia, as elsewhere in postcolonial countries, were searching for new identities and sense of community. However, this period was also characterized by ambivalence between searching for the 'new' modernity, in other words, heirs to the world culture (Lindsay and Liem, 2012), and the intensification of official moral indignation (Barendregt et al, 2017). For instance, during the Old Order era (*Orde Lama*) from 1945 to 1965, it was almost unimaginable to produce forms of youth expression based on Western cultures. Soekarno, the first president of the Indonesian Republic, was keen to protect national culture; as a result, he imprisoned groups of young musicians known as *Koes Plus*—these musicians, who covered Beatles songs, were seen as 'too Western' and would contribute to the moral decadence of young Indonesian generations in the future (Farram, 2006; Mulyadi, 2009). To cut a long story short, in the course of the Old Order era, Soekarno dictated forms of youth culture that would best represent Indonesian national identity and keep the spirit of unfinished national revolution (*Revolusi Belum Usai*) as part of the political zeitgeist.

Despite the cultural atmosphere changing significantly during the New Order era (*Orde Baru*) from 1966 to 1998, building a coherent national identity suitable for grand narratives of development and modernization remained. Thus, youth subcultures once again became the object of the regime's moral indignation. As an illustration, a rock band called God Bless was not permitted to appear on national television because all its band members had long hair and were considered by the regime as not representing national identity (Mulyadi, 2009; Baulch, 2011). Similar forms of control also manifested in the banning of youth cultural products such as pop *cengeng* (Yampolsky, 1989) and rap music (Bodden, 2005). In summary, it can be argued that youth subcultural expression was under the hegemonic control of Indonesia's military-based authoritarian regime.

As happened elsewhere, authoritarian regimes will always face not only political challenges but also cultural resistance led by young people; this also happened in Indonesia at the end of 1990s (Lee, 2011). Music-based subcultures such as punk, metal, and underground emerged and found their moment as a form of resistance against the almost totalitarian practices of the New Order regime. As explained by Barendregt and van Zanten (2002), Wallach (2005), and Martin-Iverson (2012), in the case of DIY underground scenes, many young musicians-cum-activists played significant parts in the anti-New Order protest movement, calling for structural and cultural changes toward more democratic lifestyles.

In the post-Reform era, music-based subcultures as a form of resistance do not necessarily take the shape that they used to from the early 1990s through to the aftermath of the Reformasi (Indonesia) movement. As some scholars argue, neoliberal logic and conditions have, ironically, provided new forms of resistance through the means of commodification (Luvaas, 2009; Martin-Iverson, 2012; Sutopo et al, 2020) and DIY musicians have also conducted themselves toward a similar paradox. Unfortunately, the DIY ethos performed by youth subcultures has gradually become a means of consumption rather than a productive avenue for political voicing. This is evident in the rapidly growing music festival scene in Yogyakarta that is often sponsored by cigarette companies, popular clothing brands, or beverage corporations. Hence, the ethos of autonomous, independent, and rebellious youth subculture has arguably been commodified by neoliberal logic that further expands the idea of resistance itself. Unlike 20 years ago, when the DIY ethos was still deemed peripheral and underground, the value and ideology of independent music-making have now become dominant discourses in the subcultural scene. Even so, arguably, it does not mean that political articulation is not performed by DIY musicians who joined subcultural groups in Indonesia. In short, it has transformed into new ways since the Indonesian government began to embrace a creative economic policy as part of its new developmentalism agenda (Fahmi et al, 2016; 2017).

Do-It-Yourself musicians, subculture, and life biographies in the post-Reform era

In his book *Documents of Life 2: An Invitation to a Critical Humanism*, Plummer (2001) suggests the importance of interconnection between historical moments and individual biographies. Thus, in order to understand how individuals construct subjective meaning, researchers need to take into consideration the elements of moving subjects between the development of DIY Indonesian musicians' life cycles and the ways in which external situations influence this. A constant reference to historical change is thus one of the great values of the biographical approach (Plummer, 2001, p 40). In order to explore the dynamic interpretation of DIY musicians' subcultures, in the following sections I tell the story of my participants' experiences moving from amateur to professional careers under particular conditions of the post-Reform era.

Amateur careers

Ableh, Warboy, Jungkat, and Yudha were all born in the mid-1980s and came from middle-class families. They grew up during the New Order and post-Reformation eras; thus, they experienced two different cultural and political atmospheres, characterized by a transition from repression to freedom of expression. As explained earlier, the era of reform was a period when global popular culture was introduced to Indonesian youth. In particular, pre-digital media such as magazines, radio, zines, and television were prominent (Sen and Hill, 2000; Wallach, 2005). Thus, the four informants' participation in music-based subcultures started from their passion as fans and hobbyists. Warboy, for example, started to find cool music through Nirvana's album *Smells Like Teen Spirit*, which later led him to study in music school in Yogyakarta. Jungkat experienced something similar when his brother from Sumatra Island introduced him to grunge and Guns N' Roses, which encouraged him to form a band with his best mate in high school. Similar stories came from the two other informants as well. Passion for popular music steered them each to take learning and playing music seriously, not only through formal music education but also more importantly through music communities. These were important moments for them, in particular to taste the experience of joining a music subculture. Ableh and

Warboy joined the jazz community while Jungkat and Yudha joined the underground metal community. I contend that the term 'subculture' for my informants refers to these music communities (*komunitas musik*) which had a distinctive character of Yogyakarta as a city of culture in the pre-digital era. Before investing in DIY music identity, the early internalization of subculture among the informants was influenced by the combination of intersecting micro-macro elements of significant and generalized others (Perinbanayagam, 1975) manifested in family, friends, community, and global popular culture. As an imported concept, 'subculture' was translated differently during the participants' formation of primary versus secondary habitus (Wacquant, 2016). Subjectively, they first interpreted subculture as similar to global popular culture insomuch as it was considered 'cool' and 'modern' (McGuigan, 2009). This element of coolness was used to construct participants' youth identities under conditions of transition from authoritarian to democratic eras (Heryanto, 2008). Subculture, as a representation of global popular culture, thus functioned as a bridge to the next step of 'musicking' (Small, 1998) as these young men became amateur musicians. At this point, the meaning of subculture changed into what they called '*komunitas musik*'. Their experiences and stories show that they became active and reflexive members of an 'imagined' global subculture instead of seeing themselves as passive or marginalized consumers.

Komunitas musik, as I described earlier, has similar qualities of 'subcultural substance' as suggested by Hodkinson (2002). Members of both the jazz and underground communities shared similar codes not only represented through appearance, but more importantly, through shared community values. In the case of the underground metal community in Yogyakarta, I have argued that three important shared values are *otentisitas* (authenticity), *kemandirian* (autonomy), and *komunitas* (community) (Sutopo and Lukisworo, 2020; Sutopo et al, 2020). Members typically shared similar historical narratives at the local level, which often led them to acknowledge some musicians as senior members and others as youngsters in the community. They also shared what they called '*cara berkomunitas*' (ways to behave and act as members of the music community), which, as I have explained elsewhere, are characterized by hierarchical relationships (Sutopo and Nilan, 2018) and are interconnected nationally and globally. As youngsters, Ableh, Warboy, Jungkat, and Yudha made use of the music community as a space to learn the material and symbolic aspects of 'musicking' (Small, 1998), for instance, building up their music skills, learning '*cara berkomunitas*', developing social networks, and finding a source of belonging. In short, they learned a variety of tangible and intangible skills suitable for building and developing their DIY music careers. Their personal stories reflect macro conditions in the post-Reform era, which normalized the neoliberal 'rules of the game', as manifested in the underinvestment in public services such as education and employment (White, 2016). Thus, subculture as '*komunitas musik*' was interpreted by the participants as one of the spaces in which to develop reflexive strategies of survival.

For Ableh and Warboy, *komunitas musik* jazz provided them with regular activities called jam sessions, which were very important in nurturing their embodied musical skills. In particular, live jam sessions in public spaces provided 'real time' experiences of simultaneously dealing with audiences and learning to improvise on the stage. Jam sessions were also regularly held internally among community members and were usually located in one of the members' home studios. In these spaces, youngsters had chances to reflexively share anything related to music and non-musical experiences with senior musicians and fellow youngsters alike. Thus, internal and public jam sessions were not only focal to accumulating relevant skills but also symbolically significant for developing community values, which later became a source of 'imagined communities' when members moved on to the professional stage of their music careers.

For Jungkat and Yudha, '*komunitas metal*' did not necessarily provide regular activities like the jam sessions. However, it supported the youngsters and other metal members with an 'actual' space to hang out (*nongkrong*) regularly. *Komunitas metal* became central as a space for subcultural rituals, which consisted of sharing everything related to metal music, including ways of mastering distinct metal repertoires. In Yogyakarta, these subcultural rituals also became a source for youngsters to explore identities as metalheads in addition to giving them the freedom to express their individuality. As explained elsewhere (see Baulch, 2002; Wallach, 2005; Sutopo et al, 2020), at a certain level, metalheads' values are still characterized by their strength to resist not only state and market, but also *norma umum* (society's norms). Thus, contrary to post-subculture strands which celebrate the pleasure of consumption (see Redhead, 1990; Thornton, 1995), underground metal spaces and rituals facilitated, similar to the jazz community, the nurturing of values such as *otentisitas* (authenticity), *kemandirian* (autonomy), and *komunitas* (community). In *komunitas metal*, gigs in underground spaces became the most important event in which to not only practice subcultural rituals, but also to give and receive symbolic recognition as metalheads. Often, these underground metal gigs not only became meeting spaces for the local scene, but also for members of larger translocal and international scenes (Peterson and Bennett, 2004). Thus, *komunitas metal* at the local level took these events seriously not only because they were a matter of local pride but also because they were an effort to showcase their participation in the larger global metal music community (Kahn-Harris, 2006) or to orient themselves 'elsewhere', to borrow a term from Baulch (2003). In addition, the value of 'local pride' was also crucial for metal bands when they had to play gigs in different cities around Indonesia. Arguably, it was not only a matter of constructing distinction but also a matter of developing and strengthening the 'imagined communities' of metal Indonesia. It is important to note, however, that different from the 'imagined community' of *komunitas jazz*, which was more individualized, the metal community rigorously maintained their communal identities and values.

At the amateur stage, it can be argued that dimensions of resistance and fluid subcultural identity (see Clarke et al, 1976; Bennett, 1999) were interchangeably appropriated by Ableh, Warboy, Yudha, and Jungkat in building and developing their music careers to a professional level. They reflexively reinterpreted and made use of subcultural networks and identities within the dynamics of their temporal and spatial situations. In particular, their reflexive practices reveal the ambivalent and contradictory conditions of young people's lifeworlds in the post-Reform era. On the one hand, they had relatively more freedom to express cosmopolitan values (Luvaas, 2009). On the other hand, societal changes had forced them to embrace individualization and DIY practices amidst new social structures (Nilan and Feixa, 2006). Thus, my participants had to rely on social networks provided by *komunitas musik* at the local, national, and global levels to develop their own DIY biographies.

Professional careers

During their professional DIY music careers, my informants interpreted music-based subcultures differently. For Ableh and Warboy, *komunitas jazz* lost its significance as a space in which to hang out and nurture relevant musical skills. However, during the moments they moved to Jakarta or Bali to develop pathways to the music and tourism industries, each was able to benefit from the affectual and embodied solidarity produced by imagined communities in those two places. These forms of solidarity manifested not only because they shared similar identities as jazz players from Yogyakarta, but also because they were struggling musicians and precarious workers who took their music profession seriously and were willing to survive in new cities. At this stage of their careers, the meaning of music subculture shifted towards sustainable intra-space connections within material and symbolic social networks, which functioned as capital to help them survive in the new music and tourism industry. Jungkat and Yudha also reinterpreted music subculture differently during the professional stage of their careers. Since they had been building their music careers in Yogyakarta and were only engaging in temporary mobility for gigs at local, national, and global levels, *komunitas metal* began to function as a form of fluid yet sustainable subcultural-network capital for them. Accordingly, *komunitas metal* had dual functions: first, as a source of profitable gigs which meant relative income for the musicians; second and more importantly, as a way to maintain solidarity with the larger imagined metal community as well as a personal sense of identity as metalheads.

Moreover, during their professional careers, Ableh, Warboy, Jungkat, and Yudha kept in touch with their affiliated *komunitas musik*. For Warboy, despite his decision to move permanently to Bali, he has maintained his connection with *komunitas jazz* in Yogyakarta. For Ableh, Jungkat, and Yudha, who remained in Yogyakarta to develop their careers, staying connected with *komunitas musik* was a must. For Warboy, his sustainable connection with *komunitas musik* in Yogyakarta was useful in maintaining the flow of mobilities among other young musicians traveling from Yogyakarta to Bali. There are regular patterns of mobility from Yogyakarta to Bali which are taken for granted as progressive career trajectories for young musicians (Sutopo et al, 2017a; 2017b). This is partly because musicians like Warboy interpret music subculture at the professional stage as a space and social network through which to maintain the production of jazz musicians in both cities. Often, Warboy has acted as a mentor for youngsters who recently moved to Bali. At an individual level, this role has helped him to maintain his professional music career in Bali's international tourism industry. As a professional session player who primarily performed in a full band and who seldom produced his own records, serving as a mentor has also enabled him to sustain as well as upskill the members of his band. This story shows the importance of reflexivity as an embodied, intangible skill (see Sweetman, 2003; Crossley, 2006; Sutopo et al, 2017b) that counteracts multilayered structural and cultural obstacles in the Indonesian culture industry.

For Ableh and Yudha, music-based subculture is no longer a space to nurture relevant music skills or build networks to achieve upward career mobility. Realistically, it helped them maintain their music careers locally. Their stable connections with the subculture enabled the upgrading of their material and cultural capital, and implicitly led to finding and expanding the 'market' for their music products. Ableh had not only remained active as a session player but also produced records with many bands alongside regular work as an MC (master of ceremony) at various events. *Komunitas music* and the young people who participated in it were a prospective space and audience respectively, whereby he could promote his music products. While for Yudha, who became a full-time musician, maintaining a connection with *komunitas metal* was very significant. He relied heavily on the youngsters and enthusiasts among metalheads to get gigs at local, national, and international levels. Besides that, he has also run an independent recording studio which mainly catered to metal bands interested in recording, mixing, and mastering their albums. Thus, in contrast to Cohen (1991), social networks are not only crucial sources of music tips and techniques; music-based subculture has also been crucial for the sustainability of Yudha's music career. Lastly, Jungkat reinterpreted the meaning of music-based subculture at a mostly personal, rather than professional, level. For him, continuous participation in the *komunitas metal* was a matter of maintaining his metalhead identity. Although he was still a professional musician, he admitted that gigs were no longer his main source of income. Instead, he had a promising job as a sociology lecturer. That said, Jungkat's subcultural background illuminated his educational career. In particular, his long-term experiences and embodied identity as a metalhead facilitated not only more fluid interactions with his students, but also helped him to give relatable examples in his 'Introduction to Sociology' course. Thus, it can be argued that he tried to maintain a balance between the identity domains of 'transition' and 'culture' (see Woodman and Bennett, 2015; Johansson and Herz, 2019).

Conclusion

Using a biographical approach, this chapter has illustrated the dynamic meaning of subculture among DIY Indonesian musicians and its connection with the socio-cultural-historical context of Indonesia in the post-Reform era. The life stories of four DIY musicians reveal the ambiguous character of subcultural careers amidst everyday political-economic realities in Indonesia. They also contribute to new knowledge in subcultural studies at the global level by contextualizing the concept of subculture within the subjective experiences of DIY Indonesian musicians in their specific temporal and spatial situations.

The biographical approach emphasizes a differentiation between stages of subculturalists' careers. I have formulated this using two stages: amateur and professional, which not only illustrate their trajectories as a continuum, but are also considered pivotal among DIY Indonesian musicians in the post-Reform era. At the amateur stage, DIY Indonesian musicians interpret music subculture as a space in which to accumulate valuable forms of material and symbolic skills suitable for building and developing into the professional stage. They have invested their time to acquire subcultural capitals that are bodily, mentally, and emotionally interconnected (see Wacquant, 2005; Crossley, 2015). In ontologically precarious subcultural music careers, being able to combine and flexibly reinterpret relevant knowledge and skills is crucial not only to master the multi-dimensions of 'musicking' (Small, 1998) but also to survive in the later professional stage. In particular, I have called attention to the key role of strategic social networks arising from music subculture, in their multiple and plural forms. In the amateur stage, DIY Indonesian musicians learn to build, share, and maintain solidarity among themselves not only at the local level but also at the translocal level (see Peterson and Bennett, 2004; Sutopo et al, 2017b). They also internalize the empirical manifestation of individualization (Beck and Beck-Gernsheim, 2002), in which relying on social networks is a must to prevent unpredictable consequences in both the present and future. Thus, music subculture plays a crucial role in the production of an alternative career for young people.

During the professional stage, DIY Indonesian musicians interpret music subculture as a space to sustain their music careers under uncertain and risky conditions of the subculture industry. In this stage, the pressure of individualization, in which individuals are encouraged to perform in terms of 'Me & Co' (Beck, 2000) and engage in the enterprise of the self (Kelly, 2013; Kelly et al, 2019), was becoming more intense. In particular, the participants were not only expected to provide 'rice on the table' for their nuclear and extended families (see Sutopo et al, 2017a) but also to nurture the subcultural values of authenticity (*otentisitas*), autonomy (*kemandirian*), and community (*komunitas*) (see Sutopo and Lukisworo, 2020; Sutopo et al, 2020). The narratives of DIY Indonesian musicians unveil the everyday politics of the post-Reform era, which I described as the politics of 'survival of the fittest'. The four participants were not only required to survive, but also to take responsibility for the survival of their family and community.

Reflecting on the life stories of DIY Indonesian musicians in this chapter, the subculture versus post-subculture debate has been reinterpreted based on the interconnection between my informants' subjectivities and the changing socio-cultural-historical context of Indonesia. Thus, instead of meticulously pointing out the fixity versus fluidity and resistance versus identity debates, DIY Indonesian musicians have reflexively appropriated both dimensions of subculture based on their specific temporal and spatial situations.

Notes

[1] For a description of the Chicago School tradition, see Williams (2011).
[2] For an historical overview on the Chicago School as a pioneer of biographical research, see Plummer (2001).
[3] All informants' names in this chapter are pseudonyms.

References

Barendregt, B. and van Zanten, W. (2002) 'Popular Music in Indonesia since 1998', *Yearbook of Traditional Music*, 34: 67–113.

Barendregt, B., Keppy, P. and Nordholt, H.S. (2017) *Popular Music in Southeast Asia: Banal Beats, Muted Histories*, Amsterdam: Amsterdam University Press.

Baudrillard, J. (1998) *The Consumer Society: Myths and Structures*, New York: SAGE.

Baulch, E. (2002) 'Alternative Music and Mediation in Late New Order Indonesia', *Inter-Asia Cultural Studies*, 3(2): 219–234.

Baulch, E. (2003) 'Gesturing Elsewhere: The Identity Politics of the Balinese Death/Thrash Metal Scene', *Popular Music*, 22(2): 195–215.

Baulch, E. (2004) 'Reggae Borderzones, Reggae Graveyards: Bob Marley Fandom in Bali', *Perfect Beat: The Asia-Pacific Journal of Research into Contemporary Music and Popular Culture*, 6(4): 3–27.

Baulch, E. (2011) 'God Bless Comeback: New Experiment with Nostalgia in Indonesian Rock', *Perfect Beat: The Asia Pacific Journal of Research into Contemporary Music and Popular Culture*, 12(2): 129–146.

Beck, U. (1992) *Risk Society: Towards a New Modernity*, New York: SAGE.

Beck, U. (2000) *The Brave New World of Work*, Cambridge: Polity Press.

Beck, U. and Beck-Gernsheim, E. (2002) *Individualization: Institutionalized Individualism and its Social and Political Consequences*, London: SAGE.

Bennett, A. (1999) 'Subcultures of Neo-Tribes? Rethinking the Relationships between Youth, Style and Musical Taste', *Sociology*, 33(3): 599–617.

Bennett, A. (2003a) 'Researching Youth Culture and Popular Music: A Methodological Critique', *The British Journal of Sociology*, 53(3): 451–466.

Bennett, A. (2003b) 'The Use of Insider Knowledge in Ethnographic Research on Contemporary Youth Music Scenes', in A. Bennet, M. Cieslik and S. Miles (eds) *Researching Youth*, Basingstoke: Palgrave Macmillan, pp 186–199.

Bennett, A. (2005) 'In Defence of Neo-Tribes: A Response to Blackman and Hesmondhalgh', *Journal of Youth Studies*, 8(2): 255–259.

Bennett, A. (2011) 'The Post-Subcultural Turn: Some Reflections 10 Years On', *Journal of Youth Studies*, 14(5): 493–506.

Bennett, A. (2013) *Music, Style and Aging: Growing Old Disgracefully?*, Philadelphia: Temple University Press.

Bennett, A. (2018) 'Conceptualising the Relationship between Youth, Music and DIY Careers: A Critical Overview', *Cultural Sociology*, 12(2): 140–155.

Bennett, A. and Kahn-Harris, K. (eds) (2004) *After Subculture: Critical Studies in Contemporary Youth Culture*, Basingstoke: Palgrave Macmillan.

Bennett, A. and Robards, B. (eds) (2014) *Mediated Youth Cultures: The Internet, Belonging and New Cultural Configurations*, London: Palgrave Macmillan.

Bennett, A. and Guerra, P. (eds) (2018) *DIY Cultures and Underground Music Scenes*, London: Routledge.

Blackman, S. (2005) 'Youth Subcultural Theory: A Critical Engagement with the Concepts, Its Origins and Politics, from the Chicago School to Postmodernism', *Journal of Youth Studies*, 8(1): 1–20.

Bodden, M. (2005) 'Rap in Indonesian Youth Music of the 1990's', *Asian Music*, 36(2): 1–26.

Clarke, J., Hall, S., Jefferson, T. and Roberts, B. (1976) 'Subcultures, Cultures and Class: A Theoretical Overview', in S. Hall and T. Jefferson (eds) *Resistance through Rituals: Youth Subcultures in Post-War Britain*, London: Routledge, pp 9–74.

Cohen, S. (1991) *Rock Culture in Liverpool: Popular Music in the Making*, Oxford: Clarendon Press.

Crossley, N. (2006) *Reflexive Embodiment in Contemporary Society*, Berkshire: Open University Press.

Crossley, N. (2015) 'Music Worlds and Body Techniques: On the Embodiment of Musicking', *Cultural Sociology*, 9(4): 471–492.

Fahmi, F.Z., Koster, S. and van Dijk, J. (2016) 'The Location of Creative Industries in a Developing Country: The Case of Indonesia', *Cities*, 59: 66–79.

Fahmi, F.Z., McCann, P. and Koster, S. (2017) 'Creative Economy Policy in Developing Countries: The Case of Indonesia', *Urban Studies*, 54(6): 1367–1384.

Farram, S. (2006) 'Wage War Against Beatle Music! Censorship and Music in Soekarno's Indonesia', *Review of Indonesian and Malaysian Affairs*, 41(2): 247–277.

Furlong, A., Woodman, D. and Wyn, J. (2011) 'Changing Times, Changing Perspectives: Reconciling Transition and Cultural Perspectives on Youth and Young Adulthood', *Journal of Sociology*, 47(4): 355–370.

Giddens, A. (1991) *Modernity and Self-Identity: Self and Society in the Late Modern Age*, Stanford: Stanford University Press.

Greener, T. and Hollands, R. (2006) 'Beyond Subculture and Post-Subculture? The Case of Visual Psytrance', *Journal of Youth Studies*, 9(4): 393–418.

Heath, S., Brooks, R., Cleaver, E. and Eleanor, I. (2009) *Researching Young People's Lives*, New York: SAGE.

Hebdige, D. (1979) *Subculture: The Meaning of Style*, London: New Accents.

Heryanto, A. (ed) (2008) *Popular Culture in Indonesia: Fluid Identities in Post-Authoritarian Politics*, London: Routledge.

Hesmondhalgh, D. (2005) 'Subcultures, Scenes and Tribes? None of the Above', *Journal of Youth Studies*, 8(1): 21–40.

Hodkinson, P. (2002) *Goth: Identity, Style and Subculture*, Providence, RI: Berg.

Hodkinson, P. (2005) 'Insider Research in the Study of Youth Cultures', *Journal of Youth Studies*, 8(2): 131–149.

Hodkinson, P. (2012) 'Beyond Spectacular Specifics in the Study of Youth (Sub)Cultures', *Journal of Youth Studies*, 15(5): 557–572.

Hodkinson, P. (2016) 'Youth Cultures and the Rest of Life: Subcultures, Post-Subcultures and Beyond', *Journal of Youth Studies*, 19(5): 629–645.

Hodkinson, P. and Deicke, W. (eds) (2007) *Youth Cultures: Scenes, Subcultures and Tribes*, London: Routledge.

Holdsworth, C. and Morgan, D. (2007) 'Revisiting the Generalized Other: An Exploration', *Sociology*, 41(3): 401–417.

Jensen, S.Q. (2018) 'Towards a Neo-Birminghamian Conception of Subculture? History, Challenges and Future Potentials', *Journal of Youth Studies*, 21(4): 405–421.

Johansson, T. and Herz, M. (2019) *Youth Studies in Transition: Culture, Generation and New Learning Processes*, Singapore: Springer.
Jones, G. (2009) *Youth*, Cambridge: Polity Press.
Kahn-Harris, K. (2006) *Extreme Metal: Music and Culture on the Edge*, New York: Berg.
Kelly, P. (2013) *The Self as Enterprise: Foucault and the Spirit of 21st Century Capitalism*, Aldershot: Gower.
Kelly, P., Campbell, P. and Howie, L. (2019) *Rethinking Young People's Marginalisation: Beyond Neo-Liberal Futures?*, London: Routledge.
Lee, D. (2011) 'Images of Youth: On the Iconography of History and Protest in Indonesia', *History and Anthropology*, 22(3): 307–336.
Lindsay, J. and Liem, M.H.T. (eds) (2012) *Heirs to World Culture: Being Indonesian 1950–1965*, Amsterdam: KITLV Press.
Luvaas, B.A. (2009) 'Generation DIY: Youth, Class, and the Culture of Indie Production in Digital-Age Indonesia', PhD dissertation, University of California.
Lyotard, J.F. (1979) *The Postmodern Condition: A Report on Knowledge*, Minneapolis: Minnesota University Press.
Maffesoli, M. (1996) *The Time of the Tribes: The Decline of Individualism in Mass Society*, New York: SAGE.
Malbon, B. (1999) *Clubbing: Dancing, Ecstasy and Vitality*, London: Routledge
Martin-Iverson, S. (2012) 'Autonomous Youth? Independence and Precariousness in the Indonesian Underground Music Scenes', *The Asia Pacific Journal of Anthropology*, 13(4): 382–397.
McGuigan, J. (2009) *Cool Capitalism*, London: Pluto Press.
Muggleton, D. (2000) *Inside Subculture: The Postmodern Meaning of Style*, Oxford: Berg.
Muggleton, D. and Weinzierl, R. (eds) (2003) *The Post-Subcultures Reader*, Oxford: Berg.
Mulyadi, M. (2009) *Industri Musik Indonesia: Suatu Sejarah*, Bekasi: Koperasi Ilmu Pengetahuan Sosial.
Nilan, P. and Feixa, C. (eds) (2006) *Global Youth? Hybrid Identities, Plural Worlds*, London: Routledge.
Perinbanayagam, R.S. (1975) 'The Significance of Others in the Thought of Alfred Schutz, G.H Mead and C. H Cooley', *The Sociological Quarterly*, 16(4): 500–521.
Peterson, R.A. and Bennett, A. (2004) 'Introducing Music Scenes', in A. Bennett and R.A. Peterson (eds) *Music Scenes: Local, Translocal, and Virtual*, Nashville: Vanderbilt University Press, pp 1–16.
Plummer, K. (2001) *Documents of Life 2: An Invitation to a Critical Humanism*, London: SAGE.
Redhead, S. (1990) *The End of the Century Party: Youth and Pop towards 2000*, Manchester: Manchester University Press.

Richter, M. (2012) *Musical Worlds in Yogyakarta*, Amsterdam: KITLV Press.

Robards, B. and Bennett, A. (2011) 'My Tribe: Post-Subcultural Manifestations of Belonging on Social Networks Sites', *Sociology*, 45(2): 303–317.

Samuel, H. (1999) 'The Development of Sociology in Indonesia: The Production of Knowledge, State Formation and Economic Change', PhD dissertation, Swinburne University of Technology.

Sen, A. and Hill, D. (2000) *Media, Culture and Politics in Indonesia*, Oxford: Oxford University Press.

Shildrick, T. and Macdonald, R. (2005) 'In Defence of Subculture: Young People, Leisure and Social Divisions', *Journal of Youth Studies*, 9(2): 125–140.

Small, C. (1998) *Musicking: The Meanings of Performing and Listening*, Middletown: Wesleyan University Press.

Springer, S., Birch, K. and Macleavy, J. (eds) (2016) *The Handbook of Neoliberalism*, London: Routledge.

Stahl, G. (2003) 'Tastefully Renovating Subcultural Theory: Making Space for a New Model', in D. Muggleton and R. Weinzierl (eds) *The Post-Subcultures Reader*, New York: Berg, pp 27–40.

Sutopo, O.R. and Nilan, P. (2018) 'The Constrained Positions of Young Musicians in the Yogyakarta Jazz Community', *Asian Music*, 49(1): 34–57.

Sutopo, O.R. and Lukisworo, A.A. (2020) 'Praktik Bermusik Musisi Muda dalam Skena Metal Ekstrem [Musical Practices of Young Musicians in the Extreme Metal Scene]', *Jurnal Sosiologi Pendidikan Humanis*, 5(2): 107–119.

Sutopo, O.R., Nilan, P. and Threadgold, S. (2017a) 'Keep the Hope Alive: Young Indonesian Musicians' Views of the Future', *Journal of Youth Studies*, 20(5): 549–564.

Sutopo, O.R., Threadgold, S. and Nilan, P. (2017b) 'Young Indonesian Musicians, Strategic Social Capital, Reflexivity and Timing', *Sociological Research Online*, 22(3): 186–203.

Sutopo, O.R., Wibawanto, G.R. and Lukisworo, A.A. (2020) 'Resist or Perish! Understanding the Mode of Resistance among Young DIY Indonesian Musicians', *Perfect Beat: The Asia Pacific Journal of Research into Contemporary Music and Popular Culture*, 20(2): 116–133.

Sweetman, P. (2003) 'Twenty First Century Dis-ease? Habitual Reflexivity or the Reflexive Habitus', *The Sociological Review*, 51(4): 528–549.

Thornton, S. (1995) *Club Cultures: Music Media and Subcultural Capital*, London: Polity Press.

Wacquant, L. (2005) 'Carnal Connections: On Embodiment, Apprenticeship, and Membership', *Qualitative Sociology*, 28: 445–474.

Wacquant, L. (2016) 'A Concise Genealogy and Anatomy of Habitus', *The Sociological Review*, 64(1): 64–72.

Wallach, J. (2005) 'Underground Rock Music and Democratization in Indonesia', *World Literature Today*, 79(3–4): 16–20.

Weinzierl, R. and Muggleton, D. (2003) 'What is Post-subcultural Studies Anyway?', in D. Muggleton and R. Weinzierl (eds) *The Post-Subcultures Reader*, New York: Berg, pp 3–26.

White, B. (2016) 'Generation and Social Change: Indonesian Youth in Comparative Perspective', in K. Robinson (eds) *Youth Identities and Social Transformation in Modern Indonesia*, Leiden and Boston: Brill, pp 4–22.

Williams, J.P. (2011) *Subcultural Theory: Traditions and Concepts*, London: Polity Press.

Williams, J.P. (2018) 'Subculture's Not Dead! Checking the Pulse of Subculture Studies through a Review of "Subcultures, Popular Music and Political Change" and "Youth Cultures and Subcultures: Australian Perspectives"', *Young*, 27(1): 1–17.

Woodman, D. and Bennett, A. (eds) (2015) *Youth Cultures, Transitions and Generations: Bridging the Gap in Youth Research*, Basingstoke: Palgrave Macmillan.

Yampolsky, P. (1989) 'Hati yang Luka: An Indonesian Hit', *Indonesia*, 47: 1–18.

PART III

Embodying Interpretive Practice

8

"That's Not Punk!" Authenticity, Older Punk Women, and the 'Doing' of Punk Scholarship

Laura Way

Though there has been an increased academic interest in ageing subculturalists, in the context of punk scholarship older punk women continue to be marginalized and academic discussions concerning ageing, gender, and punk have been limited. My PhD research which this chapter derives from sought to explore the construction and maintenance of punk identity by older women. Though not something I set out to explore, the concept of authenticity and how this was constructed by the women I spoke with emerged through the interviews highlighting an important aspect of their identity construction. If one is to take the view that identity is socially constructed then this does lend itself to thinking about questions of authenticity (Schwarz and Williams, 2020) and, indeed, this concept has experienced much attention from identity theorists since the early 20th century (Lemart, 2019, cited in Schwarz and Williams, 2020).

This chapter deals with two interrelated issues. First, drawing upon a feminist, inductivist methodology, the chapter will bring to the fore the previously marginalized voices of older/ageing punk women, focusing on how they construct and negotiate punk authenticity; adding further weight to the argument that punk needs to be conceptualized as something which is fluid and not static (Williams, 2006). The findings discussed will demonstrate how this conceptualization is shaped, and indeed sometimes constrained, by intersecting issues concerning gender and ageing; something previous work on ageing punk participants (for example, Bennett, 2006) has as yet failed to consider. The importance of understanding authenticity temporally, and not just how it is constructed in the present, will also be highlighted (Mullaney, 2012).

Second, this chapter considers the ways the fabrication of authenticity is woven throughout the actual 'doing' of punk scholarship itself. Despite increasing moves to engage in reflexivity within the social sciences (and in, specifically, subcultures research), such embracing of reflexivity has certainly not been taken up at large among punk scholarship; often limited to those scholars reflecting on their 'insider' position and/or those focused on marginalized identities within punk and/or those adopting a feminist framework. A consideration of the construction of authenticity is vital within punk scholarship, particularly when thinking about what becomes considered as empirical, methodological, and theoretical canon. This chapter will first, however, consider relevant literature pertaining to the key issues at hand (authenticity, punk, gender, ageing) before outlining the methodological detail of the research this chapter stems from and then moving onto the interpretive discussions.

Authenticity and punk

One way of approaching punk and its relationship to identity is to consider punk as a label which is used to categorize. Understanding identity through such processes of labeling and categorizing means constructions of 'insider/outsider' become important (Williams, 2006)—how does one construct themselves as a punk as opposed to whom they construct as not? This is indicative of the kind of questions that have been asked in scholarship concerning subcultures more broadly since work on postwar youth cultures by the Birmingham Centre for Contemporary Cultural Studies (CCCS), though it is important to note the differing approaches toward addressing such questions. While the CCCS approached this through seeking to 'map out' what they could see to be the key markers of a particular subculture from a more etic perspective, for example, subcultural scholars are increasingly now exploring questions concerning labels and categorizing from an emic route. Regardless of approach, it is clear to see why then a concept such as 'authenticity' would have such presence in subcultural scholarship when exploring identity, insider/outsider understandings and categorizations—who is authentic/not authentic? How is such authenticity constructed?

We see then a move away from previous realist positions to more microsociological approaches to understanding subcultures such as punk (Williams, 2006). This highlights that authenticity is not fixed or static, instead being something which is always in the process of construction. Authenticity is not something held by a subculture or about 'trying to weed out inauthentic "poseurs" through predictable disciplinary channels of commodification and ideological control' (Gordon, 2014, pp 183–184). As Peterson notes, authentic characteristics are not inherent, instead it is about 'a claim made by or for someone, thing or performance and either accepted or rejected by relevant others' (Peterson, 2005, p 1086, cited in Williams, 2006). Punk authenticity is therefore performed and 'always open to question' (Gubrium and Holstein, 2009, p 126, cited in Hannerz, 2015). Particularly relevant to my own research is scholarship concerning punk, authenticity, and ageing and/or gender, and it is this which I turn to next.

Punk, authenticity, and ageing and/or gender

Academic focus on punk women is commonly framed by how they are constructed and/or perceived as a minority, or how the women themselves feel to be a minority, within a masculine subculture (Roman, 1988; Leblanc, 2002; Griffin, 2012). Despite claims of egalitarianism, the way punk often reproduces inequalities is well-documented. With regards to gender this can include issues such as indirect or direct discrimination toward women; discouragement of women in the context of musicianship; the treating of women as novelties; abuse; sexual harassment; and the promotion of stereotypical understandings concerning gender (Leblanc, 2002; Rouse, 2019; Donaghey, 2021). Punk as masculinist is constructed in terms of male participants outnumbering females, punk resting upon particular notions of masculinity, and male dominance through male punks' expectations of and interactions with female punks (through things such as abuse, chivalry, and sexual pressures—all of which involve contradictions being experienced by punk girls) (Leblanc, 2002). The construction of punk authenticity has been demonstrated too to be gendered, constructed in ways which privilege punk men (Leblanc, 2002; Hannerz, 2015). This is reflective too of the struggles women experience more generally in trying to access valuable subcultural capital. As Holland (2018) notes: 'The most important thing to remember is that women have an extra barrier to authenticity and thus to authenticity and membership: quite simply, that barrier is that they are not men' (p 197).

With regards to punk and gender inequalities, Katharina Alexi (2020) has proposed 'punkriarchy' as a way of conceptualizing these inequalities within punk, describing this as: 'The same 3–30 male bands on every concert and festival flyer again. The same male bands on big punk zine covers since 30+ yrs. Unwanted advice for musicians on stage. Absolute silence on feminist fights for rights. Stereotypes in lyrics. Exclusive humor' (Alexi, 2020, np). Punkriarchy, then, could be seen as referring to gendered process of authentication and gatekeeping, nodding toward the way men are perceived to shape the agenda for what is deemed important within punk and, indeed, *who* is deemed important within punk. Punkriarchy offers a way of conceptualizing these issues within their punk context, as well as highlighting the way women may experience patriarchy 'within' and/or 'outside' of punk. In developing this as a concept I wish to also propose here that punkriarchy can encapsulate the way punk reproduces other inequalities, beyond those concerning gender, and punkriarchy can be conceived as the dominance of white, heteronormative masculinist values within punk. This has the potential then to be developed as a way of conceptualizing, and thus interpreting, how punk upholds such intersecting inequalities.

Before moving into a consideration of scholarship concerning ageing and punk it is important to first situate this chapter in the interpretive approach to age/ageing I took as a researcher. My emphasis was placed on age and ageing as socially constructed, rather than as fixed biological categories and processes. Societal norms, values, and institutions help to shape individual experiences and meanings of ageing (Morgan and Kunkel, 2007) and a way of doing this can be through the construction of particular age categories, for example, youth, adulthood, old age. These categories become associated with particular age-related expectations. For example, adulthood in Britain can be understood as comprising particular 'markers' (Jones and Wallace, 1992, cited in Pilcher, 1995), for example, being in stable full-time work, stable relationships, independent living, and parenthood (Blatterer, 2007). However, the importance of one's subjective understanding and experience of age/ageing should not be downplayed. I discuss this further in the methodology section of this chapter with regard to the sampling process involved in my research.

As noted in the introduction there is still a distinct lack of academic consideration of *older* punk women. In part this reflects punk scholarship's original preoccupation with punk as a youth culture, reflected in the cohorts researchers focused upon. However, an increasing recognition within scholarship of subculturalists/subculture participants who would be seen as 'post-youth' (Bennett and Hodkinson, 2012) has still left the voices of older punk women, largely, unheard. Some attention has been given to older punks (Andes, 2002; Bennett, 2006; 2012; Davis, 2006; 2012) but, where present, older punk women are a minority. Additionally, gender as part of a framework for analysis is non-existent. There are parallels here with the wider context in which women experience ageing, if we argue that women experience ageing within a patriarchal society that promotes a 'cult of youth' (Featherstone and Hepworth, 1991). The proposition that ageing women experience invisibility in punk scholarship then mirrors their invisibility within wider society and culture. If we are to be analyzing age and ageing within subcultures such as punk then doing so through feminist frameworks becomes increasingly important.

Where scholarly work on punk and ageing does exist, there has been some consideration of authenticity, particularly concerning the negotiations involved in maintaining 'authenticity' as one ages and how authenticity can be constructed temporally. Bennett (2013) found that older punks often constructed themselves (and were constructed by younger punks) as conveyors of punk knowledge—something which might be understood as a way of constructing continued authenticity. Furthermore, Bennett notes that ageing punks

> often argue that their experience of the original punk scene of the late 1970s makes for a unique understanding of punk. It is one that differs from that acquired by younger fans. ... This, in turn, may produce conflicts across different generations of fans, especially in relation to discourses of 'authenticity'. (2013, pp 123–124)

This highlights the importance of the temporality of authenticity, something Mullaney (2012) also notes in research with straight edgers who differentially constructed authenticity through selective use of the past, present, and future. Bringing 'age' into an exploration of subcultural authenticity offers a way, then, of exploring its temporal nature. Though no literature exists specifically on older/ageing punk women and authenticity, Holland's (2018) work concerning older/ageing 'alternative' women is undoubtedly relevant here. Holland offers some temporal analysis concerning the construction of authenticity; arguing that some of the women presented themselves as having been at the authentic core of a group in the past and, having worked at maintaining this, their authenticity was still deemed current. Holland (2018) recognizes not just the relationship between temporality and authenticity but also gender, and how authenticity is constructed in such a way that older/ageing women in particular face greater challenges to being seen as such. This lends further weight to the need to explore constructions of authenticity through a lens of both temporality and gender, especially in the context of punk where previously little attempts to consider both have been made.

Methodology

To elaborate the methodology underpinning the two research aspects of this chapter, it is important to recognize my positionality in line with a commitment to being reflexive and transparent. Punk has held a significant place in my life since I was first introduced to my parents' punk records as a small child. Playing in a band during my teenage years exposed me to various interactions in which I felt I struggled to be taken as seriously as my fellow bandmates (who were both men), for example. Just before embarking on the PhD research on which this chapter is based, I was becoming increasingly interested in how my relationship with punk was changing as I aged, particularly prompted by 'feeling old' when going to gigs despite not feeling this way outside of them(!). I turn now to the two overlapping methods which the discussions in this chapter emerge from—research comprising of interviews with older punk women, and my reflexive observations concerning that research journey. I will discuss each of these next.

Interviews with older punk women

First, the analysis concerning older punk women's constructions of authenticity comes from interviews with older punk women, which focused on older women's constructions of punk identities. This research pursued a feminist, inductivist approach guided by grounded theory. Induction can be defined as 'a bottom-up approach through which a researcher analyses data in order to construct a theory or model' (Constantinou et al, 2017, p 573) while grounded theory is 'grounded' in the perspectives of the research participants (Gibson and Hartman, 2014). My exploration of the construction and maintenance of identity among older punk women was grounded in their perspectives. While not developing a new grounded theory with this research, I sought to apply some of its methodological practices and sensibilities. I took influence from some of the core aspects of grounded theory such as openness, discovery, and an interactive research process (Gibson and Hartman, 2014). My identity as a feminist was important to me and the research incorporated particular core feminist concerns such as a focus on women's lived experiences, the challenging of unequal power dynamics, and the practice of 'strong reflexivity' during the research process (Nagy Hesse-Biber and Leckenby, 2004).

Prior to developing my research questions, I had familiarized myself with literature concerning gender inequalities within punk as well as on gender and ageing more broadly. Despite seeing the concept of authenticity in various titles of academic writing, this was not something I drew upon when constructing my literature review nor when writing my research and interview questions. Reading through and open-coding interview transcripts, I was struck particularly by some participants' feelings of 'imposter syndrome' and how the women I spoke with constructed what/who is punk (or not). This prompted me to look to some of the literature concerning authenticity and integrate this into my discussion of data. Like Hodkinson (2009) I am aware of the limitations to attempting to approach research from a wholly grounded approach, and in addition to what has been noted already I was conscious of being a PhD student and being expected as a part of my initial application for study, as well as the first stages of my PhD, to have familiarity with some relevant literature prior to the generation of data.

In terms of accessing older punk women to speak with, a call-out for participants was shared via social media, relevant online forums/groups, and word of mouth (snowballing)—the call-out invited any older punk women aged 30 years or over to get in touch, in response to pre-existing research which tended to concentrate on those in their teenage years or in their 20s. Some women got in touch to say that although they were not yet 30 they felt 'older', and this subjective understanding of age was taken as significant and where possible these women were included in the research. In total

I spoke with 22 older punk women—16 as a part of in-depth interviews, and six took part in much shorter, email interviews.

Reflexive observations on punk scholarship

Second, I draw upon fieldwork notes during the PhD as well as reflections/observations while venturing into punk scholarship to begin thinking through the construction of authenticity within scholarship on punk itself. Wall (2006) proposes that autoethnographies range from the 'conservative methodologically rigorous study … the personal but theoretically supported … and the highly literary and evocative' (p 154), and the second is most relevant to the approach taken in this chapter. My approach goes some way in being seen as providing a 'highly personalized account[s] that draw[s] upon the experience of the author/researcher for the purposes of extending sociological understanding' (Sparkes, 2000, p 21). Autoethnography, in being viewed as 'subjective', can be seen as the antithesis of positivist research values which involve a denial of the researcher's identity, avoidance of subjectivity, and bias (Wall, 2006). Yet including one's own experiences in their research is also aligned with a feminist approach (Ellis, 2004), and as Averett (2009) points out, autoethnography and feminist research are akin in the way they are both underpinned by the message that 'the personal is political'.

"That's not punk!": constructing punk authenticity as an older punk woman

I now consider some of the key themes which emerged from the interviews with older punk women concerning how they constructed punk authenticity, or what it meant to be punk. The holding of particular punk values was constructed as the key marker by participants, which I have discussed elsewhere (see Way, 2021). While I do not intend to repeat myself here, for the purpose of context these values were understood by my participants as: Do-It-Yourself, community, political consciousness, and subversion. Aside from the perceived holding of such values, the following emerged as important to constructing a punk identity: active participation in the punk scene, possessing 'insider' knowledge, and longevity/era. There is some commonality here with Holland's (2018) work with older 'alternative women' (exampled in the following quote) concerning what markers are constructed as important to authentic identity but importantly she also notes, among the women she spoke with, that:

> Some form of struggle and the accruing of particular knowledge (such as the maintenance of a suitable appearance, knowing the 'right' people,

using the right language, listening to the right music, going to the right places as well as being physically appropriate and able) was necessary to indicate full and proper authenticity of the group as a whole and membership of that group, all conditions which become harder as a woman ages. (Holland, 2018, p 196)

The construction of authenticity according to particular markers is done so then within discourses concerning age/ageing as well as gendered discourses. Next, I will discuss active participation in the punk scene, possessing 'insider' knowledge, and longevity/era in more detail, before briefly considering what exploring punk identity construction temporally can reveal. This chapter section on authenticity and older punk women will then close, focusing lastly, albeit briefly, on how the women themselves presented both social construction and also essentialist views of punk.

Active participation in the 'scene'

Most of the women I spoke with expressed active participation in the punk scene as important to their sense of being punk. Jess, for example, expressed this active participation, or "involvement" as she termed it, as: "[Y]ou're putting on shows, you're going to shows, you're supporting the scene and stuff like that and I think that's when you are a punk" (Interview).

In addition here to active participation being defined as organizing and/or attending gigs, which could be considered concrete examples, Jess also drew upon the more abstract notion of "supporting the scene". This could be a demonstration first of Jess positioning herself as drawing upon some insider knowledge, for example, being someone who understands what "supporting the scene" entails, or indeed, what "the scene" is. Yet drawing upon something more abstract or ambiguous in constructing what commitment and thus authenticity entails could also act as a buffer against any potential critique of not doing the 'right' thing. We will consider next why this might be necessary as an older punk woman.

Across my interviews with older punk women was an absence of explicit claims to being a punk, instead what was more common was the use of more hesitant language and phrasing. One participant even expressed concern over being perceived as an "imposter" should she explicitly claim herself to be "a punk", highlighting the role of others in constructing one's own sense of identity. This sense of gendered inauthenticity was expressed by Elizabeth when speaking about attending gigs with her partner:

'[L]ike I say he more looks the part and ... we've been sat outside before and someone's been flyering for something and they go to him

... but at the same time I did also find this when I had my friends and things. ... I still found people might go to sort of the more male counterparts with me 'cause it's usually blokes that are handing out flyers to be honest ... some female friends are seen more as the accessories.' (Interview)

Similarly, Jen said:

'[W]hen I go to gigs I think people assume that you've got a boyfriend in a band ... that you're there basically because your boyfriend's there ... people are surprised when you like know about music and have an interest in music.' (Interview)

In both of these accounts, women draw upon examples in which they perceived their authenticity to be called into question because of their being women and both of the contexts in which this takes place is while attending a gig. This could be considered then a form of referential meaning-making (something which I will return to more fully later)—Elizabeth and Jen understood themselves in comparison to how they saw others as being understood. There are also parallels and overlaps here with the 'female groupie' discourse. This groupie identity has been aimed at female fans/music producers to position them as inauthentic consumers through their othering and exclusion (Larsen, 2017). Here it can be seen how similar ideas are present within punk and can act as a way of constructing women as less 'serious' subcultural participants and/or less serious music fans. In turn this can constrain feelings of authenticity among punk women. Such challenging of women's authenticity contributes to punk as being socially (re)produced as masculine (Downes, 2007). Active participation in the punk scene as a way of demonstrating commitment and therefore fabricating an authentic punk self, as might be seen here, could be complicated by gender or, more specifically, by being a woman.

Insider knowledge

Some of the women I spoke with, despite answering a call-out for older *punk* women, said they would not call themselves 'a punk'. This could actually be seen as part of the fabrication of authenticity when taken alongside the argument that punk involves a rejection of labels. Regardless, one way individuals can position themselves as a participant of a particular subculture can be through the use of subcultural symbols (Fine, 1983) and, related to this, the use of 'insider knowledge'. Insider knowledge can be seen as subcultural knowledge and might involve, for example, the use of subculturally specific language or terminology (Widdicombe and Wooffitt, 1995). Even among the women I spoke with who did not refer to themselves as punk, presentation of 'insider' knowledge was present.

One demonstration of insider knowledge was through participants conveying their deeper understanding of what punk 'truly' was, rather than how others 'wrongly' perceived it or how it might be stereotypically viewed. Often this involved the dismissal of clothing as not a 'true' indicator of being punk. For example, Naefun said she'd consider some of her friends "punk as fuck" despite them not visually looking how one would expect a punk to look. This could serve as an example of how subculturalists sometimes confer authenticity upon those whom they see exemplifying the ideals of punk subculture (Lewin and Williams, 2009). Naefun, for example, confers this authenticity onto friends who do not 'look punk' or, indeed, even identify themselves as punks—in doing so, this places emphasis on punk as something which is not based on aesthetics but on something 'inside'.

Several participants constructed this distinction between insider/outsider knowledge regarding what punk is/was by drawing on examples involving interactions with others:

> 'People do come up to me and say you know, "You're so punk," and it's like, "Alright, ok," 'cause it's weird cause I've never kind of I never class myself as a punk.' (Deedee, interview)

> 'It's always quite interesting when I'm trying to explain that when people are like, "Aaay you've got silly colored hair, like, are you a punk rocker?" No, I, just no no.' (Katie, interview)

These examples highlight how aesthetics can be an important aspect of emic meaning-making. In these examples, Deedee and Katie draw upon what they construct as a misconception that punk is based on aesthetics, like dress, whereas those with insider knowledge are presented as knowing this to not be the case. But also, we see some of the participants drawing upon 'others' and their understandings of punk, for example, talking explicitly about punk stereotypes/how punk was often seen by wider society (this revolved predominantly around aesthetics/dress). This could illustrate to some extent referential meaning-making in their construction of their sense of identity—others' misconceptions of punk act as a point of reference, for example, in their own self-evaluation of who they are and what punk means to them.

Highlighting the importance of considering the temporality of authenticity, reflecting upon both the 'past' and the 'present' allowed the women I interviewed to construct the sense that this insider knowledge had been acquired over time. One of the participants, for example, referred to how their involvement in punk on first entry in their youth had been "superficial" until they had gone through a process over time of understanding more about what punk *actually* entailed and internalizing the values and knowledge associated with it. This led to this idea of punk now being something 'inside' of them as Kristianne expressed: "I'd say I'm a punk … but that's something that's 'in here'." I will return to this idea again later in this chapter.

Longevity and era

There can often be a preoccupation in public discourse concerning punk 'in the UK', with the 1976–1979 'era', or perhaps more specifically when you were born, being perceived as important in the fabrication of authenticity. This was present too in some of older punk women's narratives. This might at times be weaved into their own constructions of understanding punk authenticity, while at other times featuring in their construction of others' understandings of punk authenticity. Katie, for example, perceived more general society's view of who or what was punk as focused on the notion of 'being there': "I think when you talk about punk as in a public sense, people's reflections on that are much more about the late '70s, the Pistols, kind of what was determined as kind of punk music" (Interview).

Acknowledging how wider society views punk could contribute to one's own construction of punk identity and authenticity. Deedee, for example, also presented punk as having its origins in a particular era and living through that punk era as conferring punk authenticity:

> 'I guess I see punk as being an era in some ways and I was born in 77 so I was kind of a baby when kind of punk was established um so I kind of feel like I would be a bit of a fake if I called myself a punk.' (Interview)

Related to societal views and the relationship to one's own construction of punk identity/authenticity, then, Deedee is accepting a definition of punk which is exterior to herself and her own experiences and in turn letting herself by defined by these. This could be a reflection of Deedee constructing her own punk identity based on more dominant punk meanings held by wider society (and perhaps other punks). If viewing this from the work of Goffman (1990) concerning performance and identity, Deedee's positioning of herself as not a 'true' punk could be reflective of her wishing to put on a successful performance or presentation of self in line with societal and cultural expectations/dominant ideas concerning punk being associated with a particular era.

Interestingly, those who explicitly raised this question of era were those who felt they could not claim to be a punk. Among the women who were happy to define themselves as punks there was no outright claims of being capable to do so because of being born into the rightly timed cohort. But when speaking to them, it was clear that all bar one had grown up during those pivotal punk years and throughout their narratives they drew upon specific years as references as well as punk bands/singers of that specific era. Despite having replied to a call-out for 'punk women', a few of the women I spoke with even conveyed a sense of 'imposter syndrome' at not having been 'born at the right time'.

The construction of original or so-called 'true' authentic punk, as located in a particular historical period, was expressed too by Jess when speaking about her dad. Jess spoke of how her dad *was* a punk when he was younger because "he was around when the Sex Pistols and The Clash were all playing"—his punk identity was constructed as bounded in a particular time/era. There could be that sense again here too of the conferring of authenticity (Schwarz and Williams, 2020); Jess conferring authenticity upon her dad's younger self who she understood as exemplifying the ideals of punk identity (for example, being part of the 'original' punk scene).

This idea of the 'authentic original' has also been noted in research with punks by Bennett (2013) and Gordon (2014) though a difference is how the construction of this authentic original punk in their research operated to position the speaker (the participant) as authentic, for example, awarding authentic subcultural credentials to them while at the same time 'othering' those lacking the 'right' criteria. In discussing this idea both authors draw upon quotes from punk men, with no suggestion as to whether this is indeed a gendered display of authenticity construction. Based on my earlier discussion, I would suggest older punk women use this construction of an 'authentic original' similarly, couched in their own concerns of being deemed an imposter and perhaps reflecting the masculinism/male dominance performed within punk. Older punk women mostly, however, construct an 'authentic original' to confer authenticity to others, rather than themselves.

Interestingly (and related to this idea), in the early stages of data collection, I was sent a message through a social media platform by someone presenting as a woman who questioned my research criteria (my call-out for participants said I was looking for older punk women, aged 30 years and over). The message read: 'A 30-year-old punk will not stay a punk. ... Well I doubt it, good fucking luck ... the 45+ were the real ones' (personal communication). Given their apparent interest in the topic, I did ask the sender of the message if they wished to be involved in the research, but they declined to be interviewed. However, they appeared to feel strongly that only women over a higher age than what I had specified were the 'true punks' (their words). This minimum age would then locate these women within the particular era I referred to earlier and reflect this construction of an 'authentic original' again. The author of the message's reluctance to be interviewed could be indicative of them wanting to make a one-sided proclamation of 'fact' though this of course can only be an etic interpretation without the chance for emic verification.

Commitment, dress, and time

Through punk women reflecting on their 'younger' as well as their 'current' selves light was shed on how commitment was temporally located. As noted earlier in this chapter, this could entail a construction by the participants, for example, of their entry into punk as initially being based around fairly superficial notions of punk with internalization of punk values and insider knowledge being acquired over time. Another way this could be constructed was through some of the women's accounts of their relationship to dress and punk. This could particularly be concerning how punk was constructed as having an impact on how one dressed on entry into punk while younger and this now not being the case. This relationship between punk and dress, however, was further complicated by mainstream expectations concerning age(ing) and gender:

'I get treated differently especially as a mother 'cause I hate that people just assume that I'm not a good mum just because I'm not dressed like really nicely. ... I have this like internal struggle about should I just grow up and like start dressing nice and showering every day or is it just ok to carry on being me you know?' (Briony, interview)

'Certainly when the kids were at school I think that was the biggest pressure to conform, I think that's when you start to think that you have to somehow fit in more for their sake, not be too odd or too out of the loop. ... I hadn't dyed my hair since my little one was born and I used to have really brightly colored hair for years and years and I was going off to Amsterdam with ... with one of his bands and I dyed it bright pink or purple or something obscene anyway and forgot I was dropping off my brother but I had to pick [my son] up before I went and when I went down the school to pick him up with the hair he just cried and cried and completely freaked out.' (Sharon, interview)

Across the women I interviewed there was an awareness of societal expectations concerning women's looks and particularly the perception that there was greater expectations placed on women to look a certain way in order to meet motherly or familial obligations as they aged. Some of the women felt they challenged this; others expressed a negotiation between these expectations and their expression of a punk identity. Perhaps then constructing 'commitment' through other things, for example, by placing an emphasis on holding particular punk values acted again as a 'buffer' against the felt need to tone down or change dress as they got older while still constructing themselves as punk.

Punk identity: essential or a social construction?

Some social constructionists have considered the extent to which research participants themselves also adopt this understanding of identity and authenticity as constructed, rather than essentialist (Schwarz and Williams, 2020). There were varying degrees to which the women I spoke with presented a social constructionist approach to self-authenticity, and indeed 'punk' itself. There could be a construction of punk, for example, as something which was fluid, open to interpretation, that is, anyone could be punk. Yet, as noted earlier concerning insider knowledge and the internalization of punk values, this could co-exist with fabrications too of an essentialist understanding of identity, with punk being seen as something held inside of you. At times, then, a rejection of essentialist views of punk and, at others, an appeal to them. We shall see this appeal to an essentialist view of punk again in the next section concerning the interpretation of authenticity in punk scholarship itself.

Interpreting authenticity in punk scholarship itself

While much attention has been given to how authenticity is constructed by the punks who we involve in our scholarship, less has been aimed towards the construction of authenticity in punk scholarship itself. Yet it is important to recognize that the interactions involved in constructing what we come to see as authentic punk scholarship, like any in society, do not exist in a vacuum. They are played out within systems of power and inequality which we should not be blinkered to. This relates again to the concept of reflexivity and while there have been some punk scholars engaging in reflexivity, this has not been as widespread as it could be.

Punk scholarship and myth-making

Scholars (for the most part, unintentionally) create myths about cultural groups/subcultures—this happens through the (re)telling of particular narratives about a subculture, for example, with these narratives presented as a set of facts which entail the essentializing of the subculture (Williams, 2020).

Tracing this back to subcultural scholarship by the CCCS, this myth-making entails subcultures viewed as containing a certain authentic essence (Williams, 2020). Hebdige's (1998) research, for example, presented punk as a subculture with particular defining features and stylistic markers. Conclusions were not grounded in the (subjective) voices of the punks themselves. Instead, the semiotic analysis employed by Hebdige (1998) entailed an 'objective reality' being read and decoded by the researcher (without reflexive consideration of how such conclusions were drawn).

One example of this re(telling) of narratives concerning punk could be the recurring focus on discovering 'what is punk?', treating punk as comprising of a set of essential qualities, or values, rather than approaching punk as socially constructed. What these qualities are presented and represented as can also be problematic. Punk is often presented as upholding egalitarian views concerning gender, for example, yet the upholding of gender inequality, and the marginalization of women, can be embedded in writings on punk itself. Stewart (2019), for example, has considered this in the context of *The Philosophy of Punk* text, arguing that O'Hara (1999), by stating how men's voices are usually louder than women's in terms of challenging sexism in punk, is implying that the actual experiences of sexism are 'not as important as highlighting the actions of the male punks who oppose it in some way' (Stewart, 2019, p 214). I agree this to be the case as the celebration of the punk men's 'actions' does not appear to show any real consideration of the actual sexism at hand nor the way prioritizing the men's 'actions' over women's 'voices' is indicative of male privilege in society more broadly.

Writings on punk can also play on the notion of a 'punk is dead' discourse (for example, Robène and Serre, 2016; Butler, 2019; Grinnel, 2019), which is contrasted with a growing body of writing on 'contemporary punk'. Thinking back to the argument made earlier in this chapter concerning era and authenticity, we see this at play again here—the use of language itself, for example, 'contemporary punk', 'post-punk', can work toward a construction of authenticity as temporally located and might also be a part of this myth-making. Some of my anecdotal experiences as a (punk) doctorate student and also at the beginning of what I might term my punk scholar career have at times reflected authenticity construction framed within that notion of 'era' as highlighted in my empirical discussion earlier. When presenting my PhD research within punk academic contexts I have often received comments, for example, regarding the age range of my sample with those at the lower end of the range not being seen as 'old'—within a punk context and when raised often in relation to the women not 'being there' this relates again to that relationship between era and authenticity. Indeed, I have also received comments from those who have raised critique on the basis of the findings not reflecting their experiences of how it was 'back then' (note, these comments have always come from cis-men), something I will return to in this chapter.

Punk scholarship interacting with age and/or ageing

My observations and involvement in social media platforms for punk scholars has highlighted to me the existence of claims of 'revisionism' among 'younger scholars' and this is important to note for two reasons. First, this revisionism (looking at punk scholarship across the past 40 years or so) seems to be referring to work which challenges claims made about punk, for example, that punk was/is empowering and/or liberating for women. When points are made on such social media discussion groups in relation to this, more often than not this revisionism is seen as something to critique, and some scholars have challenged such challenging(!). Second, the link between such revisionism and 'younger' scholars is not without purpose and relates to the construction of what or who is authentic within punk scholarship—younger scholars often seen as bringing new ideas to the table (albeit not necessarily in a positive way) while 'old' scholars might be constructed as less relevant. The following two quotes came from a discussion group focused on punk scholarship—they have been paraphrased in order to prevent them being searchable:

> Early punk needs more investigating. There is a good amount of revisionism though, particularly from younger academics with different perspectives. (Anonymized post)

> There's a lot of ageism in punk scholarship today which goes unquestioned—some academics are seen as 'old' and therefore not useful to contemporary punk scholarship. (Anonymized post)

Such positioning of what counts, or doesn't count, as the concerns of punk scholarship extend as well to the relationship between punk and intersecting identities and there has been a noted disagreement between those favoring the 'traditional' theories which put class at the forefront of analysing punk and those proposing approaches to punk scholarship which is intersectional. While the existence of different approaches toward phenomena is to be expected within scholarship, the role of power needs to be considered as well as that notion of myth-making and the (re)telling of narratives concerning punk which I highlighted earlier.

I have presented my research concerning older punk women at a handful of academic events focused on punk scholarship and often received verbal comments from members of the audience which serve to discredit the experiences of the women I interviewed or, indeed, my own interpretations of the data. One criticism that has been raised has been around the ages of the women I spoke with and the notion of them all being seen as 'old' has been challenged. This resonates with this idea again of the 'authentic original' and that 'true' punks are of a certain minimum age, ignoring too the embracing of age as a social construction and participants' subjective understandings of being old(er).

Other comments in response to my presenting of my research have been along the lines of:

> 'One of your participants talked about the Manic Street Preachers ... they're not punk!'

> 'But what about older punk men? Why didn't you interview any of them?'

> 'That wasn't the experience of the punk women *I* knew.'

Here too we see the interpretation of punk along essentialized lines, for example, punk is 'this', not 'that' (shown in the first comment), and an objective claim to 'fact' (demonstrated in the last). All these comments were made by cis-men and that too is interesting to consider in terms of who constructs themselves as having the power to define what is/what is not authentic punk scholarship and/or experience. Especially interesting and relevant to that idea, I feel, is how a cis-man felt able to position himself as a greater expert of punk women's experiences than the punk women themselves (as shown in that last comment). Such comments have served as an opportunity for me to highlight again the need for feminist frameworks in approaching punk scholarship and gender as an interpretive framework, as well as noting the importance of understanding punk from the view of those who identify with it (for example, taking a social constructionist, rather than essentialist, view).

How authenticity is constructed can act as a form of gatekeeping and such gatekeeping can act to marginalize the experiences and scholarly activities of already marginalized groups/identities. The concept of a gatekeeper is commonplace within social research, referring to those who may (or indeed may not) aid the researcher in accessing potential research participants. This concept of gatekeeper has been employed too in discussing process in academia, referring to those who 'play a crucial role in defining, developing and policing' (Schurr et al, 2020, np) what counts as hegemonic knowledge within a discipline, and are also capable of deciding who has access to an academic career. Those authors point out, for example, that 'handbooks and companions, progress reports, and editorial boards are hegemonic sites of [geographical] knowledge production' (Schurr et al, 2020, np). Research also points to the way gatekeepers ensure that the work of women academics is undervalued as demonstrated in work concerning linguistics (McElhinny et al, 2003) and higher education (Jackson, 2002) more broadly, for example. Care needs to be taken so that punk scholarship does not fall foul of this same critique as well as constructing the work of academics from marginalized identities too of less value. Punk scholarship, in terms of it being interdisciplinary and relatively young as a field, has the potential to carefully consider how knowledge is constructed and start doing more of this 'work'.

Reflexivity and authenticity

Narrowing down the focus again to my own scholarly activity in thinking through the theme of authenticity in relation to punk, my fieldwork notes during my PhD research highlighted some overlap between my own understandings concerning the construction of authenticity and those of the women I spoke with. As described in the preceding section, for older punk women clothing could be an important tool in the fabrication of punk authenticity through the construction that 'true' punks 'know' that aesthetics is not a key marker of punk identity. Yet there was also an awareness of there being an outsider understanding of what 'punk' should look like and some sense of imposter syndrome among some of the women I spoke with. Looking back at my fieldnotes, it was interesting to see similar feelings expressed by myself after my first interview:

> [R]eflecting upon my choice of clothing and I had considered how to present myself beforehand which I didn't think would be the case! I opted to go for something I would wear on day-to-day basis, eg black t-shirt, rather than wearing, say, something I might wear to work. That did make me think a little about the conscious decisions I sometimes myself make regarding how I present myself in different situations and though I don't think I particularly 'look punk' I was quite eager to not be completely dismissed by the participant based on how I dressed! (Fieldnotes)

And then after the second interview:

> I guess I try to break down potential barriers which might cause me to present a formal appearance while also trying to perhaps convey something about my personality/background. For example, I don't want to alienate people based on their potential viewing of me as a punk 'outsider'—someone who just wants to study it from an academic position and is part of the 'establishment' punk often rallies against. (Interview notes)

Such reflections highlight how I, just as a number of the older punk women I spoke with, was aware of particular ideas of what punk might look like and was concerned about being seen as an imposter or being construed as an outsider and part of the establishment rather than someone who had a pre-existing relationship with punk.

Reflecting on my positionality requires me to consider too whether my gender or age were relevant to the research process and interactions with the participants. Certainly, at times I wondered whether my perceived age (or indeed perceived difference in age) by some participants might have shaped what they assumed we shared in terms of 'punk knowledge' and therefore what they felt they needed to explain (or not). Though I did at times feel I identified with experiences they presented as resulting from being a woman in a punk context—for example, feeling they were taken not as seriously as their male counterparts. This was something I felt I needed to be careful about and though I identified with their experiences in my head, I choose at the time not to voice these or over-empathize in my interactions with participants for fear of biasing the data. However, reflecting on that I wondered whether this was the right approach to take; perhaps rather than being concerned over biasing the data the more important issue would be concern with affirming their experiences through having that shared experience.

Reflecting on the limitations of my PhD research I was also very aware that despite claiming to bring the voices of marginalized punk women to the fore, my sample predominantly comprised of white punk women. In addition to this, no demographic information was gathered concerning their sexuality and no thought was given to disabled or trans women. The way I had set up the sampling (for example, by not purposively targeting to ensure diversity) in addition to the absence of particular interview themes and/or questions, was therefore problematic and, indeed, contributing to the continued scholarly marginalization of black punk women (McGraw, 2012), disabled punk women (Stewart, 2019), trans women, and non-heterosexual women (Wiedlack, 2015). Women of such various intersecting identities may make their own (and possibly very different) sense of punk subculture and identities.

Conclusion

To date, academic insights concerning punk and ageing have been very limited in terms of analysis which brings in intersection identities, such as gender. Older punk women's voices have been absent and yet exploring the theme of authenticity in this context sheds light on how both ageing and gender might shape this. Furthermore, attention too needs to be given to how authenticity is constructed within punk scholarship and among punk scholars and there is a role here for drawing more so upon feminist values in our scholarship, particularly in promoting critical reflexivity of our own work. How authenticity is constructed can act as a form of gatekeeping and those involved in punk scholarly, for want of a better word, 'systems' (for example, conference committees, editorial boards, academic networks) are key in shaping what is seen as 'punk' or not, as well as those who interact in everyday punk scholarly contexts (such as online groups). Opening up space for discussion around both of these areas is imperative in relation to Wiedlack's pertinent point that

> queer feminist and punks of color as well as the politics around racialization and non-normative genders, sexes, and sexualities have always been important parts of punk culture ... it is time to complicate the pictures, rather than renarrate the straight white punk history of white middle-classness, homophobia and racism again and again. (Wiedlack, 2015, p 10)

References

Alexi, K. (2020) 'Music and Activism: The New Feminist Movement of Punk (2010–2020), Right-Wing Populism and Punkriarchy', paper presented at the Punk Scholars Network Annual Conference, 2020.

Andes, L. (2002) 'Growing Up Punk: Meaning and Commitment Careers in a Contemporary Youth Subculture', in J.S. Epstein (ed) *Youth Culture: Identity in a Postmodern World*, Oxford: Blackwell, pp 212–231.

Averett, P. (2009) 'The Search for Wonder Woman: An Autoethnography of Feminist Identity', *Affilia: Journal of Women and Social Work*, 24(4): 360–368.

Bennett, A. (2006) 'Punk's Not Dead: The Continuing Significance of Punk Rock for an Older Generation of Fans', *Sociology*, 40(2): 219–235.

Bennett, A. (2012) 'Dance Parties, Lifestyle and Strategies for Ageing', in A. Bennett and P. Hodkinson (eds) *Ageing and Youth Cultures: Music, Style and Identity*, London: Berg, pp 95–104.

Bennett, A. (2013) *Music, Style and Aging: Growing Old Disgracefully?*, Philadelphia: Temple University Press.

Bennett, A. and Hodkinson, P. (2012) *Ageing and Youth Cultures: Music, Style and Identity*, London: Berg.

Blatterer, H. (2007) 'Contemporary Adulthood: Reconceptualizing an Uncontested Category', *Current Sociology*, 55(6): 771–792.

Butler, M. (2019) 'Punk is Dead. Or is It?' in O. Kaltmeier and W. Raussert (eds) *Sonic Politics*, London: Routledge, pp 205–215.

Constantinou, C.S., Georgiou, M. and Perdikogianni, M. (2017) 'A Comparative Method for Themes Saturation (CoMeTS) in Qualitative Interviews', *Qualitative Research*, 17(5): 571–588.

Davis, J. (2006) 'Growing Up Punk: Negotiating Aging Identity in a Local Music Scene', *Symbolic Interaction*, 29(1): 63–69.

Davis, J.R. (2012) 'Punk, Ageing and the Expectations of Adult Life', in A. Bennett and P. Hodkinson (eds) *Ageing and Youth Cultures: Music, Style and Identity*, London: Berg, pp 105–118.

Donaghey, J. (2021) 'Punk and Feminism in Indonesia', *Cultural Studies*, 35(1): 136–161.

Downes, J. (2007) 'Riot Grrrl: The Legacy and Contemporary Landscape of DIY Feminist Cultural Activism', in N. Monem (ed) *Riotgrrrl: Revolution Girl Style Now!*, London: Black Dog Publishing, pp 12–51.

Ellis, C. (2004) *The Ethnographic I*, Walnut Creek: AltaMira.

Featherstone, M. and Hepworth, M. (1991) 'The Mask of Ageing and the Postmodern Life Course', in M. Featherstone, M. Hepworth and B. Turner (eds) *The Body: Social Process and Cultural Theory*, London: SAGE, pp 371–389.

Fine, G.A. (1983) *Shared Fantasy: Role-Playing Games as Social Worlds*, Chicago: University of Chicago Press.

Gibson, B. and Hartman, J. (2014) *Rediscovering Grounded Theory*, London: SAGE.

Goffman, E. (1990) *The Presentation of Self in Everyday Life*, London: Penguin.

Gordon, A. (2014) 'Distinctions of Authenticity and the Everyday Punk Self', *Punk & Post-Punk*, 3(3): 183–202.

Griffin, N. (2012) 'Gendered Performance and Performing Gender in the DIY Punk and Hardcore Music Scene', *Journal of International Women's Studies*, 13(2): 66–81.

Grinnel, G.C. (2019) 'Punk is Dead: Notes Toward the Apocalyptic Tone Adopted by Punk Rock', *ESC: English Studies in Canada*, 45(4): 53–81.

Hannerz, E. (2015) *Performing Punk*, Hampshire: Palgrave Macmillan.

Hebdige, D. (1998) *Subculture: The Meaning of Style*, London: Routledge.

Hodkinson, P. (2009) 'Grounded Theory and Inductive Research', in N. Gilbert (ed) *Researching Social Life*, London: SAGE, pp 98–120.

Holland, S. (2018) 'Ageing Alternative Women: Discourses of Authenticity, Resistance and "Coolness"', in S. Holland and K. Spracklen (eds) *Subcultures, Bodies and Spaces: Essays on Alternativity and Marginalization*, Bingley: Emerald Publishing, pp 191–203.

Jackson, S. (2002) 'Transcending Boundaries: Women, Research and Teaching in the Academy', in G. Howie and A. Tauchert (eds) *Gender, Teaching and Research in Higher Education: Challenges for the 21st Century*, London: Routledge, pp 20–32.

Larsen, G. (2017) '"It's a Man's Man's Man's World": Music Groupies and the Othering of Women in the World of Rock', *Organization*, 24(3): 397–417.

Leblanc, L. (2002) *Pretty in Punk: Girls' Gender Resistance in a Boys' Subculture*, London: Rutgers University Press.

Lewin, P. and Williams, J.P. (2009) 'The Ideology and Practice of Authenticity in Punk Subculture', in P. Vannini and J.P. Williams (eds) *Authenticity in Self, Culture and Society*, Aldershot: Ashgate, pp 65–83.

McElhinny, B., Hols, M., Holtzkener, J., Unger, S. and Hicks, C. (2003) 'Gender, Publication and Citation in Sociolinguistics and Linguistic Anthropology: The Construction of a Scholarly Canon', *Language and Society*, 32(3): 299–328.

McGraw, G. (2012) 'Sodom's Daughters: The Removed and Forgotten Black Female of Punk Culture', *Women & Performance: A Journal of Feminist Theory*, 22(2–3): 325–333.

Morgan, L.A. and Kunkel, S. (2007) *Aging, Society and the Life Course*, New York: Springer.

Mullaney, J.L. (2012) 'All in Time: Age and the Temporality of Authenticity in the Straight-Edge Music Scene', *Journal of Contemporary Ethnography*, 41(6): 611–635.

Nagy Hesse-Biber, S. and Leckenby, D. (2004) 'How Feminists Practice Social Research', in S. Nagy Hesse-Biber and M.L. Yaiser (eds) *Feminist Perspectives on Social Research*, Oxford: Oxford University Press, pp 209–227.

O'Hara, C. (1999) *The Philosophy of Punk: More Than Noise!*, Chico: AK Press.

Pilcher, J. (1995) *Age and Generation in Modern Britain*, Oxford: Oxford University Press.

Robène, L. and Serre, S. (2016) 'Punk is Dead. Long Live Punk! A "Golden Age" of Punk in the French Music Press', *Le Temps Des Médias*, 27(2): 124–138.

Roman, L. (1988) 'Intimacy, Labor and Class: Ideologies of Feminine Sexuality in the Punk Slam Dance', in L. Roman and L. Christian-Smith with E. Ellsorth (eds) *Becoming Feminine: The Politics of Popular Culture*, London: The Falmer Press, pp 143–184.

Rouse, J. (2019) '"Punks are not Girls": Exploring Discrimination and Empowerment through the Experiences of Punk and Alt-Rock Musicians in Leeds', *Punk & Post-Punk*, 8(1): 73–88.

Schurr, C., Müller, M. and Imhof, N. (2020) 'Who Makes Geographic Knowledge? The Gender of Geography's Gatekeepers', *The Professional Geographer*, 72(3): 317–331.

Schwarz, K.C. and Williams, J.P. (2020) 'Introduction to the Social Construction of Identity and Authenticity', in K.C. Schwarz and J.P. Williams (eds) *Studies on the Social Construction of Identity and Authenticity*, New York: Routledge, pp 1–24.

Sparkes, A.C. (2000) 'Autoethnography and Narratives of Self: Reflections on Criteria in Action', *Sociology of Sport Journal*, 17: 21–43.

Stewart, F. (2019) '"No More Heroes Anymore": Marginalized Identities in Punk Memorialisation and Curation', *Punk & Post-Punk*, 8(2): 209–226.

Wall, S. (2006) 'An Autoethnography on Learning About Autoethnography', *International Journal of Qualitative Methods*, 5(2): 146–160.

Way, L. (2021) 'Punk is Just a State of Mind: Exploring what Punk Means to oOlder Punk Women', *The Sociological Review*, 69(1): 107–122.

Widdicombe, S. and Wooffitt, R. (1995) *The Language of Youth Subcultures: Social Identity in Action*, Hemel Hempstead: Harvester Wheatsheaf.

Wiedlack, K. (2015) *Queer-Feminist Punk: An Anti-Social History*, Vienna: Zaglossus.

Williams, J.P. (2006) 'Authentic Identities: Straightedge Subculture, Music, and the Internet', *Journal of Contemporary Ethnography*, 35(2): 173–200.

Williams, J.P. (2020) 'Myth and Authenticity in Subculture Studies', in B. van der Steen and T.P.F. Verburgh (eds) *Researching Subcultures, Myth and Memory*, London: Palgrave Macmillan, pp 35–53.

9

"Let's All Be Friends": Emotional Labor and Insider Research in Punk Subculture

Stanislav Vysotsky and Donna Manion

Studying subcultures is a very personal process for many scholars. This is especially true for researchers with strong connections to the subcultures that they are researching. While the standards of research in many disciplines within the social sciences are skeptical, if not wholly derisive, of close connections between researchers and the subjects of their study, the field of subcultural studies frequently draws on such dynamics to provide accurate depictions of culture and related processes not available to 'outsiders' (Bennett, 2003; Hodkinson, 2005). Similarly, the role of emotions and 'emotional labor' (Hochschild, 1983) in the research process has been highlighted by scholars interested in reflecting upon their role as researcher in light of the sociological study of emotions. Such work largely focuses on the emotions researchers experience when studying sensitive topics or engaging with especially vulnerable populations (Blackman, 2007; Dickson-Swift et al, 2009). This chapter seeks to merge these distinct strains of reflexive analysis of the research process by discussing the emotional labor involved in the process of engaging in 'insider' research on subcultures.

From its inception in the 1970s, the first wave of punk has been perceived as rebellious, nonconformist, and anti-authoritarian along with a Do-It-Yourself (DIY) ethic. From the first wave onward to later iterations, subculturalists designed their own clothes, formed their own bands, created their own record labels, ran distros,[1] and published zines.[2] While this wave of punk was distinguished with sardonic, contrarian social and political attitudes, anchored by shock value behaviors, ornaments/symbols/pins, and fashion, it paved the way for the next wave of punk, which included the more explicitly politicized and activist-oriented anarcho-punk. Punk's second wave advocated leftist and anarchist political ideologies exemplified by bands playing at anti-nuclear, Rock Against Racism, Rock Against Reagan, and Anti-Nazi League rallies (Davies, 1996). Many second wave anarcho-punk bands criticized institutions such as capitalism, government, religion, and social problems such as war, sexism, racism, classism, and global exploitation (Cross, 2004; 2010; Manion, 2007; Worley, 2012).

In our cases, we came to study aspects of punk subculture from our own participation in local scenes in the 1980s–2000s and distinct affiliations with the anarcho-punk scene. Stanislav became involved in punk subculture through skateboarding in the mid-to-late 1980s. He was first introduced to punk bands through skateboarding magazines and tapes made by one of his close friends at the time. During this skater punk period, his taste in punk tended toward a broad engagement with a variety of bands and subgenres, but it was the bands with the most explicit political content that most appealed to him; chief among them being Dead Kennedys. In the late spring of 1989, he purchased his first Crass record and anarcho-punk zine *Profane Existence* and soon after identified explicitly as an anarcho-punk. He became active in his local DIY and underground punk scene, which had a die-hard contingent of anarcho-punks. Throughout the 1990s and early 2000s, he was active in anarcho-punk scenes in Baltimore and Boston, and points in between along the east coast. He organized DIY shows in both cities and was the vocalist in the bands Culture in Decline, Krema-1, and A//Political.

In the 1980s, Donna grew up next to an air force base in a small town in central New York; she started to question why nuclear weapons were needed on this base and throughout America. When she was in 8th grade, she read a painstakingly detailed autobiography of the Hiroshima bombing. These details shocked her and led to her distaste for nuclear weapons. While in high school, she never understood the reason why others tried to attain the status quo whether it was by riches, clothes, flashy cars, and body size. She most definitely felt out of step with the world. She was horrified by television shows and movies and rejected the cultural values that mass media's propaganda attempted to transmit. Around 18, she found her first punk record, Dead Kennedy's *Fresh Fruit for Rotting Vegetables*, and a year later she bought *Feeding of the 5,000* by Crass, which appeared to agree with her way of thinking and further foster anarchist ideas. At this point in time, her participation in the community comprised solely of correspondence with other anarcho-punks in the UK and Europe culminating in trading cassettes and zines as well as engaging in the larger punk community by way of friendship books, which are artistically handmade books in which each individual had their own page to dedicate to their favorite bands along with their corresponding address (usually specially made stickers with quotes and pictures of favorite bands) so similar others could communicate. By the

1990s, her participation increased in the emergent central New York punk community. In the early 2000s, Donna was a participant in the Richmond, Virginia (RVA) anarcho/crust punk scene and organized punk shows, Ladyfest, and the RVA CLIT Fest. She also hosted ladies' nights and overall support of the local scene.

By engaging with the punk subculture as participants while pursuing studies in sociology, we were able to identify aspects in need of scholarly analysis; specifically, dynamics of misogyny, gender inequality, and antifascism (Manion, 2007; Vysotsky, 2013; 2015; 2020). Taking a reflexive approach to understanding our role as insider researchers of subcultures to which we had strong affiliations identified a number of emotional experiences, impacts, and processes. First, and foremost, the research that we engaged in was driven by personal commitment to not only study toxic dynamics such as misogyny and fascism within the punk scene, but to provide scholarly input toward solutions. Second, we found that empirical studies of internal subcultural dynamics led to disenchantment as well as emotional strain, strained interactions, and partial departure from the community. We experienced emotional dissonance and subsequent alienation that resulted from our status as peers to subcultural participants. Role strain became apparent while being subculturalists with anticipated ideals while managing our responses to the contradictory reality of behaviors and backlash. Third, as insiders, we experienced doubt regarding the validity of our findings because some subculturalists questioned the value of the research being conducted. Finally, conducting research with subcultural peers created strained interpersonal dynamics because of the dual role of the researcher as active participant. We tried to navigate these emotional strains while maintaining 'objectivity' in gathering empirical evidence. We found that we had to manage not only our emotional states but fellow subcultural participants' expectations and emotions. Along with attempts to propose, enact, and engender subcultural solutions, we reflexively tried to moderate our own and mitigate others' expectations in order to conduct impression management and further allow for our own research and subcultural participation.

Insider research

In the quest for objectivity, there is often an expectation within the social sciences to conduct research with a certain amount of detachment from the subject of study. It is expected that researchers will be outsiders who engage in a structured, preferably quantitative analysis of the phenomena under study (Mills, 1959; Merton, 1972; Young, 2011). Qualitative researchers, particularly those studying deviance and subcultures, have increasingly taken an 'insider' approach by studying subcultures in which they are active participants (Roseneil, 1993; Ferrell, 1996; Bennett, 2003; 2003; Hodkinson,

2005; Ferrell et al, 2015; Taylor, 2011). Merton described the relative benefits of the 'insider principle' of research as follows:

> Only through continued socialization in the life of a group can one become fully aware of its symbolisms and socially shared realities; only so can one understand the fine-grained meanings of behavior, feelings, and values; only so can one decipher the unwritten grammar of conduct and the nuances of cultural idiom. (Merton, 1972, p 15)

Insider research offers a number of key benefits that are unavailable to the detached 'outsider' researcher including access, understanding, rapport, (sub) cultural capital, as well as knowledge and insight that can only be gleaned from direct experience.

Studying subcultures frequently requires gaining access to people and spaces that operate outside of the purview and view of mainstream society. While it is possible for outsiders to find individuals and places, the insider possesses distinct knowledge that gives them easier access to subcultures that may be denied to an outsider (Ferrell, 1996; 2001; Bennett, 2003). An insider researcher can utilize 'subcultural capital' (Thornton, 2013) to gain entry into spaces where an outsider may be unwanted or approached with antagonism or mistrust (Hodkinson, 2005). Researchers who have a background or connection to their field of study frequently have the necessary 'cultural competency' to interact with participants based on mutual language and experiences within a shared culture (Roseneil, 1993; Hodkinson, 2005). Because of their own experiences with the field that they are studying, insider researchers are better able to identify who is a dependable and genuine representative, which facilitates access to participants and spaces unavailable to outsiders (Roseneil, 1993; Hodkinson, 2005).

Once the researcher has gained access to the subculture, their insider position also facilitates effective interviews of participants. Insider researchers frequently are able to build rapport and trust with participants because of shared or similar experiences, which allow them to be viewed as equals and reduces the imbalance of power common in the research process. Researchers often enter the field with their status as a scholar clearly known, which may intimidate or alienate potential interviewees. Insiders, however, possess a familiarity with the subculture that can reduce the social distance between participants and researchers, even if it doesn't completely eliminate dynamics of power (Roseneil, 1993; Hodkinson, 2005; Chavez, 2008; Ross, 2017).

The insider perspective also provides an advantage in research design because their experiences facilitate the ability to choose an appropriate method of study, critically assess interview responses and appropriately probe for additional information and interpret findings in a manner that reflects the position of the group being studied. By engaging with a subculture directly, a researcher is better able to understand which methods and frames of analysis are the most appropriate for developing an understanding of the subject being investigated (Roseneil, 1993; Bennett, 2003; Hodkinson, 2005; Brannick and Coghlan, 2007). Insider researchers are able to accurately assess the appropriate field to enter and frequently avoid the difficulties of false starts, pilot studies, and application of inappropriate methods of analysis (Hodkinson, 2005; Brannick and Coghlan, 2007; Chavez, 2008). As a result of their own experiences with the subject they are studying, insiders are able to assess the validity of participants' responses (Bennett, 2003; Hodkinson, 2005). Finally, the insider researcher can draw on their own intimate knowledge of the subject being studied to uniquely apply a scholarly perspective to their own experiences as well as those of their interviewees or other research subjects (Roseneil, 1993; Hodkinson, 2005; Chavez, 2008; Ross, 2017).

As this brief review on insider research suggests, much of the qualitative literature focuses on practical and interpretive issues. However, as we reflected on our own experiences as insider researchers with many years of involvement in the subculture that we studied at the time of conducting research, we found that these issues were not comprehensive. Our position as insiders provided many of the benefits discussed earlier, but also generated unique emotional experiences that complicated the research process. Therefore, we found it necessary to consider the emotional labor of insider research as well.

Emotional labor and research

Hochschild's (1983) concept of emotional labor focuses not only on researchers' and their subjects' experienced emotions but on analyzing and attempting to control researchers' and participants' emotions. Although emotional labor is a well-established conceptual framework for analysis in sociology, the application of the concept to the process of research is more controversial in a field dominated by a realist orientation (Fox, 2008). However, researchers who employ this frame reflexively on their work have indicated benefits along with disadvantages of this tool (Ellis, 1991a). Hochschild (1983) explains the purpose and importance of the researchers' ability to engage in emotional labor, by suppressing inappropriate emotions and, at the same time, promoting appropriate sentiments in order to foster 'the proper state of mind in others' (p 7). This perception of emotional labor takes on a symbolic interactionist and social constructivist perspective, whereby emotions are contingent upon time and culture, including subcultures. This tool is essential with respect to studying not only sensitive topics, such as sexism or racism, but to engage with especially vulnerable populations (Blackman, 2007; Dickson-Swift et al, 2009), such as subcultural participants. Researchers indicate that emotional reflexivity, or introspection as noted by Ellis (1991b), is not only a tool of emotional labor for research but a strategy to both illuminate and confront veiled issues within a studied community (Hochschild, 1983; Ellis, 1991a; Blackman, 2007; McQueeney and Lavelle, 2017). Scholars have also posited that emotional reflexivity involves processes of self-introspection and/or an interactive-introspection component, which includes the inherent process of continuously analyzing both researchers' and subjects' emotions by utilizing diaries/journals, participant observation, intensive interviews, and oral histories (Ellis, 1991b; Blix and Wettergren, 2015).

Emotional reflexivity is about power and risk (Ellis, 1991a; Rowling, 1999; Blackman, 2007; Romocea, 2014; Blix and Wettergren, 2015; McQueeney and Lavelle, 2017), as monitoring emotional reactions can be a difficult process. It is the integration of the individual, their social location, and social structure that influences the emotional process. By considering individual and structural variables, research subjects' behaviors are positioned within larger social contexts. Researchers must be aware of their own and subjects' status and power. Sociology of emotion scholars (Dickson-Swift et al, 2009; Blix and Wettergren, 2015; McQueeney and Lavelle, 2017) also explain the way researchers undertake impression management in the process of meeting others' expectations of themselves. Blix and Wettergren explain the ways they, themselves, had to adjust their interactional and emotive styles (for example, holding back personal feelings) to negotiate status while conducting research on elite institutions, which culminated in surface acting.

McQueeney and Lavelle (2017) offer three steps to transform emotional labor into a tool to analyze both their own and subjects' emotions within a larger social context. The first step requires the researcher to develop a way to contextualize emotions in which researchers become aware of their own reactions to their own and participants' social location in a subculture reflective of dominant culture and its consequential inequalities. This includes an attempt to defer or mask reactions and try to understand subjects' positions and their origins. Subjects' social locations generate insight into their worldview, in which a participant may hold sexist or racist views. Just as interviewees may have perceived us as troublemakers, we may have perceived them as not meeting the anarcho-punk standards culminating in our view of them as fake or status seekers. The next step involves using emotions to unmask power in the research process as investigators' power and status may not match up to the subjects'; therefore, self-reflexivity works to delve deeper into power dynamics such as how and perhaps to answer why some participants may not want to answer questions or be resistant to the interview. The third tool involves linking emotions to researchers' and participants' biographies. Personal histories are important as it can elucidate subjects' lives, including individual histories. Additionally, hidden inequalities can be discovered as McQueeney and Lavelle (2017) found that dynamics of power were evident within the setting that their research subjects occupied. This reveals the intersections of inequality affecting both researchers' and subjects' daily lives and worldviews.

Notably, much of the literature on emotional labor in research is written by researchers who are not part of a subculture that they are studying. Our position as insider researchers, therefore, provides a unique perspective. In the next section, we will discuss many of the issues of emotional labor that arose in our experiences studying a subculture that we actively participated in while conducting research. Our experiences reinforce much of the extant literature on emotional labor, yet also indicate ways in which these emotional processes are unique to the experience of insider researchers.

Emotional labor as insider researchers

The process of conducting insider research within and with subcultural groups in which we were active participants generated a unique set of emotional responses and processes. These experiences emerged as part of our emotional labor in the research process. This unique position created conditions that generated several distinct emotional situations and responses. We came to our research topics from positions of experience and deep commitment to punk. However, the experience of studying a subculture that we so strongly connected to also engendered a degree of disenchantment, emotional dissonance, and doubt. The dynamics of engaging simultaneously as scholars and as peers also created strain with some participants.

Experience and commitment

We chose to study aspects of anarcho-punk subculture because of our own participation within it. At the time of our data collection and research, each author had over 20 years of experience as an active participant in the punk scene and identified as an anarchist punk. Our choices of topics to study reflected the intersection of activism and identity within the subculture. The issues that we explored were of primary interest to us because of our intimate knowledge of their importance to the subculture as a whole and their relevance to sociological analyses of gender, race, and social movements.

As active participants, we were able to leverage our existing social networks and subcultural capital in order to recruit participants and gain access to subcultural spaces that would otherwise be unavailable to outsiders. Since we were a part of this subculture, we were aware of the nuances of situations, how to interact with other subculturalists, the subcultural values, and emotional labor required for not only our own but research participants' emotions. This entailed a number of scenarios that reflected our authentic emotional reactions and bonds with our research subjects rather than the deep and surface acting that is engaged in by outsider researchers.

Insider researchers have the unique benefit of experience that facilitates construction of appropriate interview questions as well as interactions that decrease social distance and flatten power imbalances between researchers and participants (Roseneil, 1993; Hodkinson, 2005). We found that our experiences allowed for easier access to the field as well as building an appropriate pool of interview subjects. As participants, we had a more intimate understanding of the people whom we interviewed. Stanislav was able to develop an interview schedule that addressed many of the issues involved in contemporary antifascism from an activist's perspective. Unfortunately, the interview questions were so focused on experiences of militant antifascists, especially those with a background in the anarchist punk scene, that they were at times confusing to the non-militant, non-punk participants in his research. In one case, an interviewee who was identified as a non-militant antifascist and who didn't have a background in punk subculture interpreted a question about the role of the state as being about the state government for which they worked. Conversely, the militant antifascists whom Stanislav interviewed frequently used question prompts to discuss in detail their experiences and build rapport with him that is discussed later.

Donna felt that she gained subcultural capital because, over time, subculturalists knew her not only through her research conducting interviews at a crust fest in Philadelphia, Pennsylvania, but also by observing her interactions with higher status individuals to set up RVA punk shows, and her work as a DJ. By being a DJ, she was put on the various label lists for free music to play on radio shows and became a contact point for setting up touring bands' shows. Interactionally, at shows, her friends pointed out her increase in status in which the scene elite knew who she was, talked to her, and were overall friendly to her. At some point, these very same people would approach her and say, "Oh, you're Donna. I have heard so much about you and what you are doing." This never occurred to her before her research, as she was usually dismissed at events. Further, subculturalists began to talk about the issue of sexism, even if not much had been done to ameliorate it in the RVA scene. She also felt as if she became the token barometer for sexism in RVA as people would apologize if they felt that she heard sexist comments. Paradoxically, she realized that people had a fear that they may say something inappropriate with regard to sexism in front of her. While becoming more worried about sexism, she talked about it at an increasing rate and ultimately confronted or 'called out' individuals who had sexist attitudes and behaviors regardless of their scene status and, in return, due to their power along with her lesser power, she gained the label of 'big mouth' or 'troublemaker'. Although bittersweet reactions existed to her project, this offered Donna the confidence and ensuing networks to pursue organizing a fest in RVA that was only organized previously in Minneapolis, called Combatting Latent Inequality Together (CLIT Fest). To be considered to be part of the fest, each band had to include at least one female member. There were also workshops on sexism and its concomitant issues confronting the punk scene. In subsequent years, this fest burgeoned in cities such as Chicago, Los Angeles, and Portland, among others.

Donna took many memories from this—both bad and good—due to sexism and the lack of roles for women in this subculture. Her participation in the subculture led her to a heightened, albeit temporary, status and a sense of efficacy knowing that she participated in this subculture in a way that was important to her and similar others. However, there were many times that she was challenged as to the reasons why she studied this particular issue. She also learned that due to the lack of roles for women, it created competition and barriers between punk women in the anarcho-punk subculture. She realized this issue also exists not only in the general punk community but in other subcultures and dominant society due to a lack of female representation in high status positions in organizations which results in other ensuing issues reflective of inequality, such as tokenism, cooptation, or stereotyping.

The rapport and relationships that we developed through our research were in large part the product of the authentic expressions of subcultural identity and values that we engaged in as insider researchers. When subjects in our studies talked about distressing and sensitive issues, we were empathetic to our participants because of our shared subcultural experiences. Within the anarcho-punk subculture, expressions of concern about sexism or fascism are expected from participants; therefore, our own attention to these issues was very strong. Instead of the dynamic of surface and deep acting employed by the somewhat detached outsider researcher, our interactions reflected our genuine concerns with the subject and our subcultural peers. As Hochschild (1983) explains, deep acting occurs when researchers expose their feelings and interact with research participants with the totality of their personality, while surface acting refers to researchers exhibiting emotions that are expected within a cultural or situational context. This possibly leads to emotional dissonance as researchers or participants may not internally feel the displayed emotions but feel the need to act in certain ways. Both deep acting and surface acting are dependent upon cultural, subcultural, and situational emotive rules with regard to what to be concerned about, the level of concern, and the display of emotions (Rowling, 1999; Nylander et al, 2011; Blix and Wettergren, 2015). Rather than engaging in the dynamic of deep and surface acting in the interview process, both of us expressed genuine emotional reactions because this conforms to the anarcho-punk subculture's norms of authenticity and legitimacy. In doing so, we were able to bridge the divide between researcher and interviewee in a manner reflective of dynamics of friendship that is unique to insider investigators (Ross, 2017).

Stanislav's approach to studying militant antifascism with participants in the anarchist punk scene generally facilitated building close ties with his research subjects. Not only was his choice of subject a reflection of his identity and political activism at the time of the study, but also a product of his interactions with antifascists through the punk scene. Because of this commitment, his interactions with research participants were frequently much more like those of a peer activist and subculturalist than a 'detached' scholar. The insider knowledge gave him the ability to speak the language of his research subjects and align with their emotional states. Building rapport with interviewees was almost instantaneous because he was recognized as a veteran member of the anarcho-punk subculture and an affiliate of the antifascist movement. This was easily visible through his presentation of self, which was marked by clothing and tattoos that indicated his subcultural and ideological affiliations. It is common for insider researchers who share many attributes with their research subjects to switch between the professional demeanor of researcher and the familiar interactions of a compatriot (Chavez, 2008; Ross, 2017). This dynamic became clear for Stanislav during the interview process as he switched between roles as interviewer and subcultural peer. Interviews were conducted in a professional tone as questions were read from the schedule. These same interviews with relative strangers would frequently progress into interactions more akin to conversations between friends because of the similarities of experience and affinity that he shared with his research subject. Many post-interview debriefs lasted hours as conversations ranged from movement dynamics and strategy to subcultural experiences and discussions of bands and show experiences. The bonds formed during this research extended well beyond the duration of the project. Because of the shared subcultural identification and activism of the researcher and participants, many interviewees became friends with whom Stanislav connected long after the end of interviews and fieldwork.

For Donna, rapport was more of a struggle initially as many did not know who she was, and, for those who in fact knew her, her legitimacy was questioned as she deviated from age and body size norms. She found the importance of her research questions were met with mixed reactions to the research project. She incurred a different reception for her subject of study than Stanislav as antifascism was deemed to be a more important subject than sexism. She hypothesized this may be due to punk being a hypermasculinist subculture that may not want to confront male privilege. At times, she felt at odds with other female members of the subculture due to masculinist norms inherent in this subculture. This, in turn, affected women to want to fit in their proscribed role of femininity (being passive, meeting beauty and sizeist standards, and not wanting to confront male privilege). Many women in the scene may have been surface acting to conform to the standards that punk men wanted while Donna, herself, rebelled against them, both intentionally and unintentionally. Incidentally, while some thought her research was a waste of time and were critical of it, others, outright, wanted to be interviewed. After her persistence and passion for her research and its accompanying social issues, people began to know and trust her, albeit she was perceived as a troublemaker by some. Her semi-structured interview schedule allowed for tangential deviations by participants. Subsequently, some long-lasting friendships were engendered by this research process. Additionally, rapport was also made with some of the interviewees due to some participants in her research sample wanting to take part in this study. In turn, this led to her results being inferred to only her sample rather than a larger population of anarchist/crust punks. While arguing for the importance of her research and illuminating the social problem of sexism in this community for two whole years, her deep acting led to a higher amount of stress and exhaustion. For Donna, there were expectations regarding issues in the scene surrounding various manifestations of sexism. She was expected to be the spokesperson for equality in this regard while having vast knowledge of the subject at hand. Thus, subsequent effects occurred. This led to keener insight and further concentration on Donna's part regarding various issues of misogyny in the scene. She was concerned about sexism for an entire year which actually led to other activities such as ladies' nights and a fest that concentrated on women in this anarcho-punk community. While being a token spokesperson for these issues, many would argue with her, expecting her to teach them about this type of inequality while also performing a mother-like role in the scene. Other people placed her in a default role of being an informal spokesperson for sizeism and women's various body issues. People approached her many times about body/size issues and she felt as if she had to share her 'wisdom' with younger female punks. At times, after her defense of her Master's thesis research project and the CLIT Fest, she felt that she proved her point; however, a year or two later, she felt that her community had not fostered any changes with regard to sexism. Both researchers' roles created some dynamics of strain because some of the people with whom we interacted were unclear of our roles as a result of the authentic expressions of our beliefs and emotions where they would have expected a more detached demeanor from a scholar. These dynamics led to further emotional strain and exhaustion for both authors.

Disenchantment, dissonance, and strain

Emotions are not only part of the research process; emotional labor elicits negative and positive consequences as a result of doing extended field research. Researching sensitive topics is known to bring emotional strain (Blix and Wettergren, 2015). Ellis (1991a) cautions against over-involvement and against 'going native'; however, we approached our work as already native because of our involvement in the anarcho-punk subculture. We experienced several negative emotional outcomes that stemmed from our unique position as insider researchers. Both the subject of study and the interactive dynamics with research participants generated feelings of disenchantment, strain, and dissonance for us because of our role as researchers. Due to our experiences in this research process, we felt vulnerable and emotionally strained from awkward interactions with peers, which culminated in a partial departure from the subculture we were studying.

Conducting insider research on the anarcho-punk subculture exposed the 'hidden' aspects of its dynamics and created a greater awareness of negative elements within it (Blackman, 2007). While we had an awareness of many of the internal and external criticisms of the anarcho-punk subculture, such as this subculture being comprised of idealistic delinquents, armchair anarchists with little understanding of theory or history, and just strange, misunderstood individuals, the process of studying it from within placed these aspects in stark relief upon scholarly reflection and analysis of our data and experiences. While Stanislav primarily engaged with individuals who were antifascist activists inside and outside of their scene, his in-depth engagement with this topic demonstrated the surface commitment of others in the subculture. Additionally, upon reflecting on the primacy of antifascism within the anarcho-punk scene, he found it sadly lacking among some of the core bands and individuals at the foundation of the subculture (Cross, 2004; Worley, 2012; Lohman and Worley, 2018). Donna noted examples of only superficial commitment to anti-misogyny in the anarcho-punk community. Her subculturalist peers vocalized support of anti-sexism; however, she found it to be a feigned and fostered support that contrasted with a plethora of subtly sexist behaviors evidenced on a daily basis, such as talking over and being dismissive of anarcho-punk women, excluding women from punk bands, hyper-valuating and legitimizing men in the scene, subjectively objectifying women, and participating in good old boy's networks, among other issues (Manion, 2007).

The primary form of strain that resulted from engagement with this research was between us and other participants in the subculture. As alluded to earlier, we were treated with suspicion because of our desire to engage in research on what is generally a 'closed' community. This resulted in a great deal of gatekeeping by participants, which challenged our sense of self and subcultural identity. Gatekeeping and access led to emotional labor, and was noted to be an issue in the research process (Rowling, 1999; Blackman, 2007; Romocea, 2014). We had to develop rapport and trust with various gatekeepers in order to gain field access. Blix and Wettergren (2015) have noted that distrust can lead to denial of access to the research field, culminating in a disruption of the research process and a high amount of stress for the researchers. If we were not perceived as legitimate, we likely would have been treated very differently as punks within the field. Those authors further noted techniques gatekeepers may employ to keep researchers at bay. Elitist participants with large amount of power, for example, 'tend to be vigilant not to expose themselves or their groups to critique that could question their positions or privileges' (Blix and Wettergren, 2015, p 690).

While the anarcho-punk subculture presents itself as egalitarian and desires to change the world, it is a very closed community even to its own participants. In order to obtain research participants, Donna initially posted a request for research participants on a prominent anarcho-punk message board, Profane Existence, that culminated in one administrator asking her, 'Who are you? Why have we not seen you on this page before? Why don't we know who you are?' Donna was intimidated by these questions as she initially mistakenly thought that people would be more open to her research due to this being a subculture that wanted to change the world for the better. Donna presumed that many of the participants on the message board were waiting for her response because she was treated as an imposter, or worse, an outsider. No one responded until she responded the next day, where she claimed that she was indeed an anarcho-punk.

Similarly, Stanislav's credentials were questioned by potential participants. Although he entered the field with a great deal of subcultural capital stemming from over 15 years of subcultural and political activism, his status as a scholar generated questions about the motivation behind his research. While his work was grounded in a practice of 'militant ethnography' that works with social movements in their favor (Juris, 2007), he was still treated with suspicion and had to leverage his subcultural and social capital to maintain positive relationships with participants. In both cases, we had to repeatedly prove ourselves to potential participants in order to not only conduct our research, but also to establish its legitimacy.

Both Donna's and Stanislav's intentions of studying their respective scenes were questioned and were treated with suspicion with a fear that their research would leave a negative depiction of their communities. Donna noted being treated as a whistleblower with regard to her research on misogyny in the anarcho-punk subculture. Initially, when she told two friends, a heterosexual couple, about her research, the male, who had very high status and privilege in this community, told her, "Forget that ... just have sex," which led to his girlfriend's scowl. While he thought it was not a worthwhile endeavor, his girlfriend agreed with Donna. This resulted in Donna perceiving this male individual differently due to his purported commitment to combating racism and fascism, but not sexism.

Similarly, Stanislav's intentions were questioned by would-be research participants who wondered if his research would be used to suppress their movement or paint it in a negative light. Others were unsure of his commitment to the principles discussed earlier because of this dual role as subcultural activist and researcher. Furthermore, many of these misgivings were expressed to others, and shared with Stanislav by trusted associates who knew him well.

Also, both authors noted their legitimacy in the scene was questioned. As noted, when Donna told the couple already mentioned about her study of sexism, that very same male individual made it difficult for her to be active in this community and questioned her competency, legitimacy, and commitment to anarcho-punk, pushing Donna to simultaneously question his commitment to the subculture in turn. Stanislav also found that his credibility as an activist and researcher was being questioned, as well as the depth and value of the relationships that he had developed through the research process.

Strained interactions with other subculturalists resulted from these issues. Donna noted that her friends requested to participate in her study because several of them were involved with the wider punk subculture but did not identify as anarcho-punks. Because of this research sample boundary, she had to reject requests by some of her friends to participate, which caused hurt feelings. In one case, she had to turn away two members of a well-known thrash band because they did not identify as anarcho-punks. These types of interactions caused a great deal of tension between Donna and individuals within the scene who did not understand the nuances of her research decisions. Additionally, Stanislav's relationships with the people who were told by participants about their misgivings about him were strained because they were placed in the awkward position of either siding with him and defending the research or against him in criticizing his work. Such dynamics clearly impacted the relationships that we had with not only the research subjects of our study, but with the wider subcultural field in which we operated as well as with friends and acquaintances in the scene.

Researchers have found if academics do not manage self-care, emotional exhaustion may occur, leading to the researchers' withdrawal from the culture or subculture they are studying. Many researchers indicated that self-care was an important emotional component to their research process (Rowling, 1999; Nylander et al, 2011; Blix and Wettergren, 2015). Our relational experiences in the field led to feelings of emotional dissonance for both of us. The disenchantment and strain resulted in our questioning not only the purported principles of the anarcho-punk subculture, but the value of continued participation within it. Both authors found a chasm between being and doing anarcho-punk. They both found that many purported that they were anarcho-punks but did not necessary act in a way that upheld the values of this subculture. While we still identify as anarcho-punks and adhere to many of the ideological positions associated with that identity, neither author is active within their scene or the wider subculture.

Conclusion

Our experiences as insider researchers generated emotional responses and dynamics that reflect those identified by other scholars, as well as unique experiences that stem from our position as insider researchers with close personal ties to the subject of our studies and research participants. By taking a reflexive approach in thinking about our research experiences, we are able to identify key emotional situations (Ellis, 1991a; 1991b). The process of studying a subculture within which we were already embedded first and foremost generated a strong commitment to our work and the subjects of our respective studies. Our close ties to our research also produced disenchantment, dissonance, and strain that ultimately resulted in both authors distancing themselves from the anarcho-punk subculture.

As insider researchers, we were in unique positions regarding maintaining impression management in the field (Dickson-Swift et al, 2009; Blix and Wettergren, 2015; McQueeney and Lavelle, 2017). Our experience generally involved a greater degree of expression of our authentic beliefs and emotions because of our personal ties to the field of study and participants (Chavez, 2008; Ross, 2017). We frequently found ourselves attempting to negotiate a dual identity as researchers and active participants that provided benefits while also creating a number of key drawbacks with regard to interpersonal interactions.

While many researchers experience emotional strain because of the subject of their studies or the necessity to maintain professional distance in situations that were emotionally stressful (Blackman, 2007; Dickson-Swift et al, 2009; Blix and Wettergren, 2015; McQueeney and Lavelle, 2017), we found that it developed from situations where our work generated conflict within ourselves and with members of the subculture. By analyzing the 'hidden' aspects of the research process (Blackman, 2007), we came to view aspects of the subculture as fundamentally contradictory. By studying sexism and antifascism, we came to understand that much of the anarcho-punk subculture is performative in its commitment to values of challenging sexism and fascism in the culture at large and within the subculture itself. Further, our experiences with some members of the subculture were marked by suspicion and derision, which in turn led to their questioning our status as legitimate subculturalists. Partially as a result of the disenchantment and strain that we experienced conducting this research, both authors exited formal participation in the subculture. Unlike 'scene rejectors' who wholesale left the subculture because it cannot be reconciled with adult responsibilities (Davis, 2006), our exit from subcultural participation was the result of a deeper commitment to the egalitarian values than what was being expressed by anarcho-punks with whom we interacted as part of the research process. Ironically, consistent with Bennett's (2006) analysis that ageing punks retain many of the values of the subculture, it is precisely because we believe in the ideological elements of anarcho-punk that we could not participate in it.

The research that we conducted demonstrates that there are numerous benefits to engaging in insider research on subcultures and social movements consistent with the findings of other scholars in these fields (Merton, 1972; Green, 1993; Roseneil, 1993; Bennett, 2003; Hodkinson, 2005) and indicates that there are positive emotional outcomes that are associated with this position. However, this chapter also demonstrates that there are a number of negative emotional dynamics that may also arise from conducting this type of work. Further scholarship and reflection are necessary to gauge the generalizability of these emotional dynamics beyond this subculture and our distinct experiences, as well as to identify other aspects of emotional labor within both insider and outsider research.

This chapter also indicates the interpretive aspects of conducting insider research. As we sought to construct meaning through interviews with anarcho-punks, we experienced distinct emotional reactions to our interactions with our research participants. These emotions were in part the product of our insider status as anarcho-punks as we experienced these interactions and interview responses through our own understanding of the principles and values of anarcho-punk. In turn, our attempts to make meaning from these dynamics influenced our perception of the subculture. Over time, our sense of the subculture shifted from a positive to negative interpretation. This process underscores the importance of the reflexive aspect of conducting insider research wherein the researcher must consider their role and relationship to the subject of their study and how their interactions and emotions impact their understanding (Chavez, 2008; Ross, 2017).

Notes

[1] A distro is when records, CDs, and tapes are purchased from record labels and resold at punk shows or, especially today, online.
[2] Short for fanzine, zines were previously handmade magazines but now online, highlighting band interviews, record reviews, area scene updates, tour updates, and articles on political and social issues.

References

Bennett, A. (2003) 'The Use of Insider Knowledge in Ethnographic Research on Contemporary Youth Music Scenes', in A. Bennett, M. Cieslik and S. Miles (eds) *Researching Youth*, New York: Palgrave Macmillan, pp 186–200.

Bennett, A. (2006) 'Punk's Not Dead: The Continuing Significance of Punk Rock for an Older Generation of Fans', *Sociology*, 40(2): 219–235.

Blackman, S.J. (2007) ' "Hidden Ethnography": Crossing Emotional Borders in Qualitative Accounts of Young People's Lives', *Sociology*, 41(4): 699–716.

Blix, S. and Wettergren, A. (2015) 'The Emotional Labour of Gaining and Maintaining Access to the Field', *Qualitative Research*, 15(6): 688–704.

Brannick, T. and Coghlan, D. (2007) 'In Defense of Being "Native": The Case for Insider Academic Research', *Organizational Research Methods*, 10(1): 59–74.

Chavez, C. (2008) 'Conceptualizing from the Inside: Advantages, Complications, and Demands on Insider Positionality', *The Qualitative Report*, 13(3): 474–494.

Cross, R. (2004) 'The Hippies Now Wear Black: Crass and the Anarcho-Punk Movement, 1977–1984', *Socialist History*, 26: 25–44.

Cross, R. (2010) '"There Is No Authority but Yourself": The Individual and the Collective in British Anarcho-Punk', *Music and Politics*, 4(2): 1–20.

Davies, J. (1996) 'The Future of "No Future": Punk Rock and Postmodern Theory', *Journal of Popular Culture*, 29: 3–25.

Davis, J.R. (2006) 'Growing Up Punk: Negotiating Aging Identity in a Local Music Scene', *Symbolic Interaction*, 29(1): 63–69.

Dickson-Swift, V., James, E., Kippen, S. and Liamputtong, P. (2009) 'Researching Sensitive Topics: Qualitative Research as Emotion Work', *Qualitative Research*, 9(1): 61–79.

Ellis, C. (1991a) 'Emotional Sociology', *Studies in Symbolic Interaction*, 2: 123–145.

Ellis, C. (1991b) 'Sociological Introspection and Emotional Experience', *Symbolic Interaction*, 14: 23–50.

Ferrell, J. (1996) *Crimes of Style: Urban Graffiti and the Politics of Criminality*, Lebanon, NH: Northeastern University Press.

Ferrell, J. (2001) *Tearing Down the Streets: Adventures in Urban Anarchy*, London: Palgrave Macmillan.

Ferrell, J., Hayward, K.J. and Young, J. (2015) *Cultural Criminology: An Invitation*, London: SAGE.

Fox, N.J. (2008) 'Post-Positivism', in L.M. Given (ed) *SAGE Encyclopedia of Qualitative Research Methods*, Thousand Oaks: SAGE, pp 659–664.

Green, P (1993) 'Taking Sides: Partisan Research on the 1984–1985 Miners' Strike', in D. Hobbs and T. May (eds) *Interpreting the Field: Accounts of Ethnography*, Oxford: Oxford University Press, pp 99–117.

Hochschild, A.R. (1983) *The Managed Heart: Commercialization of Human Feeling*, Oakland: University of California Press.

Hodkinson, P. (2005) '"Insider Research" in the Study of Youth Cultures', *Journal of Youth Studies*, 8(2): 131–149.

Juris, J.S. (2007) 'Practicing Militant Ethnography with the Movement for Global Resistance in Barcelona', in S. Shukaitis, D. Graeber and E. Biddle (eds) *Constituent Imagination: Militant Investigations. Collective Theorization*, Chico: AK Press, pp 164–176.

Lohman, K. and Worley, M. (2018) 'Bloody Revolutions, Fascist Dreams, Anarchy and Peace: Crass, Rondos and the Politics of Punk, 1977–84', *Britain & the World*, 11(1): 51–74.

Manion, D. (2007) *Roles and Attitudes of Males and Females in The Anarchist Punk Community*, Richmond: Virginia Commonwealth University, https://scholarscompass.vcu.edu/etd/791

McQueeney, K. and Lavelle, K. (2017) 'Emotional Labor in Critical Ethnographic Work: In the Field and Behind the Desk', *Journal of Contemporary Ethnography*, 46(1): 81–107.

Merton, R.K. (1972) 'Insiders and Outsiders: A Chapter in the Sociology of Knowledge', *American Journal of Sociology*, 78(1): 9–47.

Mills, C.W. (1959) *The Sociological Imagination*, Oxford: Oxford University Press.

Nylander, P., Lindberg, O. and Bruhn, A. (2011) 'Emotional Labour and Emotional Strain among Swedish Prison Officers', *European Journal of Criminology*, 8(6): 469–483.

Romocea, O. (2014) 'Ethics and Emotions: A Migrant Researcher Doing Research among Romanian Migrants', *Sociological Research Online*, 19(4): 176–189.

Roseneil, S. (1993) 'Greenham Revisited: Researching My Self and My Sisters', in D. Hobbs and T. May (eds) *Interpreting the Field: Accounts of Ethnography*, Oxford: Oxford University Press, pp 177–208.

Ross, L.E. (2017) 'An Account from the Inside: Examining the Emotional Impact of Qualitative Research Through the Lens of "Insider" Research', *Qualitative Psychology*, 4(3): 326–337.

Rowling, L. (1999) 'Being In, Being Out, Being With: Affect and the Role of the Qualitative Researcher in Loss and Grief Research', *Mortality*, 4(2): 167–181.

Taylor, J. (2011) 'The Intimate Insider: Negotiating the Ethics of Friendship When Doing Insider Research', *Qualitative Research*, 11(1): 3–22. https://doi.org/10.1177/1468794110384447

Thornton, S. (2013) *Club Cultures: Music, Media and Subcultural Capital*, Polity Press.

Vysotsky, S. (2013) 'The Influence of Threat on Tactical Choices of Militant Anti-Fascist Activists', *Interface: A Journal for and about Social Movements*, 5(2): 263–294.

Vysotsky, S. (2015) 'The Anarchy Police: Militant Anti-Fascism as Alternative Policing Practice', *Critical Criminology*, 23(3): 235–253.

Vysotsky, S. (2020) *American Antifa: The Tactics, Culture, and Practice of Militant Antifascism*, London: Routledge.

Worley, M. (2012) 'Shot by Both Sides: Punk, Politics and the End of "Consensus"', *Contemporary British History*, 26(3): 333–354.

Young, J. (2011) *The Criminological Imagination*, Cambridge: Polity Press.

10

Intimacy, Exchange, and Friendship as Sensitizing Concepts: Interpreting and Teaching Subcultures through Ethnographic Fieldwork

Shane Blackman and Laura Barnett

This chapter is a joint production bringing together a PhD supervisor and post-PhD early career researcher focused on exploring Herbert G. Blumer's (1969 [1954]) 'sensitizing concepts' developed within the symbolic interactionist approach. Our sensitizing concepts are intimacy, exchange, and friendship, which form the basis to understand and interpret data from a series of ethnographic studies on young people and subcultures. We look across our separate research studies and research sites and select examples from fieldwork as part of a joint research imaginary that brings together sociological analysis and the teaching of subcultures.

On this basis, we suggest that sensitizing concepts allow meaning to emerge containing the words and thoughts of research participants, which can then be open to the practice of interpretation. We begin this chapter by first outlining our research biographies to contextualize our backgrounds, highlighting our experience in the study of subcultures. Second, we explain our research positionality, related to the Chicago School of sociology and Blumer's theory of sensitizing concepts. Third, we specify our pedagogic approach to teaching subcultures through fieldwork and interpretation. In the final section, we introduce a series of ethnographic data vignettes focusing on intimacy, exchange, and friendship that sensitize students to the practice of interpretation.

Background and context: Barnett's and Blackman's research studies

Laura Barnett was an undergraduate taught by Shane Blackman who then became his PhD supervisee and subsequently, academic colleague teaching sociological approaches to research for final year undergraduates. We draw on our shared knowledge and commitment to research through this academic journey by doing ethnographic studies on young adults' roles in subcultural groupings in the fields of education, alcohol, drugs, deviance, poverty, and youth cultural style. We investigate subcultures through fieldwork and teaching.

Laura : In this chapter I refer to data collected as part of my PhD scholarship at Canterbury Christ Church University. My thesis was titled: 'Pleasure, Agency, Space and Place: An Ethnography of Youth Drinking Cultures in a Southwest London Community' (Barnett, 2017). The study involved three years of fieldwork alongside young people, subcultural groups, and community members to explore youth alcohol consumption values and practices, and community responses to them. The research entailed fieldwork with approximately 50 underage drinkers in schools, youth centers, and drugs/alcohol services; fieldwork alongside a core group of 30 young adult drinkers, also with other young adult drinkers in bars, clubs, and pubs; and fieldwork with community members including neighbors, teachers, youth workers, drug/alcohol workers, police, and street pastors in a variety of settings.

Shane: In this chapter, I refer to data from two studies. Firstly, my PhD, completed in 1990, at the Institute of Education, University of London, later published as *Youth: Positions and Oppositions – Style, Sexuality, and Schooling* (Blackman, 1995). The research was an ethnographic study of young people within Marshlands Comprehensive School in the South of England. The sample consisted of over 120 girls and boys aged 15 to 17, including four major groups: Mod Boys, New Wave Girls, Boffin Boys, and Boffin Girls. When I undertook the study, I was 22. The young people were studying for examinations. The second study, published in 1997 as *'Destructing a Giro': A Critical and Ethnographic Study of the Youth 'Underclass'*, was funded by the Home Office and took place in Brighton under the title '108 Project' (Blackman, 1997). There were approximately 100 young people (21 percent women and 79 percent men) who visited and stayed at the seafront drop-in center.

The Chicago Schools and Blumer's 'sensitizing concepts'

The ethnographic studies of the Chicago School of sociology under Robert E. Park and Ernest W. Burgess, and the subsequent work of the

'Second Chicago School' from the 1950s to 1960s have been integral to our methodological and theoretical approaches to ethnography because of the Chicago School's emphasis on participatory fieldwork. From W.I. Thomas, Charles S. Johnson, and Frederic M. Thrasher to Paul G. Cressey, Vivien M. Palmer, Frances R. Donovan, E. Franklin Frazier, and Helen MacGill Hughes, on to Howard S. Becker, Erving Goffman, Alfred R. Lindesmith, and Anselm L. Strauss, we read their work on the basis that these Chicago School researchers' methodological struggles in the past were ours in the present. We felt close to the Chicago School and their broad focus on ethnography and deviance within subcultural contexts.

Not only have the Chicago Schools informed our methodological and theoretical approaches to ethnographic research, but their work has informed our positionalities. We identify the key link between both schools through Norman Denzin's (2001, p 243) suggestion that Robert Park was 'a founding "figure" of symbolic interactionism' and that it was Herbert Blumer who first coined the term 'symbolic interactionism' in 1937 (Blumer, 1969 [1954], p 1) at the University of Chicago. On this basis, our chapter employs Patrick Williams' (2011, p 38) assertion that 'symbolic interactionalism can offer us a useful framework for subcultural scholarship'. To apply this approach to our ethnographic fieldwork, we employ Blumer's (1969 [1954], p 147) notion of 'sensitizing concepts' to the practice of interpreting data under the larger pedagogical concept of the 'subcultural imagination' informed by C. Wright Mills (Blackman and Kempson, 2021). Or as Best (2006, p 7) emphasizes, Blumer 'insists the sociologist must attend to the empirical'. In other words, using sensitizing concepts in teaching will connect students to sociological thinking through fieldwork and interpretation.

We see ethnographic data as closely related to Barney G. Glaser and Anselm L. Strauss' (1967) grounded theory through inductive analysis, where the search is for patterns and themes which emerge through interpretation on an interactive basis. David Matza (1969, pp 24–26) in *Becoming Deviant* argues that it is possible to see the early emergence of the grounded theory approach within the work of Park and Burgesses graduate researchers, but of course, the theory bloomed in the 1950s under the Second Chicago School. As Blumer (1969 [1954], p 152) argued, sensitizing concepts are an integral part of 'naturalistic research' within ethnography. Glenn A. Bowen (2006, p 14) sees sensitizing concepts as 'an interpretive device' for sociologists, which according to Kathleen M. Charmaz (2003, p 259), 'provide starting points for building analysis, not ending'. Our chapter provides an open conceptual framework to interpret data through three sensitizing concepts: intimacy, exchange, and friendship. We regard intimacy as having a research relationship underpinned by mutual care and trust, where there is openness and respect for personal vulnerabilities

(Busier et al, 1997). Marcel Mauss' (1950 [1935]) gift exchange theory has informed our definition of exchange as a sensitizing concept, which we regard as the processes of giving, receiving, and reciprocating within ethnographic research to create, strengthen, and maintain social relations to ultimately build trust between ourselves and our research participants. We share Corrine Glesne's (1989, p 46) view of friendship as being more than rapport; participants are equal actors in establishing and maintaining mutual relationships through confidence and trust, as well as 'liking, feeling, affection for one another, [which] implies a sense of intimacy and mutual bonding'. We recognize that our sensitizing concepts strongly relate to research relationships, which in turn informs our interpretive practice of subculture. For example, Charmaz (2014) explains that research relationships are complex and can affect strategies for data collection. Moreover, through the process of developing methodological self-consciousness, we can be reflexive about and examine issues relating to power, identity, subjectivity, and marginality of both ourselves and our research participants, which can inform our relations, approaches, worldviews and potentially enrich research interpretation and analysis (Charmaz, 2017).

Our sensitizing concepts are not definitive or prescriptive; they rest on relevance and can be seen as related to James Clifford's (1986, p 7) idea that 'ethnographic truths are thus inherently *partial*-committed and incomplete'. As Becker (1988, p 16) notes, Blumer's idea of sensitizing concepts 'pointed to something we observed but could not yet define adequately'. Thus, for Blumer (1969 [1954], pp 148–150), the task of sensitizing concepts is not about being 'definitive' but 'providing clues and suggestions'. Van den Hoonaard (1997, p 5) argues that 'the defining characteristic of Barney Glaser and Anselm Strauss "grounded theory" directed towards the discovery of theory from data, is a direct descendent of Blumer's sensitizing concepts'. Here we provide the groundwork for interpreting research data to enable students to address the feasibility and trustworthiness of our analysis: using fieldwork examples to guide learners towards being open about what is happening, and towards effective interpreting and theorizing. We suggest that our sensitizing concepts are accessible and practical in the context of teaching, whereby students can practically take them on as they are learning about ethnographic work. This is attributed to the sensitizing concepts of intimacy, exchange, and friendship, which act as starting points for building a possible framework for interpretation, which could be seen as a grounded theory approach to data analysis through the subcultural imagination, bringing observation and theory closer. Following Blumer (1969 [1954], pp 146–147), we set out our ethnographic fieldwork vignettes as 'instances' showing 'relevance' under the theoretical headers of our three sensitizing concepts in an open context, to allow for multiple interpretation for us and our students.

Teaching subculture and interpretation: some hesitations

Here we introduce our approach to teaching and interpretation influenced by the naturalistic stance of the Chicago School from Nels Anderson to Howard Becker, where biography became an entry point for research and teaching (Roberts, 2006, p 18). Initially, we were drawn to Ben Green and Christine Feldman-Barrett's (2020) ideas of 'insider research' and 'insider teaching', which we used to introduce an interpretation of subcultures to students. However, we then felt that these set artificial limitations on teachers who lacked subcultural knowledge and research experience. Robert K. Merton (1972, p 11) suggests that insiders may have increased 'access to knowledge' and even present 'insider truth', but the dangers of 'ethnocentrism' or the extravagant claims of an 'insider epistemology' (p 25) work on 'the credentialism of ascribed status ... where understanding becomes accessible only to the fortunate few or many who are to the manner born' (p 14), or to paraphrase Merton, the issue becomes: can only subculturalists understand subcultures? To their credit, Green and Feldman-Barrett (2020, p 12) are cautious about advancing 'insider teaching' because of the danger of teachers 'becoming a subcultural spokesperson'. We share this hesitation and feel that there are flaws in this binary position of insider and outsider because as Clifford J. Geertz (1974, p 29) has written on the subject of 'natives', 'you don't have to be one to know one', which he followed up with 'we are all natives now' (Geertz, 1983, p 151). For us, the critical context of sociological teaching relates to Mills' (1959) emphasis on the use of the 'intellectual life' whereby teachers, like researchers, may construct knowledge with students and participants based on reflexivity and imagination. In presenting our fieldwork instances to students, we invite them to engage in a dialogue, encouraging them to bring their own knowledge, values, and experiences to expand the social realities of the subcultures under study.

We aim to draw on a teacher's subcultural background or knowledge to ensure that through the presentation of our ethnographic examples, there is an open context for students and researchers to assess, critique, and appreciate that fieldwork on subcultural grouping is not restricted by or dependent upon the teacher's experience. For us, teaching is about play, testing, and suggesting, which corresponds to Robert Park's (1941, p 39) idea that student learning should always be 'an adventure which was taking us beyond the limits of safe and certified knowledge into the realm of the problematic and unknown'.

In contrast, Lucy Robinson and Chris Warne (2020, p 232) highlight 'the significance of the personal experience of our subcultural identification when teaching punk'. For them, teaching about punk through biography and the take-up of Dick Hebdige's approach to subculture enables the teacher to be critical at a political level and encourages students to be themselves. The punk pedagogy advocated by David Beer (2014) and Gareth D. Smith, Mark Dines, and Tom Parkinson (2017) is informed by Neil Postman and Charles Weingartner's (1969) 'Teaching as a Subversive Activity' and linked to the origins of cultural studies derived from Raymond Williams' *Radical Project* whereby 'decanonized knowledge' on youth and subculture can challenge cultural elitism (Blackman, 2000). Similarly, our teaching content related to gender, subcultural identity, personal vulnerability, racist discrimination, or social class inequalities can be based on what Les Back (2012) calls 'live sociology' in the classroom, where moments captured from the field can illustrate the promise of theory or bring concepts to life. This is what makes sociology social, and research methods populated by people. While there is no substitute for first-hand observation of our ethnographic descriptions and interpretation, we want to avoid the totalizing position of having to possess a prerequisite to teach an aspect of sociology, including subcultures.

Many students come into higher education with prior knowledge about subcultures because of their access to key sociological texts from secondary schooling at GCSE and Advanced levels, and they may have had some prior experience of subcultures through their degrees of participation in them. Therefore, our fieldwork examples enabled students to use their prior knowledge and experience in helping them to make sense of and interrogate our accounts. Through ethnography, lived experience is infused with opportunities for discussion. Importantly, personal experience and subjectivity are at the heart of ethnography both in the field and in the teaching context (Stevenson and Lawthom, 2017). Never more so than with Charles Johnson's (1923, p 56) *The Negro in Chicago*, we hear the voices of the oppressed and their everyday ordinariness, through the method formalized by Clifford Shaw's (1930, p 21) 'own story' and 'the life-history' of *The Jack-Roller*. The classroom becomes a fieldwork site where interpretation is created. In our module *Research and Society*, research projects are more than just coursework; they (potentially, at least) embody critical pedagogy rooted in the sociological imagination and Mills' focus on social justice. For students who are dealing with personal troubles, including forms of discrimination or vulnerabilities, these research projects can be *therapeutic* insofar as they provide deeper and more nuanced understandings of the injustice students feel or perceive (Williams, 2016). But therapy is not all, the sociological imagination ties these personal troubles to public issues in ways that can change students' outlook on life, affecting their future beliefs and actions. Working together, the ethnographic process can become a series of moments that are as subjectively empowering as they are pedagogically instructive.

When using examples of friendship, intimacy, and exchange in classroom settings with students, we as teachers can return to the original site of data collection. As a result, in the teaching context, it is possible to describe an incident or an encounter using fieldwork descriptions, voices, or artefacts. Thus, the classroom becomes the site of fieldwork where assignments are more than essays. They are part of a critical pedagogy whereby interpretation can follow through the articulation of 'personal troubles to public issues', where students identify real-life experiences with ethnography to catch critical moments of wider social and cultural understanding. This increases the likelihood that in teaching, we may be brought back to the moment of data collection. We are transported to a variety of emotional experiences such as excitement, thrill, sadness, or fear. This allows us to pedagogically re-live our fieldwork to enable students to see the potential in their biography and experience. In turn, through discussion, students can make their assessment of our actions and interpretations.

In the teaching context, we explain how research participants trusted Laura and me as researchers. This trust relationship is then transferred to the teaching context and students become aware that the interpretation and assessment of data can be transferred to them. Our emphasis on observing, listening, questioning, and reciprocity makes sociological research tangible and approachable. This can only be effective if students imagine that the research storyline is feasible, and that interpretation is plausible. Then, they may be able to make their own interpretations. Through critical and interactive dialogue, we seek to share with our students new perspectives collectively underpinned by trust (Brookfield, 2015). Moreover, in their assignments, students can use what has been taught in their undergraduate program to critique, interpret, and understand the relevance of their biographies and personal knowledge. On this basis, Williams (2016, p 175) argues: 'In the classroom, students took the chance to critically assess the nature of social and cultural hierarchies within which they live.' Thus, where reflexivity in the classroom is supported by the sociological imagination, as teachers we take forward the approach and excitement of the Chicago School studies to demonstrate that past work has contemporary relevance to today's research and teaching contexts. This sustains the legacy of Vivien Palmer's (1928, p 203) *Field Studies in Sociology*, which expressed the sociologist's 'imagination' and aim to 'be creative'.

Using ethnographic examples for interpretive practice

In this section, we tie ethnographic examples of fieldwork with subcultural groups to three sensitizing concepts: intimacy, exchange, and friendship. While there is a degree of overlap between these themes, we thought it valuable to critically reflect on and explore how fieldwork is informed by Mills' promise of theory. Selected ethnographic vignettes are introduced and explored based on the sensitizing concepts for students, researchers, and teachers to assess how young people are presented in subcultural groups or settings, alongside how observation and explanation take place. It is possible to address, for example, the role of the researcher and how participants related to them. Similarly, it is possible to examine the visibility of females within subcultures and consider gender in practice. This invites students to think about the gendered relations within fieldwork friendships, enabling them to explore sociological theory (Skeggs, 2001). The sensitizing concepts are codes that offer a tentative sociological interpretation, where students and teachers can explore meaning, findings, and theory. Here we bring students and teachers into the web of analysis to creatively explore and critique our and their interpretations.

We follow Carole McGranahan's (2014, p 28) pedagogic strategy where 'research based on ethnographic fieldwork were given to ... students'. At the same time, we created for our students an awareness of subcultural identities as potential themes to explore in the *Research and Society* module. Attendance was required over a series of weeks, including lectures and interactive workshop discussions. Through the teaching of research methods, we aimed to cultivate ethnographic sensibility among our undergraduates using the sensitizing concepts of intimacy, exchange, and friendship. To achieve this, we thought it necessary for two types of transparency, first, for students to see us as teacher-ethnographers actively seeking explanations from data, and second, for students to assess material transparently delivered to them to read and interpret.

In practice, the sensitizing concepts derived from ethnography were brought into the classroom to explore the actions, practices, and values for interpretation of subcultural markers and identities. This allowed students to explore the meaning of how fieldwork took place and, through interpretation, students could begin to respond as sociologists to think about the insights of subcultural theory and how research is undertaken. In agreement with Given (2008, p 2) that sensitizing concepts are 'important methodological devices with which to enter the world of meanings of a researched population', we contend our sensitizing concepts expand our knowledge and assist with the interpretation of subcultural worlds.

Intimacy within fieldwork
Vignette 1, Shane, 'Dishing out the spuds'
When in Brighton studying the homeless and unemployed, I was recruited by a social services manager to work in a Day Centre to serve lunch. My task was to dish out potatoes, boiled or roasted, to each customer. I remembered Mauss' (2007 [1947], p 41) comment that 'fieldworkers too often fail to study the consumption of food'. As I served the hungry people, I began to recognize individual young adult men and women. There would subsequently be a bit of chatting and smiling persuasion to

gain extra portions. I could see winks and grins and hear laughter, which is where I first detected moments of sensitivity with the participants. This level of food bribery through intimacy was about gaining favors for survival. I felt this and was sure they knew it. After weeks of sitting, chatting, and drinking tea, coffee, or hot chocolate, I was aware of how little food they ate which impacted on their health and confidence. It reinforced their sense of poverty and being without. We spent much time talking about how others saw them as different, deviant, 'aggressive beggars', which informed my interpretation of what it means to be regarded as a subcultural 'underclass'. At the Chicago School, Helen MacGill Hughes (1940, p 211) always put priority on human emotional experiences, reflecting on narratives of despair and sensitivity with a keen eye on kindness.

Some of the young homeless had been brought into close contact with the police and the courts, and through both social and youth workers, they were aware that they were identified as a 'criminal subculture'. Even if they had not committed any crime, their 'style of life' appeared to attract unwanted attention. Their experience of being 'pigeon-holed' as 'scruffy' or thought of as being part of a traveler subculture weighed on their minds. This is the personal and human side of ethnography where participants felt 'embarrassed', 'ashamed', and 'labeled' (Becker 1973 [1963], p 73). But at the same time, working with participants brought emotional problems for the researcher. Garthwaite (2016, p 31) has noted that fieldwork was 'incredibly heart-breaking, draining and frustrating'. Critically, 'dishing out the spuds' enabled improved contact and communication with the young homeless as they saw me in different roles. During the fieldwork many of the young homeless spent time thinking about money because they had none; what type of style of clothes, boots, or trainers they would buy. Perhaps, one of the key aspirations of young people here was to participate in consumer culture; to buy a drink, go to a club, be fashionable and play music, but they found these pleasures were out of reach (Blackman, 1997).

Vignette 2, Laura, "Have you ever tried weed, Miss?"

When researching at a local drug and alcohol service, The Rafters, I was introduced to high school students who had been identified by their teachers as 'requiring intervention' to help them with their drug/alcohol 'misuse'. These young people were signed up for The Rafters' six-week program led by two male coordinators, which I attended weekly. Despite teachers nominating students to attend, they felt stereotyped for being asked to go for the program. Nonetheless, they were happy to be out of school and 'went along with it'. The community space where the program took place was welcoming. At the start of each session, we had lunch together. This was one of the opportunities to chat and get to know each other. We seemed to get on well and this strengthened as the weeks went on, as people shared details about their lives. I noticed how the young people addressed me as 'Miss' in the same way they did their teachers, despite me telling them I wasn't a teacher or drug/alcohol worker but a researcher. When it came to the third session about cannabis, the young people enjoyed telling stories about their consumption. During a break, a couple of male students asked me: "Have you ever tried weed, Miss?" I told them a story about when I was a teenager and how my boyfriend offered to introduce me to weed for the first time and would take me through it so I wouldn't 'whitey' (vomit). I said how I was anxious about trying it (just as they said they had been) and how I wanted to have someone I could trust with me, if I were to do it. I continued to explain that a couple of days after my boyfriend's offer, he came to meet me one evening, clearly stoned. He was paranoid, shouting, "The Feds are after me" and ran three miles home in his getaway, leaving me alone and baffled. There were no police officers in sight. I laughed: "How could I trust him to take me through it after that?" We continued chatting about the story and they interjected with bemusement: "What a dick!" They empathized when I explained that I hadn't felt the need to try weed after that and enjoyed the buzz of drinking with friends. At the end of that week's session, the young men departed with a wave: "See you next week, Laura."

These ethnographic descriptions show how intimacy in fieldwork, through seemingly ordinary, everyday interactions and dialogue with research participants, can carve out opportunities to further explore subcultural concepts and establish research relationships. In these moments, intimate exchanges were personal and subjective but maintained through mutual trust and openness. This resonates with what Robert E. Park (1941, p 8) wrote of Frances Donovan's *The Sales Lady* (1929), she 'has been able to enter sympathetically and understandingly into the experiences of the persons whose lives she depicts'. With students in the classroom, then, we were able to speak about entering and understanding the 'social world' of the participants, with its own ways of acting, talking, and thinking, through customs, meanings, and purposes (Cressey, 1932). This led to discussions about how we can attempt to explore social worlds by assessing emotional comments from, and stereotypes and stigma faced by, the homeless and other subcultural groups. We can then relate these to sociological concepts including leisure, inequality, and 'underclass', alongside the power of labelling a group as a deviant subculture (Becker, 1973 [1963]). Notions of power, stereotypes, and stigma are sociological concepts that the students recognized and related to. We then analyzed these together theoretically using the work of key theorists of the Chicago School, such as Goffman's (1963) work on *Stigma*, to encourage students to offer a critical interpretation of subculture and to debunk myths using theory. Intimacy as a sensitizing concept could then reveal to students how 'natural' dialogue could be part of their fieldwork, helping them to understand how the layers of interpretation could be developed and then used in writing research.

Exchange within fieldwork
Vignette 3, Laura, 'Token gestures'

While researching at a local community youth center, I faced the challenge of establishing rapport with the 'Alternative' youth-subcultural group who attended. The Alternative group's style was inspired by punk and emo subcultures; they listened to and played punk, heavy metal, and rock music; consumed a variety of drugs and alcohol; and many identified as gay, lesbian, bisexual, and pansexual. Considering the 'mainstream' and heterosexual markers of my own identity, the feelings of being an outsider were prominent during fieldwork, so I found it hard to relate to them, and them to me. I struggled to build rapport with the young people because we seemingly had little in common and they weren't forthcoming in discussions about their drug/alcohol use. This was apparent when I overheard the young people talking to youth workers whom they had established relationships with. They were even less forthcoming with me when they spotted my field diary. As pointed out by the youth center manager, many researchers like me had been to the youth center looking to 'take what they needed' and disappeared. It became apparent that I needed to invest more time in getting to know them and earn their trust. For months I went to the youth center and just hung out with the young people. I played pool, joined in with crafts, listened to them play music and computer games, and we spoke about school and home life. I sat in the reception as the young people came in, and when some didn't have the 50 pence entry fee, I popped the money into the deposit box. As time went on, I enjoyed my time at the youth center and noted how the Alternative young people engaged with me more as we shared moments. Over time, they enquired about my research with genuine interest and didn't mind when the field diary reappeared. One young male, Luke, recommended that I "should read about a guy called Paul Willis' work," whom he learned about in his sociology classes. He also invited me to join a group of the Alternative young people outside of the youth center to "really see what goes on" with their drug use. Months later following our interactions, small gestures, and tokens of exchange, when it came to 'formally' recording interviews with the young people, I felt elated when they volunteered to take part. I recalled Howard Becker's (2020) reflections on Alfred Lindesmith: 'The two big people for Lindy at Chicago were Herb Blumer and Edwin Sutherland. Blumer was a great advocate of getting close to the people you did research on.' The emphasis on field studies and 'Own Story' enabled Lindesmith to understand biographical narratives within the context of social normality. Similarly, for me, the participants became transparent and open in their discussions with me. I recorded in the field diary how the fieldwork had completely turned on its head, and how I had made genuine fieldwork friends.

Vignette 4, Shane, 'Being asked for favors'

Being brought into people's lives is what we do in our daily lives. Our friends, acquaintances, and colleagues may request something from us. To do something. This is the practice of everyday life as explored by Michel de Certeau (1984) and Raymond Williams (1989 [1958]), wherein we help each other through ordinary processes, both traditional and creative. This also takes place in ethnographic research. The applied nature of fieldwork results in exchanges and requests which can vary from an exchange of feelings to an exchange of opinions and views through humor and storytelling. Importantly, in ethnography as a researcher, you can disagree with your research participants, they can challenge you, and vice versa. Ethnographers get asked direct questions by the researched, and the researcher must respond. During fieldwork there can be minor exchanges between oneself and the researched, including a cigarette, a cup of tea, use of a mobile phone, listening to music on a smartphone, an alcoholic drink, a glass of water, a joint, a book, a badge, or a scarf. When studying mods as part of my PhD fieldwork, a young mod, known as Hat, asked if I could buy a copy of Stan Cohen's (2002 [1972]) *Folk Devils and Moral Panics* for him. The book had been used in a sociology and history lesson at school by the head of history. I agreed, and Hat (the mod research participant) paid for it. This was a symbolic subcultural exchange. Some weeks later it happened again when another mod asked me to purchase Dick Hebdige's (1979) *Subculture: The Meaning of Style*. This I duly did. Being asked for favors could also be seen as a type of test that participants put before the researcher. Are you up to this?

In these ethnographic vignettes, exchange as a sensitizing concept brings awareness that ethnographic research is live, direct, and immediate. Reflecting on the issue of obligation in Mauss' gift relationship, Roda Madziva (2015, p 14) suggests that the research relationship is a gift-exchange, and very sensitively observes that 'my participants were able to give me something more valuable and long-lasting than what I was able to give them'. While we feel that this is correct, from our perspective, special gifts exchanged during research may vary greatly in diversity and depth. In the classroom, our students witnessed from the ethnographic vignettes young people reaching out for sociological understanding related to their cultural practice and schoolwork. Initially, our students thought that being asked for favors or exchanging tokens/gestures in research could be seen as a dual-axis but concluded that these were positive outcomes that consolidated field relations. The exchange relationship enabled students in the classroom to assess trust-building and power relations between the researcher and the researched. In the classroom, students became aware that we were giving and not just receiving. It was not merely subcultural 'knowledge transfer', it went to the heart of reciprocity, as explained by Thrasher (1928, p 245) and Frazier (1940, p 27). We could explain how putting yourself out there and showing commitment to and awareness about participants are part of naturalistic research and are motivational for participants who are attempting to understand the research process and, in a certain sense, seeking to assist the researcher. Arguably, participants and the researcher are sharing a type of subcultural imagination and students in the classroom are observing this by seeking an interpretation. Discussing exchange as a sensitizing concept with students then enables us to explore researcher positionality with our students, examining how it not only informs fieldwork approaches and relations but also the interpretations that we offer to subculture. We went on to encourage our students to be reflexive about their identities when debating how their identity markers, including class, gender, ethnicity, and so on, can inform how they interact with and interpret subcultural groups. In turn, through the sensitizing concept of exchange, we have also been able to prompt critical debates with our students around notions of insider and outsider research on the identities of the subcultural groups we study.

Friendship within fieldwork
Vignette 5, Shane, "Shane's with us!"

When traveling with research participants—on a bike, on a scooter as a pillion passenger, on a bus, on a train or in a car—as a researcher, I got an incredible feeling of presence. I found pleasure from walking with participants and being part of their subcultural actions—at a pub, café, club, gig, or festival, in the street, going into a shop, a house or a flat, playing football, going to the cinema or the beach. There is something exciting about being out with your research participants after midnight, even slightly deviant for an academic! When out one winter evening walking with some of the New Wave Girls' subcultural group to attend a music and drinks party, we could hear noise and sound blasting out from a house. We stood by a garden fence and peered into one of the rooms of the house and we could see boyfriends (some of whom were ex-boyfriends) of the New Wave Girls involved in close contact with sixth-form girls. It looked like a tight squeeze for the party goers as we gazed at them.

We stood there for ages. It was around 10:30pm. The girls were upset and thought the behavior of their boyfriends was a betrayal; they did not like the way they "touched each other". This turned into humor as the girls were laughing and joking about their boyfriends at the party. At one point the humor became "roarkus" and we all fell over on the pavement, scrambling over one another and the fence. The giggling and chortling had become addictive. Then the laughing turned into action when the girls decided to both ring the bell and knock on the door: *bang bang!!!* Quickly, a couple of their boyfriends appeared on the threshold, and the sixth-form girls could be seen behind them. The boyfriends welcomed the New Wave Girls and me, saying "Come in", but to the amazement of their boyfriends, the New Wave Girls shouted at them and said they would not be attending this event. So, they left. The boyfriends were silent as the girls turned their backs and walked off. One of the boyfriends, Rick, said: "Shane you can come in if you like? Plenty of music and beer!" One of the New Wave Girls, Jenny, said: "No way, Shane's with us!" and I said goodnight to the lads! Everyone was chatting as we walked to a house of one of the girls. For me, this was a cathartic moment during fieldwork, where I had been assigned a place, a position, and a type of loyalty.

Vignette 6, Laura, "We can't leave you on your own"

As part of my fieldwork, I conducted participatory research alongside young adults in pubs, bars, and nightclubs, and notably, much of this research was undertaken with my existing friends. While ethnographic research alongside friends brought about rich fieldwork experiences and unexpected data collection opportunities, this dynamic between myself as a 'researcher' and my friends as 'participants' brought about challenges relating to fieldwork and thesis writing. On one fieldwork occasion, I started the night with two friends, Stephanie and Amelia. We walked into the town center together to have food and drinks at a bar to celebrate Stephanie's friend's birthday. On the walk to the bar, Stephanie and Amelia kept telling me it was going to be a 'quiet night' because they had work in the morning. When it got to 11:45pm, Stephanie's work friend begged us to join their group in going to a nightclub, wanting to make the most of free entry before midnight. I told Stephanie and Amelia I would join the group because it would make a great fieldwork experience and they would have each other to safely travel home together. I reassured them that I would make my way back and get a family member to pick me up. However, Amelia firmly insisted with Stephanie's backing: "We can't leave you on your own." This was not up for negotiation. Even though I was going to join another group of people who were Stephanie's friends, had a means of getting home safely, and wasn't engaging in alcohol consumption, it was apparent on this occasion that friendship trumped fieldwork. This was grounded in both the broader research findings that women on nights out employed risk-management strategies to stay safe (Barnett, 2017), and that as an 'intimate insider' (Taylor, 2011), the deep-rooted values of friendship, including the values of intimacy and support, and the emotional bonds between us, were central to maintain.

Through these ethnographic vignettes, we were able to invite students to reflect upon their own gendered experiences in forming and sustaining friendships, drawing upon ideas relating to loyalty, excitement, fun, closeness, the meaning of friendship, and so on. In the classroom, we found that students gained the feeling and sense that we were actively involved with our subcultural participants. A major issue in ethnography is that researchers must make decisions in fieldwork. Both vignettes allow students to reflect on issues of power, pleasure, and belonging in a transparent manner. Students were invited to explore these reflections further; to think critically about the ethical considerations arising from friendships in fieldwork. When interpreting data with students in the classroom and focusing on friendship as a sensitizing concept, we found it useful to introduce our students to 'double reflexivity' (Blackman and Commane, 2012), where the researcher engages in reflexivity, first in relation to data collection and then, second, through analysis of that data in the interpreting and writing process. This offers visibility to textual production and the management of fieldwork relations. The sensitizing concept of friendship allowed students to question and think about research friendships and power relations, and how these need to be explained in sociology. There is a need to think about Becker's (1967) question: 'Whose Side Are We On?'

Conclusion

Sensitizing concepts are important for interpretation because they are the links between observation, data, and theory. Doing data analysis is a craft requiring effort, thought, and imagination. The ethnographic-subcultural examples explored under each sensitizing concept have been used within the classroom setting with our students—we went back and forth between context, data example, and emerging analysis.

In presenting our ethnographic examples through the sensitizing concepts of intimacy, exchange, and friendship, we hope that we have been able to invite the reader, as we do our students, to apply their sociological imagination to these vignettes. Doing so encourages and supports us in developing and critically debating understandings and interpretations of subculture by reflecting upon and incorporating biographies, knowledge, and experiences. Sociological theory could also be applied to illuminate new ways of thinking about subculture and ethnography. To this end, we could say that we share Paul Atkinson's view:

> [W]e can all surely have ideas and work with ideas. We can have ideas about the social phenomena we study, and we can all work with ideas.

We can pick up ideas from the literature we read, and we can assimilate ideas into our research interests. So, data are stuff to think with, and ideas are the tools we use. (2017, p 8)

This is a philosophy that we have towards our ethnographic research and teaching, and the relationship between them.

Sensitizing concepts of intimacy, exchange, and friendship are practical tools that guide students through a grounded theory approach to data analysis—students addressed the different ways to code data, studying different types of conversational data, fieldnotes, and observations. Certain phrases or ideas from research participants can be identified from ethnographic work, which can sit alongside the researcher's critical understanding of the field and literature. The researcher can then develop a partial language of description whereby interpretation of young people's actions in subcultures can be understood. Students can then see how this language links to previous studies, theories, and concepts, or more generally, the literature on young people and subcultural identification. We explored the following in classroom discussions with students: how specific approaches are used in fieldwork, how data emerges, how types of data are created, and how they might fit together or not. We asked: What is missing? What works? Through using Blumer's idea of sensitizing concepts as a type of initial code, we could ensure that data interpretation in the classroom heightened students' sociological imagination.

In this chapter, we have shown how the sensitizing concepts of intimacy, exchange, and friendship have developed through our research journeys to shape our knowledge and interpretation of, and contribution to, the study of subculture. We have provided an account of how these sensitizing concepts have been inspired by generations of researchers from the Chicago School, who have informed our research biographies and approaches to ethnography and fieldwork. Through this account, we have articulated and shown the relevance and legacy of their work in a contemporary context. Much like the Chicago School sociologists, through our research and teaching, we have demonstrated how we have taken our sensitizing concepts and shared them within our teaching contexts, not only to inform our pedagogic approach to teaching subculture within the discipline of sociology but also to invite our students to become researchers of subculture. Through the presentation of ethnographic research data, we encouraged our students to progress knowledge by reflecting upon and challenging our thinking. Creating a critical dialogue in this way with our students helps to extend our knowledge and commits us to think about subculture in new ways with our students through joint endeavors of reflexivity and applying our sociological imaginations. We contend and hope that other researchers and teachers can also develop and commit to new ways of thinking about and interpreting subcultures through some of the research and teaching approaches outlined in this chapter.

Acknowledgments

We would like to thank Howard Becker for his conversations, Patrick Williams for his suggestions, the students on the module that we taught, and the research participants from our ethnographic studies.

References

Atkinson, P. (2017) 'Introduction: Granular Ethnography', in P. Atkinson, *Thinking Ethnographically*, London: SAGE, pp 1–13.

Back, L. (2012) 'Live Sociology: Social Research and its Futures', *The Sociological Review*, 60: 18–39.

Barnett, L. (2017) 'Pleasure, Agency, Space, and Place: An Ethnography of Youth Drinking Cultures in a Southwest London Community', PhD dissertation, Canterbury Christ Church University.

Becker, H.S. (1967) 'Whose Side Are We On?', *Social Problems*, 14(3): 239–247.

Becker, H.S. (1973 [1963]) *Outsiders*, New York: Free Press.

Becker, H.S. (1988) 'Herbert Blumer's Conceptual Impact', *Symbolic Interaction*, 11(1): 13–21.

Becker, H.S. (2020) Personal communication.

Beer, D. (2014) *Punk Sociology*, London: Palgrave Macmillan.

Best, J. (2006) 'Bulmer's Dilemma: The Critic as Tragic Figure', *American Sociologist*, 37: 5–14.

Blackman, S. (1995) *Youth: Positions and Oppositions—Style, Sexuality, and Schooling*, Aldershot: Avebury Press.

Blackman, S. (1997) '"Destructing a Giro": A Critical and Ethnographic Study of the Youth "Underclass"', in M.R. London (ed) *Youth, the 'Underclass' and Social Exclusion*, London: Routledge, pp 113–129.

Blackman, S. (2000) '"Decanonised Knowledge" and the Radical Project: Towards an Understanding of Cultural Studies in British Universities', *Pedagogy, Culture, and Society*, 8(1): 43–67.

Blackman, S. and Commane, G. (2012) 'Double Reflexivity: The Politics of Fieldwork and Representation within Ethnographic Studies of Young People', in S. Heath and C. Walker (eds) *Innovations in Researching Youth*, London: Palgrave Macmillan, pp 229–247.

Blackman, S. and Kempson, M. (2021) 'The Subcultural Imagination: Critically Negotiating the Co-Production of "Subcultural Subjects" through the Lens of C. Wright Mills', *Sociological Research Online*, 28(1): 1–15.

Blumer, H. (1969 [1954]) *Symbolic Interactionism*, Hoboken: Prentice Hall.

Bowen, G. (2006) 'Grounded Theory and Sensitizing Concepts', *International Journal of Qualitative Methods*, 5(3): 12–23.

Brookfield, S. (2015) *The Skillful Teacher: On Technique, Trust, and Responsiveness in the Classroom* (3rd edn), San Francisco: Jossey-Bass.

Busier, H.L., Clark, K.A., Esch, R.A., Glesne, C., Pigeon, Y. and Tarule, J.M. (1997) 'Intimacy in Research', *International Journal of Qualitative Studies in Education*, 10(2): 165–170.

Charmaz, K. (2003) 'Grounded Theory: Objectivist and Constructivist Methods', in N.K. Denzin and Y.S. Lincoln (eds) *Strategies for Qualitative Inquiry* (2nd edn), Thousand Oaks: SAGE, pp 249–291.

Charmaz, K. (2014) 'Grounded Theory in Global Perspective: Reviews by International Researchers', *Qualitative Inquiry*, 20(9): 1074–1084.

Charmaz, K. (2017) 'The Power of Constructivist Grounded Theory for Critical Inquiry', *Qualitative Inquiry*, 23(1): 34–45.

Clifford, J. (1986) 'Introduction: Partial Truths', in J. Clifford and G. Marcus (eds) *Writing Cultures*, Berkeley: University of California Press, pp 1–26.

Cohen, S. (2002 [1972]) *Folk Devils and Moral Panics*, Oxford: Martin Robertson.

Cressey, P.G. (1932) *The Taxi-Dance Hall*, Chicago: University of Chicago Press.

de Certeau, M. (1984) *The Practice of Everyday Life*, Berkeley: University of California Press.

Denzin, N. (2001) 'Symbolic Interactionism, Poststructuralism and the Racial Subject', *Symbolic Interaction*, 24(2): 243–249.

Frazier, F. (1940) *Negro Youth at the Crossways*, New York: Schocken Books.

Garthwaite, K. (2016) *Hunger Pains: Life Inside Foodbank Britain*, Bristol: Policy Press.

Geertz, C. (1974) 'From the Native's Point of View: On the Nature of Anthropological Understanding', *Bulletin of the American Academy of Arts and Sciences*, 28(1): 26–45.

Geertz, C. (1983) *Local Knowledge*, London: Fontana.

Given, L.M. (2008) *The Sage Encyclopedia of Qualitative Research Methods*, Thousand Oaks: SAGE. doi: 10.4135/9781412963909.

Glaser, B.G. and Strauss, A. (1967) *The Discovery of Grounded Theory: Strategies for Qualitative Research*. Chicago: Aldine.

Glesne, C. (1989) 'Rapport and Friendship in Ethnographic Research', *International Journal of Qualitative Studies in Education*, 2(2): 45–54.

Goffman, E. (1963) *Stigma: Notes on the Management of Spoiled Identity*, London: Penguin Books.

Green, B. and Feldman-Barrett, C. (2020) ' "Become What You Are": Subcultural Identity and "Insider Teaching" in Youth Studies', *Teaching Higher Education*, 27(1): 39–53.

Hebdige, D. (1979) *Subculture: The Meaning of Style*, London: Methuen.

MacGill Hughes, H. (1940) *News and the Human Interest Story*, Chicago: Chicago University Press.

Madziva, R. (2015) 'A Gift Exchange Relationship? Reflections on Doing Qualitative Research with Vulnerable Migrants', *Families, Relationships and Societies*, 4(3): 465–480. doi:10.1332/204674313X1387282768155.

Matza, D. (1969) *Becoming Deviant*, Hoboken: Prentice-Hall.
Mauss, M. (1950 [1935]) *The Gift: The Form and Reason for Exchange in Archaic Societies*, London: Routledge.
Mauss, M. (2007 [1947]) *Manual of Ethnography*, New York: Berghahn Books.
McGranahan, C. (2014) 'What is Ethnography? Teaching Ethnographic Sensibilities without Fieldwork', *Teaching Anthropology*, 4: 23–36.
Merton, R.K. (1972) 'Insiders and Outsiders: A Chapter in the Sociology of Knowledge', *American Journal of Sociology*, 78(1): 9–47.
Mills, C.W. (1959) *The Sociological Imagination*, New York: Oxford University Press.
Palmer, V. (1928) *Field Studies in Sociology: A Student's Manual*, Chicago: University of Chicago Press.
Park, R. (1941) 'Methods of Teaching: Impressions and a Verdict', *Social Forces*, 20: 36–46.
Postman, N. and Weingartner, C. (1969) *Teaching as a Subversive Activity*, New York: Dell.
Roberts, B. (2006) *Micro Social Theory*, London: Palgrave Macmillan.
Robinson, L. and Warne, C. (2020) '"Can You Really Get Away with that at Work?": Recent Experiences of Teaching and Learning Hebdige', in The Subcultural Network (ed) *Hebdige and Subculture in the Twenty-First Century: Through the Subcultural Lens*, London: Palgrave Macmillan, pp 231–252.
Skeggs, B. (2001) 'Feminist Ethnography', in P. Atkinson, A. Coffey, S. Delamont, J. Loflanda and L. Lofland (eds) *Handbook of Ethnography*, London: SAGE, pp 426–442.
Smith, G.D., Dines, M. and Parkinson, T. (2017) *Presenting Punk Pedagogies in Practice*, London: Routledge.
Stevenson, A. and Lawthom, R. (2017) 'How We Know Each Other', *Anthrovision*, 5(1): 1–20.
Taylor, J. (2011) 'The Intimate Insider: Negotiating the Ethics of Friendship when Doing Insider Research', *Qualitative Research*, 11(1): 3–22.
Thrasher, F. (1928) 'How to Study the Boys' Gang in the Open', *Journal of Educational Sociology*, 1(5): 244–254.
Van den Hoonaard, W.C. (1997) *Working with Sensitizing Concepts*, London: SAGE.
Williams, J.P. (2011) *Subcultural Theory*, Cambridge. Polity Press.
Williams, J.P. (2016) 'Connecting Personal Troubles and Public Issues in Asian Subcultural Studies', in S. Blackman and M. Kempson (eds) *The Subcultural Imagination: Theory, Research and Reflexivity in Contemporary Youth Cultures*, London: Routledge, pp 167–177.
Williams, R. (1989 [1958]) 'Culture is Ordinary', in *Resources of Hope*, London: Verso, pp 3–18.

PART IV

Conclusion

11

Approaching, Contextualizing, and Embodying Interpretive Practice in Subcultural Studies

J. Patrick Williams and Samuel Judah

When the subculture concept first entered the social-scientific vocabulary in the 1920s, the Chicago School of sociology was invested in studying the everyday lives of marginalized and deviant groups of people living in and around modern cities. Indeed, the metropolis (and its demands on inhabitants) may be seen as a key social phenomenon that shaped the emergence of the subculture concept. In the 1970s, the Centre for Contemporary Cultural Studies (CCCS) reinvigorated subcultural theory through its studies on working-class British youth subcultures by drawing attention to the growing influence of media and consumer cultures for explaining the rise of new styles and practices. The significance of these early theoretical frameworks can still be seen in contemporary studies that use plug-and-play versions of subcultural theory rooted in the study of problem-solving, resistance, or consumption (for example, Barrett, 2017; Mohammadi, 2022). Now well into the 21st century, subcultural theories are also adapting with the times and have been extended or reworked in connection to the many cultural, economic, environmental, political, social, and/or technological changes and challenges experienced within late modernity (for example, Woo, 2015; Christopher et al, 2018; King and Smith, 2018; Ferrell et al, 2019). What might these changes and challenges mean for the future of subcultural studies?

The preceding chapters in this volume have made plain the significance of interpretive practice for answering such a question. How we *approach* sociocultural phenomena conceptually, how we *contextualize* research questions, populations, data, and analysis, and how we *embody* both ourselves as researchers and the individuals and groups whose actions bring subcultures to life, are fundamental processes that shape the very heart of subcultural studies. Whether implicitly or explicitly, contributors have shown that the value of subcultural theory is clearest when we understand subculture as a *sensitizing* concept in interpretive practice. As Blumer argued:

> Theory is of value in empirical science only to the extent to which it connects fruitfully with the empirical world. Concepts are the means, and the only means of establishing such connection, for it is the concept that points to the empirical instances about which a theoretical proposal is made. (Blumer, 1969, p 143)

In this regard, 'subculture' is not something that should have fixed or rigid boundaries, nor need it exist primarily as a formal concept that is applied in a deductive fashion. Instead, the concept is most useful when grounded in empirical data and checked in terms of the meanings or practices to which it is applied. 'Subculture' can sensitize scholars to specific (and varied) types of social and cultural phenomena and processes. A sensitizing concept, 'which gives the user a general sense of reference and guidance in approaching empirical instances', differs from what Blumer called definitive concepts, which 'refer precisely to what is common to a class of objects, by the aid of a clear definition in terms of attributes and fixed benchmarks' (Blumer, 1969, pp 147–148).[1] We can see this approach in action, for example, in Fennell's (2020) study of BDSM subculture, which challenges normative discourses that depict BDSM as shameful, dirty, or sinful and instead shores up the subcultural values of leisure and enjoyment. Her analyses and interpretation create room for participants to subjectively define concepts like 'sex', which itself reveals important 'hotly debated' values and identities within the BDSM community and between it and mainstream society. Woo (2015) argued that subculture is a valuable concept not because of any general theory or operationalized definition, but because 'it has face validity [and is] phenomenologically real for members'.

We extend these insights to bring the researcher into the interpretive frame as well—subcultural theories function to the extent that researchers use them to sensitize themselves to cultural phenomena that are either experienced as subcultural by research participants, or that otherwise help them frame empirical findings within a larger field of subcultural scholarship. Sensitivity to academic as well as lay meaning-making practices can facilitate important insights into how subcultures are articulated in everyday life, whether in terms of reflexivity and self-actualization (Lewin and Williams, 2009), non-normativity (Gelder, 2007), alternativity and marginalization (Holland and Spracklen, 2018, p 1), and so on. These are reiterative approaches in which 'subculture' is always contextualized, often modified, and sometimes even bracketed or discarded (for example,

Williams and Kamaludeen, 2017) to improve sociological understandings of relevant phenomena in everyday life.

As discussed in Chapter 1, this volume explores how scholars approach, contextualize, and embody interpretive practice in their subcultural research. Collectively, the contributors share an interest in utilizing the subculture concept in connection with youth- and/or music-related phenomena. These are common topics in subcultural studies, but do not adequately represent the gamut of scholarship using the subculture concept. Therefore, in this concluding chapter we want to situate this work within the larger field of contemporary research to see what we can learn about the trajectories of subcultural theory. To identify a broad range of relevant research, we conducted academic literature searches for the term 'subculture' multiple times in 2021 and 2022, limiting our search to the last three years and browsing the first 30 results for reputable peer-reviewed journal articles or conference proceedings that contained the term in the title. Usually about one-fourth of the results were outside our focus, either in terms of publication outlet (encyclopedia entries, predatory conferences or publishers) or discipline (for example, biological research). The remaining three-quarters covered a range of disciplinary and interdisciplinary projects. We selected ten publications to review more closely, which are listed from most recent to oldest (see Table 11.1).

The publications cover a diverse range of empirical topics that, like the chapters in this volume, include music—such as jihadi rap, grime, and emo—as well as youth-oriented phenomena like gaming. Extending well beyond these areas, however, studies also deal with gender and sexuality, consumer culture, involuntary celibacy, memes, and school shootings. They cover numerous regional contexts—from the Global North/West (for example, the US and UK) to the South/East (for example, Brazil, Japan, India, China, Japan)—as well as transregional online spaces. Following from Chapter 1 (see Figure 1.1), our sample also features various disciplinary approaches spanning business and consumer studies, literature and film studies, linguistics, criminology, psychology, sociology, and cultural studies. In what follows, we analyze these publications using the same framework by which the chapters in this volume have been organized—approaching, contextualizing, and embodying subcultures—to further explore its relevance for the larger field of subcultural studies. Socratic-style questions to guide this discussion include: How do these studies implicitly assume emic and/ or etic perspectives, and how does the answer problematize the issue of *approaching* subcultures? How do these studies *contextualize* both empirical phenomena and the interpretive traditions they use to frame subcultures and subcultural analyses? How or to what extent do these studies account for researcher reflexivity in the process of interpretation, and how do they account for increasingly diffuse and mediated modes of action, participation,

Table 11.1: Ten recent peer-reviewed studies (2018–2022) with 'subculture' in the title

Year	Authors	Title
2022	Jensen et al	'Rap, Islam and Jihadi Cool: The Attractions of the Western Jihadi Subculture'
2022	O'Malley et al	'An Exploration of the Involuntary Celibate (Incel) Subculture Online'
2021	Snodgrass et al	'Indian Gaming Zones as Oppositional Subculture'
2021	Shamoon	'Class S: Appropriation of "Lesbian" Subculture in Modern Japanese Literature and New Wave Cinema'
2020	Farrell et al	'On the Use of Jargon and Word Embeddings to Explore Subculture within the Reddit's Manosphere'
2020	Tan and Cheng	'Sang Subculture in Post-Reform China'
2019	Koch and Sauerbronn	'"To Love Beer above All Things": An Analysis of Brazilian Craft Beer Subculture of Consumption'
2019	Fatsis	'Grime: Criminal Subculture or Public Counterculture? A Critical Investigation into the Criminalization of Black Musical Subcultures in the UK'
2018	Raitanen and Oksanen	'Global Online Subculture Surrounding School Shootings'
2018	Trnka et al	'Understanding Death, Suicide and Self-Injury among Adherents of the Emo Youth Subculture: A Qualitative Study'

and identification that *embody* subcultures today? Such questions are becoming increasingly prominent within the practice of contemporary subcultural research, and we tackle them in what follows. Finally, we make some concluding remarks about how we might best make sense of scholarly interpretive practice as subcultural studies seeks to maintain its relevance to a growing range of empirical topics and analytical perspectives in our contemporary age.

Approaching interpretive practice

In Part I of this volume, contributors demonstrated that whether we see some phenomenon as subcultural or otherwise has a lot to do with the interpretive practices of the people involved in naming it as such (Bennett, Chapter 3). It is often the case that scholars will decide ahead of time whether to approach a phenomenon as subcultural, for example due to academic training or prior research. Or, scholars may prefer concepts to emerge from the data in a grounded theoretical fashion (Charmaz, 2006). As Haenfler

(Chapter 2) discusses, individuals who self-identify as straight edge frame that phenomenon in various ways—as a subculture, a scene, a lifestyle, or a movement—while Haenfler himself, who is simultaneously a sociologist and a self-identifying straight edger, prefers the portmanteau 'lifestyle movement'. His approach is based partly on scholarly considerations (Haenfler et al, 2012), but also takes into account other insiders' definitions. Most of the chapters in this book showcase researchers accounting for such conceptual decision-making. And because most contributors self-identify (or did in the past) as participants in the subcultures they are studying, they are reflexively aware of both emic and etic approaches to interpretive practice. Looking at the ten articles listed in Table 11.1, however, we see an overwhelming reliance on etic interpretive frames—that is, the researchers decide to use the subculture label without much (if any) consideration of congruence between their own definitions and the conceptions of those they are studying. Thus, the first point regarding *approaching* subcultures has to do with *who* decides whether to use the term subculture in the first place. Of the ten studies, only Trnka et al (2018) use a method to recruit participants based on self-identification, and even then, the authors report that 80 percent of would-be respondents 'strictly refused the invitation for an interview immediately' (Trnka et al, 2018, p 338), suggesting that the youths approached had some concerns about the researchers' definitions of themselves and emo culture.

A second point is *how* the subculture concept is used. Eight of the ten studies approach their research topics in terms of social problems and about half use deviance, violence, and/or criminality to frame their interpretations. The studies tend to conceptualize subcultures in one of two ways. On the one hand, subcultures serve social, cultural, and/or psychological functions that ameliorate or solve shared problems. Tan and Cheng's (2020) study of *sang* (丧) subculture and Snodgrass et al's (2021) study of young Indian videogame players explore cultural dissonances and strains experienced by young people vis-à-vis 'mainstream conceptions of the good and proper life' (Snodgrass et al, 2021, p 773). Fatsis (2019, p 451) frames subculture as collective ideological resistance to 'the "endless pressure" of living in stultifying urban environments that are shaped by a lack of opportunities and negative experiences', while Shamoon (2021, p 27) explores how the 'exploitative representation' of *shōjo bunka* (少女文化 or 'girls' culture') in mainstream Japanese literature and film throughout the mid-20th century has unintentionally facilitated the growth and empowerment of LGBTQIA+ subcultures in more recent years.

On the other hand, subcultures are sometimes approached as problems that mainstream society needs to deal with. Raitanen and Oksanen (2018) investigate the circulation of social media content among subcultural 'fans' of school shootings. While noting that consuming such content does not link directly to one becoming a school shooter, the research nevertheless frames some consumers of such content as potentially dangerous. Rather than posing a risk to others, participants in the emo culture, according to Trnka et al (2018, p 337), pose a risk to themselves. The study frames self-identifying emo kids as victims of a 'peer contagion' that increases the chances of depression, self-harm, and suicide due to the subculture's trading in 'symbols of death, dying, suicide, and the mutilation of body parts'. In a few other studies, both approaches are visible together. As examples, two studies on incel subculture and the manosphere[2] focus on males who 'experience significant personal distress' in mainstream relationships and therefore gravitate toward subcultures in 'attempts to find meaning in their alienation' (O'Malley et al, 2022, p 3), yet who also 'promote hate and have sometimes been linked with hate crimes, radicalization, extremism and terror attacks' (Farrell et al, 2020, p 222).

Only two studies approach subcultural phenomena without a focus on social problems. Jensen et al (2022) deal with a phenomenon that is at face value highly problematic in the West—Islamic jihad—yet their focus on 'the styles and symbolic repertoires' (p 431) of jihadi hip hop defuses the religious radicalness of the topic. Meanwhile, Koch and Sauerbronn (2019) explore the craft beer subculture in Brazil by focusing on how productive and consumptive activities affect social cohesion. Following from the work of Schouten and McAlexander (1995), they promote subculture as 'an analytic category that can lead to a better understanding of consumers and the manner in which they organize their lives and identities' (Schouten and McAlexander, 1995). Both of these studies align more with CCCS and post-subcultural emphases on consumption and style than with the problem-solving version of subcultural theory developed by American delinquency scholars and now dominant in criminology.

To the extent that this random sample of recent research could be generalizable, it suggests that a significant proportion of scholars approach the subculture concept from an etic rather than emic standpoint. Many researchers do not appear to personally identify with the subcultures they are studying. Further, while some take an empathetic approach by way of participant-observational studies that provide them with insider perspectives, many use subculture to refer to problematic worldviews, beliefs, and practices, or populations that mainstream society ought to be concerned with.

Contextualizing interpretive practice

As suggested in Chapter 1, the history of subcultural studies has been written largely in terms of the West/Global North, with the Chicago and Birmingham Schools framed as foundational communities of practice. Their scholarship produced concepts that pegged subcultures to the study of class, marginality, delinquency, culture, resistance, and style, among others. In recent decades, however, subcultural studies has grown and developed in at least two ways. The first is empirical, as those core concepts have been deployed in an increasingly diverse set of contexts around the world. This has been done by Western/Northern scholars who work as expatriates or conduct research overseas, as well as by scholars from non-Western/Southern countries, many of whom receive postgraduate training at universities in English-speaking countries before returning home to scholarly careers. Whatever the case, the idea is that subcultural theory is often learned in canonical form and then applied internationally as an interpretive frame in new, local contexts (for example, Hazlehurst and Hazlehurst, 2018; Bestley et al, 2021). Studies of heavy metal and punk in South, Southeast, and East Asia, for example (Liew and Fu, 2006; Hannerz, 2016; Quader, 2016; Xiao, 2016), have tended to be concerned with Western subcultural concepts such as hegemony, resistance, subcultural capital, authenticity, and the like. The second way in which subcultural studies has developed is conceptual, as scholars have taken account of the specificities of and changes in contemporary societies and cultures. We can say that subcultural theories are used globally, though not in a homogeneous manner. Alongside canonical ideas, new interpretive frames and concepts have emerged and become increasingly salient as scholars deal with empirical diversity—not only in terms of regional, national, and local contexts, but also in terms of a broadening of concerns, from personal identities to labor to careers to the platformization of subcultural practices.

Part II of this volume provided crucial insight into the contextualization of the subculture concept through contributors' discussion both of new empirical instances and of context-specific concepts. On the one hand, we saw that Chapters 4 and 7 kept the classic CCCS notion of resistance at the heart of their research. This may not be surprising given that the music genres and subcultures being studied are themselves imported from the West. Yet, El Zein (2016, p 91) argues that 'the activities that readers of [CCCS] literature are encouraged to notice are (exclusively) the ones that can be seen to indicate resistance'. Her point more generally is about the portability of British subcultural theory into other geographies and cultures and the extent to which the interpretation of empirical data, regardless of context, is influenced by the hegemony of Western theories. Chapters 4 and 7 implicitly agree with and respond to this criticism through the development of context-relevant theory and concepts. Guerra introduces cosmopolitanism alongside resistance to explain how Portuguese punk comes to mean something unique compared broadly to the history of punk cultures in the UK or US. Sutopo also goes beyond resistance by using biography, temporality, and space as micro-sociological lenses through which to view how Indonesian Do-It-Yourself musicians maintain personal careers in the face of various social and economic obstacles.

El Zein's (2016) work is part of a larger move among non-Western scholars to openly question the extent of Western biases upon which subcultural theories rest. In their introduction to a volume on Arab subcultures, Sabry and Ftouni (2016, p 2) ask some important questions, including whether we can 'uncouple the term "subculture" from the specificity of its etymological roots and its appropriations in research in the UK and the US, or [whether] "subculture" is a universal category that discloses itself in similar ways, regardless of the differences in historical moments or cultural geographies'. They go on to suggest that, despite its lexical roots in the English language, it would be a mistake to essentialize the concept in terms of a single 'set of concepts and modes of inquiry emergent from within Euro-US academe' because this would overlook 'the revisions, transitions and translations that subcultural studies [has undergone elsewhere]' (p 5). In Chapter 5, Shin notes that Japan and China each had recognizable youth subcultures before the concept, as proposed by the CCCS, was introduced to the academies in those countries. Thus, to some extent Shin's argument is like that of the CCCS—youth subcultures were a conjunctural product of a number of social and cultural process that affected those countries, including Korea's democratization movement and China's economic reform policies, which opened up both countries to globalization processes in the 1970s. However, Shin's analysis also shows that class, ideology, and hegemony have never been required components of Asian subcultural theory. Similarly, Xiao and Dong (Chapter 6) conduct an analysis of punk in China that explicitly brackets prior analyses of resistance and authenticity and instead proposes contextually relevant concepts from Chinese philosophy—doing nothing and the hermit lifestyle—to retheorize punk practices.

Like the efforts made by contributors to emphasize the significance of context, research more broadly appears to be increasingly international, but mixed in terms of its skepticism of subcultural theory's core concepts as scholars consider how to fruitfully expand or reconfigure its interpretive potential. Of the ten publications we sampled, half are situated outside the anglophone world, with studies from Brazil, China, Czech Republic, India, and Japan. Further, four out of ten rely exclusively on data from internet or social media contexts (though most were English-based media). Several of the studies use the term subculture as a kind of generic tag for non-mainstream values, interests, or practices and then treat the topic as one that is problematic to normal society. A couple of publications explicitly critique traditional subcultural approaches. Tan and Cheng (2020, p 86), for example, write that, 'unlike subcultures in the West, *sang* subculture does not constitute a form of political resistance, but expresses instead an inchoate feeling of loss among Chinese youths'. Yet those authors nevertheless interpret those expressions though a British cultural studies lens via Raymond Williams' concept of 'structures of feeling'. More generally speaking, a broad mix of criminological, cultural studies, functionalist sociological, linguistic, and psychological traditions are present in the sample—most citing predominantly Western sources. On the one hand, the American and British roots of subcultural studies remain apparent, with most of the studies referring to them either implicitly (through topic and framing) or explicitly (through citations). On the other hand, the variety of topics, contexts, and disciplinary frames suggests that subcultural studies is, like the limbs of a tree, branching and flowering in numerous directions. Finally, *contextualizing* goes beyond making inter-regional comparisons alone. Part II of this volume represents a set of unique insights from non-anglophone scholars on phenomena outside the Global North/West, yet they simultaneously demonstrate a grounded sensitivity to different layers and nuances of context itself as they draw attention to contextual parameters around localized historical, political, and economic landscapes. In this sense, contextualization is relevant to all the chapters in the book—an unsurprising point when we know that all interpretive practices are predicated on situated meanings.

Embodying interpretive practice

A final theme that this volume brings to light concerns *embodiment* in subcultural research. By embodiment, we do not refer to some sort of limited focus on the physical body in and of itself. Rather, embodiment conceptualizes the body as both subjectively experienced and objectively identified in ways that are emergent and negotiated (Crossley, 2006). Embodiment thus refers to how individuals as raced, classed, gendered, sexed, cultured, and otherwise marked or unmarked persons make sense of the world around them (Waskul and Vannini, 2016). We see two ways in which the notion of embodiment is pertinent to contemporary subcultural studies. The first, as demonstrated in various chapters in this volume, has to do with researchers' self-embodiment as a reflexive resource for interpretive practice. The second, which becomes evident when reviewing the external literature we gathered, focuses on (dis)embodiment as subcultural scenes and practices proliferate on digital/social media platforms.

Embodied researcher reflexivity is both methodological and epistemological in nature. Davies (1999, p 7) observes researchers' 'necessary connection to the research situation and hence their effects upon it'. Reflexivity involves researchers accounting for themselves in embodied and relational terms, which is more likely to be explicitly accounted for when doing 'insider' or autoethnographic research (Hodkinson, 2005; Williams and Zaini, 2016). Blackman and Kempson (2021) conceive of researcher embodiment through the concept of the 'subcultural imagination', derived from C. Wright Mills' sociological imagination, which grounds researchers to history and context, as well as to their and participants' biographies, identities, emotions, and experiences. Embodiment represents a particular subcultural subjectivity—a reflexive resource that plays an integral role in the interactions between researchers and subcultural participants. It is interaction, embodied in social (inter)actions, that encourages the co-production of subcultural knowledge (Blackman and Kempson, 2021). Reflexivity also calls attention to the more emergent, emotive, and empathetic aspects of research embodied as feelings (Palmer, 1926; Hodkinson, 2005; Measham and Moore, 2007). Green and Feldman-Barrett (2020) suggest that acknowledging the embodied nature of interpretive practice reconciles many of the assumed differences between the CCCS's focus on structural, material conditions and the Chicago School's focus on subjectivities and interaction.

A number of chapters in this volume explicitly demonstrate how reflexive researcher embodiment bolsters interpretive practice (see also Thanem and Knights, 2019). Haenfler (Chapter 2) and Bennett (Chapter 3), for instance, articulate how their embodied experiences as sociologists with participatory biographies in music cultures have affected their understandings of youth (sub)cultural phenomena over the years. Whereas these two authors keep their reflections at the conceptual level, the chapters in Part III focus explicitly on embodiment, reflexivity, and interpretation at emotional and interactional levels. In Chapter 8, Way demonstrates how embodying both subcultural and researcher identities are critically *intersectional*—and she shows how aged and gendered embodiments affect how the notion of 'authenticity' is shaped not only within the subculture but within subcultural scholarship. Vysotsky and Manion (Chapter 9) take a deep-dive into the emotional labor that they had to undertake as not only researchers but also subculturalists at the same time, and their chapter depicts how both insider participation and insider research is uniquely embodied at the nexus of ideology, intrapersonal community relationships, and emotional experiences. Lastly, Blackman and Barnett (Chapter 10) present multiple iterations of embodiment—from embodying fieldwork, to embodying reflexive subcultural recounts through description, to embodying dynamic and dialogical 'insider teaching' in the classroom—and each of these is shown to bolster the co-production of knowledge between scholars and their students, an increasingly prominent theme in subcultural studies (Green and Feldman-Barrett, 2020).

Comparing these chapters to our sample, we see a clear difference in the extent to which scholars engage with their own embodied practices. For example, Koch and Sauerbronn (2019) discuss the shift from outsider to insider status during their research, but most studies frame subcultural phenomena from etic standpoints that distance the researcher from their object of study. Fatsis (2019) communicates empathy with the grime subculture but remains absent from the study. Jensen et al (2022) go a step further by clearly linking their own *personal* interests in hip hop to the research project, yet that interest is largely invisible in their analysis. Other studies such as Farrell et al (2020) and Trnka et al (2018) are notably more clinical in their approaches. The scholars are completely disembodied from the research, while embodying research subjects as collections of troubled individuals. We should emphasize that our discussion of researcher embodiment and reflexivity is not meant to serve as a generic attack on non-reflexive, objectivist, or outsider research. A basic tenet of interpretivism is that there is no single 'Truth' to be found in the social world. Rather, our point thus far is to highlight the extent to which the broader contemporary field of subcultural research, at least as represented in our small sample, is comprised of scholarship in which researchers tend to be invisible (that is, disembodied) and non-reflexive. Such differences can also be seen in Williams' (2016) comparison of two simultaneous research projects, one in which the researchers reflexively embodied themselves and the other in which they did not.

The concept of embodiment is not intended to refer only to the researcher role, of course. Traditionally, scholarship has embodied subcultures by emphasizing things such as participants' socio-material conditions (for example, nationality, race, class, gender, and location) and everyday practices (for example, sartorial styles, music or media tastes, consumptive behaviors, and social networks). In other words, the subcultural body has often played an objectified role. In the 21st century, however, research has paid increasing attention to new technologies and sociocultural practices that challenge classic conceptions of subcultures as locally bounded and internally homogeneous. Of the ten articles we sampled, only two report on local, face-to-face subcultural scenes and only one embodies subcultural participants in a narrow, homogeneous fashion (Trnka et al, 2018). The rest approach subcultures through media, whether music (Fatsis, 2019; Jensen et al, 2022), literature (Shamoon, 2021), video games (Snodgrass et al, 2021), the internet (Raitanen and Oksanen, 2018; Farrell et al, 2020; O'Malley et al, 2022), or social media (Tan and Cheng, 2020). The internet and social media studies in particular highlight the diversity of disparate and distributed populations and networks of users that inhabit various online spaces. A few studies lump individuals or communities with diverse interests, experiences, and contexts together under the 'subculture' label. As quoted earlier, for example, Tan and Cheng's (2020) study of *sang* in China is less about embodying a politics of resistance through style, but rather about affective identification and catharsis. Farrell et al's (2020) research suggests a shared culture at times, but otherwise there is not much that embodies participants in rigid or uniform ways. Embodied practices in many of the sampled studies are reduced to the sharing of values, beliefs, and opinions on digital-mediated platforms, and even these are often heterogeneous (for example, Raitanen and Oksanen, 2018, pp 203–204).

The large proportion of studies that focus on mediated subcultures show that subcultural research extends beyond a traditional *collective* logic to include what Bennett and Segerberg (2012) call a *connective* logic. Their concept, though proposed in terms of contemporary social movements, is nevertheless helpful in sensitizing us to changes in subcultural phenomena as well. Collective logic is reminiscent of traditional research that clearly defined subcultures in terms of shared values and practices and that distinguishes them from so-called mainstream or dominant cultures (for example, Copes and Williams, 2007). Connective logic, on the other hand, 'applies increasingly to life in late modern societies in which ... group ties are being replaced by large-scale, fluid social networks' (Bennett and Segerberg, 2012, p 748) and situated social action in the co-presence of significant others is being replaced with multimodal representations of selves, styles, and value-orientations that are managed through hashtags and algorithms (Williams and Judah, 2023). Yet, even when viewed through the concept of connective logic, morality, style, resistance, identity, and other traditional concepts remain important interpretively. Subcultures continue to be forged, cultivated, sustained, or changed through participants' embodied engagements across both physical and digital realms, and analytic practices should remain sensitive to the nuances of (dis)embodiment in contemporary subcultural phenomena.

Conclusion

The world is a very different place than it was when either the Chicago or Birmingham Schools theorized subcultures. The differences have been fueled by globalization, which is characterized by the increasingly fast and complex flows of people, technology, money, information, and ideas (Appadurai, 1990). In many cases, subcultures have been and are *enabled by* or *created through* globalization processes. At the same time, subcultures may be understood as articulated collective or connective *responses to* them. Subcultural theories emerged within the US and UK to study what appeared then to be coherent cultural formations situated in problematic relations with dominant or conventional culture. Those traditions are visible in the contributions collected in this volume. All the contributors have paid homage in one way or another to them. Yet, scholars increasingly use the subculture concept to interpret a much broader range of phenomena around the world. As the geographical and disciplinary diversity of subcultural research grows, will its interpretive potential? We believe so, but with such potential comes risk. We can see that the term is sometimes used in a purely descriptive fashion to refer to phenomena that are assumed to be real in taken-for-granted sort of ways. Meanwhile, 'successive generations of scholars have ... attempt[ed] to reformulate the "subculture" concept with the aim of making it a useful analytical tool for emerging phenomena'

(Berzano and Genova, 2015, p 160). Might the concept be stretched beyond what it is analytically capable of handling? This is a loaded question, because it of course depends on how the term is made meaningful in context. For some scholars, this already happened in the late 20th century. For others, the concept still has more to offer. But it will be necessary for scholars to reflect on their interpretive practices to ensure that subculture is used to improve understandings of the social world and/or to ameliorate problems in it, and not simply function as a generic reference to cultural difference.

The variety of topics and analytic frames discussed in this volume suggests that subculture continues to be used across the social sciences and humanities to study a range of distinct, non-normative, and/or marginal cultural phenomena. Not only is there continued use of Chicago and Birmingham traditions, but those theories are being developed or modified to study more international and interdisciplinary topics. In short, we see a continuation of the 'diffusion'—but not the 'defusion'—of the subculture concept (Clarke, 1976). Despite this volume focusing primarily on scholarship about youth and/or music subcultures, it has brought some important questions to light for subcultural theory more generally. Is it helpful to invoke the subculture concept without defining it or delineating it from other concepts? Does or should subculture refer to violence, consumption, problem-solving, shared values, style, personal identity, or some combination of these? (How) Is subculture useful for analyzing contemporary phenomena that may not be easily interpreted using classic theory and concepts? In addressing these questions, the contributions to the volume have highlighted the importance of how we approach, contextualize, and embody interpretive practice in our subcultural research.

Notes

[1] The CCCS's theory of subculture, while I think somewhat sensitizing in its original intent, has typically been framed by critics as definitive in nature, not least because of the insistence on class, style, and ideology as 'necessary' components.
[2] The research defines the manosphere as a men's interests subculture that has been linked to violent crime. Incels are typically understood to be one of many subcultural communities that operate within the manosphere.

References

Appadurai, A. (1990) 'Disjuncture and Difference in the Global Cultural Economy', *Theory, Culture & Society*, 7(2–3): 295–310.

Barrett, R. (2017) *From Drag Queens to Leathermen: Language, Gender, and Gay Male Subcultures*, Oxford: Oxford University Press.

Bennett, W.L. and Segerberg, A. (2012) 'The Logic of Connective Action: Digital Media and the Personalization of Contentious Politics', *Information, Communication & Society*, 15(5): 739–768.

Berzano, L. and Genova, C. (2015) *Lifestyles and Subcultures: History and a New Perspective*, London: Routledge.

Bestley, R., Dines, M., Guerra, P. and Gordon, A. (2021) *Trans-Global Punk Scenes: The Punk Reader* (vol 2), Bristol: Intellect Books.

Blackman, S. and Kempson, M. (2021) 'The Subcultural Imagination: Critically Negotiating the Co-Production of "Subcultural Subjects" through the Lens of C. Wright Mills', *Sociological Research Online*, 28(1): 58–72. doi: 10.1177/13607804211006112.

Blumer, H. (1969) *Symbolic Interactionism: Perspective and Method*, Berkeley: University of California Press.

Charmaz, K. (2006) *Constructing Grounded Theory: A Practical Guide through Qualitative Analysis*, Thousand Oaks: SAGE.

Christopher, A., Bartkowski, J.P. and Haverda, T. (2018) 'Portraits of Veganism: A Comparative Discourse Analysis of a Second-Order Subculture', *Societies*, 8(3): 55–75.

Clarke, J. (1976) 'Style', in S. Hall and T. Jefferson (eds) *Resistance through Rituals: Youth Subcultures in Post-War Britain*, London: Hutchinson, pp 175–191.

Copes, H. and Williams, J.P. (2007) 'Techniques of Affirmation: Deviant Behavior, Moral Commitment, and Subcultural Identity', *Deviant Behavior*, 28(3): 247–272.

Crossley, N. (2006) *Reflexive Embodiment in Contemporary Society*, Maidenhead: Open University Press.

Davies, C.A. (1999) *Reflexive Ethnography: A Guide to Researching Selves and Others*, London: Routledge.

El Zein, R. (2016) 'Resisting "Resistance"', in T. Sabry and L. Ftouni (eds) *Arab Subcultures: Transformations in Theory and Practice*, London: Bloomsbury, pp 87–112.

Farrell, T., Araque, O., Fernandez, M. and Alani, H. (2020) 'On the Use of Jargon and Word Embeddings to Explore Subculture within the Reddit's Manosphere', in *12th ACM Conference on Web Science*, New York, NY: ACM, pp 221–230.

Fatsis, L. (2019) 'Grime: Criminal Subculture or Public Counterculture? A Critical Investigation into the Criminalization of Black Musical Subcultures in the UK', *Crime, Media, Culture*, 15(3): 447–461.

Fennell, J. (2020) 'It's Complicated: Sex and the BDSM Subculture', *Sexualities,* 24(5–6): 784–802.

Ferrell, O. C., Johnston, M.W., Marshall, G.W. and Ferrell, L. (2019) 'A New Direction for Sales Ethics Research: The Sales Ethics Subculture', *Journal of Marketing Theory and Practice*, 27(3): 282–297.

Gelder, K. (2007) *Subcultures: Cultural Histories and Social Practice*, London: Routledge.

Green, B. and Feldman-Barrett, C. (2020) '"Become What You Are": Subcultural Identity and "Insider Teaching" in Youth Studies', *Teaching in Higher Education*, 27(1): 39–53.

Haenfler, R., Johnson, B. and Jones, E. (2012) 'Lifestyle Movements: Exploring the Intersection of Lifestyle and Social Movements', *Social Movement Studies*, 11(1): 1–20.

Hannerz, E. (2016) 'Emplacing Punk: Subcultural Boundary Work and Space in Indonesia', in J. Lee and M. Ferrarese (eds) *Punks, Monks and Politics: Authenticity in Thailand, Indonesia and Malaysia*, Washington, DC: Rowman & Littlefield, pp 91–104.

Hazlehurst, K. and Hazlehurst, C. (2018) *Gangs and Youth Subcultures: International Explorations*, London: Routledge.

Hodkinson, P. (2005) '"Insider Research" in the Study of Youth Cultures', *Journal of Youth Studies*, 8(2): 131–149.

Holland, S. and Spracklen, K. (eds) (2018) *Subcultures, Bodies and Spaces: Essay on Alternativity and Marginalization*, Bingley: Emerald Publishing.

Jensen, S.Q., Larsen, J.F. and Sandberg, S. (2022) 'Rap, Islam and Jihadi Cool: The Attractions of the Western Jihadi Subculture', *Crime, Media, Culture*, 18(3): 430–445.

King, A. and Smith, D. (2018) 'The Jack Wills Crowd: Towards a Sociology of an Elite Subculture', *The British Journal of Sociology*, 69(1): 44–66.

Koch, E.S. and Sauerbronn, J.F.R. (2019) '"To Love Beer above All Things": An Analysis of Brazilian Craft Beer Subculture of Consumption', *Journal of Food Products Marketing*, 25(1): 1–25.

Lewin, P. and Williams, J.P. (2009) 'The Ideology and Practice of Authenticity in Punk Subculture', in P. Vannini and J.P. Williams (eds) *Authenticity in Culture, Self, and Society*, Aldershot: Ashgate, pp 81–100.

Liew, K.K. and Fu, K. (2006) 'Conjuring the Tropical Spectres: Heavy Metal, Cultural Politics in Singapore and Malaysia', *Inter-Asia Cultural Studies*, 7(1): 99–112.

Measham, F. and Moore, K. (2007) 'Reluctant Reflexivity, Implicit Insider Knowledge and the Development of Club Studies', in B. Saunders (ed) *Drugs, Clubs and Young People*, London: Routledge, pp 13–25.

Mohammadi, F. (2022) 'Real Muslim Caves: Exploring an Emerging Religious Youth Subculture Among Young Canadian Muslims', *Religious Studies and Theology*, 41(1): 93–110.

O'Malley, R.L., Holt, K. and Holt, T.J. (2022) 'An Exploration of the Involuntary Celibate (Incel) Subculture Online', *Journal of Interpersonal Violence*, 37(7–8): NP4981–NP5008.

Palmer, V.M. (1926) 'Field Studies for Introductory Sociology: An Experiment', *Journal of Applied Sociology*, 10: 341–348.

Quader, S.B. (2016) 'Forms of Capital in the Dhaka Metal Scene', *Metal Music Studies*, 2(1): 5–20.

Raitanen, J. and Oksanen, A. (2018) 'Global Online Subculture Surrounding School Shootings', *American Behavioral Scientist*, 62(2): 195–209.

Sabry, T. and Ftouni, L. (2016) *Arab Subcultures: Transformations in Theory and Practice*, London: Bloomsbury Publishing.

Schouten, J.W. and McAlexander, J.H. (1995) 'Subcultures of Consumption: An Ethnography of the New Bikers', *Journal of Consumer Research*, 22(1): 43–61.

Shamoon, D. (2021) 'Class S: Appropriation of "Lesbian" Subculture in Modern Japanese Literature and New Wave Cinema', *Cultural Studies*, 35(1): 27–43.

Snodgrass, J.G., Dengah, H.J.F., Upadhyay, C., Else, R.J. and Polzer, E. (2021) 'Indian Gaming Zones as Oppositional Subculture', *Current Anthropology*, 62(6): 771–797.

Tan, K.C. and Cheng, S. (2020) 'Sang Subculture in Post-Reform China', *Global Media and China*, 5(1): 86–99.

Thanem, T. and Knights, D. (2019) *Embodied Research Methods*, Los Angeles: SAGE.

Trnka, R., Kuška, M., Balcar, K. and Tavel, P. (2018) 'Understanding Death, Suicide and Self-Injury among Adherents of the Emo Youth Subculture: A Qualitative Study', *Death Studies*, 42(6): 337–345.

Waskul, D.D. and Vannini, P. (eds) (2016) *Body/Embodiment: Symbolic Interaction and the Sociology of the Body*, New York: Routledge.

Williams, J.P. (2016) 'Connecting Personal Troubles and Social Issues in Asian Subculture Studies', in S. Blackman and M. Kempson (eds) *The Subcultural Imagination: Theory, Research, and Reflexivity in Contemporary Youth Cultures*, Abingdon: Taylor & Francis, pp 167–177.

Williams, J.P. and Zaini, M.K.J. (2016) 'Rude Boy Subculture, Critical Pedagogy, and the Collaborative Construction of an Analytic and Evocative Autoethnography', *Journal of Contemporary Ethnography*, 45(1): 34–59.

Williams, J.P. and Kamaludeen, M.N. (2017) 'Muslim Girl Culture and Social Control in Southeast Asia: Exploring the Hijabista and Hijabster Phenomena', *Crime, Media, Culture*, 13(2): 199–216.

Williams, J.P. and Judah, S. (2023) 'Organizing Subcultural Identities on Social Media: Instagram Infrastructures and User Actions', in D. vom Lehn, W. Gibson and N. Ruiz-Junco (eds) *People, Technology, and Social Organization: Interactionist Studies of Everyday Life*, London: Routledge, pp 101–118.

Woo, B. (2015) 'Nerds, Geeks, Gamers, and Fans: Doing Subculture on the Edge of the Mainstream', in Alexander Dhoest, Steven Malliet, Jacques Haers, and Barbara Segaert (eds) *The Borders of Subculture*, London: Routledge, pp 17–36.

Xiao, J. (2016) 'Striving for Authenticity: Punk in China', *Punk & Post-Punk*, 5(1): 5–19.

Index

A

activism 31, 34, 35, 59, 64–68, 70, 75–76, 85, 86, 99, 156, 159, 162
aesthetics 46, 60, 136, 144
affect (as concept) 60, 115, 171, 199
age 28, 127–146
alcohol 21–37, 102, 103, 169, 176, 178, 179, 181
anarchist 32, 83, 151, 156, 157, 159, 160
authenticity 26, 29, 35, 45, 48, 49, 60, 62, 67, 68, 80, 81, 82, 83, 93–105, 113, 114, 118, 127–146, 156, 158, 160, 164, 195, 196, 198
authoritarianism 104, 111, 113, 150
authority 48, 95, 97

B

Becker, Howard S. 170–172, 178, 182, 184
Bennett, Andy 44, 61, 130–131, 138, 198
biography 112–117, 155, 168, 178, 182, 183, 195, 197, 198
Birmingham School *see* Centre for Contemporary Cultural Studies
Blackman, Shane 8, 44, 169, 197
Blumer, Herbert 168, 169–171, 178, 183, 190

C

capitalism 34, 61, 62, 66, 68, 80, 81, 82, 85, 151
Centre for Contemporary Cultural Studies (CCCS) 3, 6, 9, 10, 11, 41, 42–43, 44, 45, 60, 63, 67, 76, 77, 81, 83, 95, 105, 107, 108, 109, 128, 141, 189, 194, 195, 196, 198, 200, 201
Chicago School 3, 6, 8–9, 11, 60, 108, 118, 168, 169–170, 172, 174, 176, 177, 178, 183, 189, 194, 198, 200, 201
class (as concept) 6, 8, 11, 24, 25, 27, 29, 35, 42, 43, 60, 80, 83, 88, 95, 96, 99, 102, 107, 108, 110, 112, 142, 146, 169, 173, 180, 194, 196, 197, 199, 201
  culture 80, 83, 88
  lower-class 8, 43
  middle-class 27, 43, 45, 110, 112, 146
  underclass 176, 177
  upper-class 83, 110
  working-class 9, 24, 42, 43, 45, 60, 96, 108, 189
Cohen, Stanley 9, 43, 96, 179
collective
  action 4, 23, 25, 61, 97, 200
  challenge 21, 22, 25, 26, 32, 33, 35
  representation 5, 82
  see also identity, collective; resistance, collective
consumerism 9, 10, 25, 26, 43–45, 49, 60, 80, 81, 82, 85, 114, 176, 189, 191, 194, 199, 201
cosmopolitanism 61–64, 65, 69, 70, 115, 195
counter-culture 48, 79, 88
counter-school culture 42–43
COVID-19 48, 50–51, 93
crime 176, 194, 201

D

delinquency 6, 7, 8, 161, 194
deviance 6, 7, 8, 9, 15, 26, 30, 41, 84, 98, 99, 108, 152, 169, 170, 176, 177, 180, 189, 193
digital
  culture 42, 53, 84–85, 108
  interaction 23, 84–85
  media 12, 41, 47–48, 49, 50, 53, 61
  platforms (including domain, site, space) 23, 37, 49, 50, 52, 64, 197, 199, 200
  technology 47, 50
internet 28, 59–70, 84–85, 196, 199
  pre-digital 47, 49, 50, 51, 112, 113
discourse 10, 26, 41, 78, 80, 83, 85, 86, 112, 131, 134, 135, 137, 141, 190
discrimination 129, 173
Do-It-Yourself (DIY) 3, 11, 14, 15, 59–70, 100, 104, 107–118, 150, 151
drugs 21–37, 169, 176, 178

205

E

embodiment 9, 23, 25, 28, 30, 97, 114–117, 197–200
  (dis)embodiment 197, 200
emotional labor 150–165
  and deep acting 158, 160
  and surface acting 155, 157, 158, 159
emotionality 97, 117, 150–165, 174, 176, 177, 182, 192, 198
  see also reflexivity, emotional; emotional labor; affect
environmentalism 25, 26, 49, 52

F

fascism 26, 31, 65, 152, 157, 158, 159, 161, 162, 164
feminism 25, 35, 127–133, 143, 145–146
femininity 159
fragmentation 44, 51, 60–61, 70
friendship 158, 160, 180–182

G

gaming 36, 191, 192, 193
gay 101, 178
genre 23, 28, 29, 47, 60, 69, 70, 77, 81, 83, 151, 195
Global South 59–70, 94
globalization 13, 59, 196, 200
Goffman, Erving 137, 170, 177

H

Hebdige, Dick 9, 42, 44, 45, 60, 76, 84, 96, 141, 172, 179
Hodkinson, Paul 61, 69, 109, 113, 132, 153–154

I

identity
  collective 6, 22, 23, 25, 33
  personal 26, 201
  social 98, 99, 102
  see also insider perspective/knowledge; outsider
ideology 9, 25, 35, 82, 96, 98, 111, 128, 151, 159, 163, 165, 193, 196, 198, 201
insider 9, 23, 109, 128, 181
  perspective/knowledge 26–35, 37, 45, 133, 134, 135–137, 139, 140, 193, 194
  research 37, 45, 150–165, 172, 180, 197, 198
  teaching *see* pedagogy

L

leisure 6, 25, 26, 33, 177, 190
lesbian 178, 192
lifestyle (as concept) 21, 22, 23, 24–26, 29–33, 35–36, 44, 63, 193
  movement 22, 26, 33–35, 36, 193

M

mainstream
  appropriation 45
  clothing 103, 139
  culture 8, 9, 12, 27, 29, 44, 75, 81, 85, 95, 98, 102, 104, 178, 193, 200
  politics 51
  society 8, 22, 84, 104, 105, 153, 190, 193, 194
marginality 3, 6, 8, 12, 24, 27, 62, 76, 83, 93, 113, 127, 128, 141, 143, 144, 145, 171, 189, 190, 194, 201
Marxism 9, 43, 45, 80, 81, 108
masculinity 35, 129, 130, 135, 138, 159
media 9, 46–48, 49–52, 59, 60, 61, 70, 78, 84–85, 94, 112, 189, 196, 199
  mainstream/mass 46, 78, 80, 84–85, 151
  studies 61, 84, 199
methods
  autoethnography 133, 197
  biography 108–110, 172–174
  ethnography 6, 22, 37, 43, 94, 162, 168–183
  interviews 23, 37, 59, 64, 67, 68, 80, 127, 131–133, 145, 153–160, 165, 178, 193
  rapport 153, 156–160, 161, 171, 178
Mills, C. Wright 170–174, 197
moral panic 46, 51, 179
Muggleton, David 9–10, 41, 43, 44, 46, 49, 76
music (genres)
  death metal 28
  electronic dance 25
  grime 191, 192, 198
  hardcore 21, 22, 23, 25, 26, 27–29, 30, 31, 37, 46, 49, 67
  heavy metal 81, 178, 195
  hip-hop 46, 65, 81, 194
  house 81
  indie 75, 93
  jazz 109, 113, 114–115, 116
  popular 41, 47, 48, 81, 87, 107, 111, 112
  rap 46, 81, 111, 191
  rave 25, 41, 46
  rock 48, 62, 63, 70, 110, 111, 151, 178
  techno 81

N

neoliberalism 62, 111, 113
neo-tribe 10, 25, 41, 61, 76, 77
news (casts, media) 51, 52, 60
newspaper 51, 80, 88
non-normative 3, 12, 146, 190, 201
normative 30, 190
norms 114, 130, 158, 159

O

opposition 6, 8, 9, 10, 27, 29, 33, 88, 97, 99, 192
state 31, 33, 59, 62, 114

INDEX

outsider 26, 28, 99, 104, 144, 145, 153, 157, 158, 162, 165, 172, 178, 180, 198, 199

P

pedagogy 84, 168–183
  insider 172–174, 198
philosophy
  Chinese 94, 96, 98, 99, 102, 104, 105, 196
  Greek 3–4, 98
  hardcore 67
  punk 102, 141
police 62, 96, 97, 169, 176, 177
policy
  change 23, 25, 33
  economic 112, 196
  government 86
  makers 82
pop(ular) culture 36, 75, 79, 81, 82, 93, 112, 113
postcolonial 110
Postmodernism 44, 49, 77, 78, 108
post-Subculture 10, 24, 44, 49, 52–53, 70, 76, 77, 107, 108, 114, 118
post-war 9, 42, 43, 48, 60, 128
problem(s) 32, 34, 48, 66, 97, 100, 176
  social 8, 151, 160, 193, 194
  subculture as problematic 8, 172, 193, 194, 196, 200
  subculture as problem-solving 9, 60, 65, 108, 189, 193, 194, 201
protest 26, 31, 33, 44, 66, 82, 85, 88, 95, 96, 97, 101, 111

Q

queer 35, 146

R

racism 26, 31, 65, 66, 146, 151, 154, 155, 162, 173
reflexivity 4, 11, 25, 35, 42, 60, 96, 108, 109, 112–118, 128, 131–133, 140–145, 146, 150, 152, 164–165, 171, 172, 174, 180, 182, 183, 190, 191, 193, 197–199
  emotional 154–156
religion 10, 26, 30, 103, 151, 194
resistance (as concept) 6, 10, 11, 13, 14, 15, 24, 27, 31, 33, 34, 35, 59, 60, 62, 64–68, 70, 81, 94, 93–105, 107, 111, 115, 118, 189, 194, 195, 196, 199, 200
  class and 43, 108
  collective 13, 29, 60
  covert 102
  cultural 34, 111
  groups and 33
  ideological 193
  passive 100
  as practice 94, 95, 98, 99
  Resistance through Rituals 9, 107, 108, 115, 201
  subcultural 36, 82, 96
  symbolic 24, 96

S

scene (as concept) 10, 21, 22, 25, 26, 27–29, 35–36, 61, 193, 197, 199
  hardcore 22, 28
  metal 28, 114
  music 11, 22, 109, 111, 112, 114
  punk 22, 24, 27, 28, 59–70, 93, 95, 101, 131, 133, 134–135, 138, 150–165
  straight edge 30, 32, 34
sensitizing concepts 6, 36, 168–183, 190, 200, 201
sexism 31, 141, 151, 154, 155, 157–160, 161, 162, 163, 164
social media 12, 21–37, 45, 59, 62, 64, 65, 70, 132, 138, 142, 193, 196, 197, 199
  Facebook 23, 27, 37, 51, 52, 64
  Instagram 21–37, 50
  online forum 132
  TikTok 52
  Twitter 47
  YouTube 37, 47, 49, 51, 52
social
  movements 22, 23, 25, 26, 30–33, 35–36, 70, 80, 101, 102, 156, 162, 165, 200
  networks 59, 64, 65, 69, 102, 113, 115, 116, 117, 156, 199, 200
style (as concept) 9, 11, 12, 24, 25, 28, 29, 30, 35, 42, 44, 45, 46, 49, 50, 52, 53, 59, 60, 61, 70, 93, 95, 96, 100, 101, 103, 141, 155, 169, 176, 178, 189, 194, 199, 200, 201
  clothing and 9, 22, 25, 30, 33, 49, 62, 66, 96, 102, 103, 111, 136, 139–140, 144, 150, 151, 159, 176
  emotive 155
  and music 28, 46, 60, 61, 103, 178
  see also Hebdige, Dick
subculture (as concept)
  history of 3–16, 24–26, 41–45, 76–78
subcultural
  capital 76, 116, 153
  career 12, 69, 107–118
  identification 159, 172, 183
  identity 115, 158, 161, 173, 175
  imagination 170–174, 180, 197
  knowledge 136, 172, 198
  resistance 36, 82, 96
  ritual 9, 42, 43, 96, 114
  values 5, 8, 25, 26, 65, 68, 69, 79, 81, 85, 99, 102, 103, 104, 111, 113, 114, 115, 118, 130, 133, 137, 139, 140, 141, 150, 151, 153, 156, 158, 163, 164, 165, 169, 175, 181–182, 190, 194, 196, 199, 200, 201
subcultures (named)
  anarcho-punk 151–165
  art punk 28

BDSM 6, 190
crust punk 28, 83, 152, 157, 160
emo 46, 178, 191, 192, 193, 194
global punk community 62, 64, 69, 70, 95, 102, 105
hardcore punk 21, 22, 26
hippie 46, 48, 49, 50, 95
involuntary celibate (incel) 192, 194, 201
metal 114–117
mod 24, 95, 179
post-punk 141
punk rock 83, 93, 136
otaku 76–77, 85, 87–88
rocker 24, 49, 50, 95
sang (丧) 192, 193, 196, 199
shojo bunka (少女文化) 193
skinhead 24
straight edge 21–37
teddy boys 95
symbolic
  action 25, 96, 101
  interactionism 6, 35, 154, 168, 170
  struggle 70

symbols 9, 22, 24, 60, 64, 102, 103, 104, 108, 113, 114, 117, 135, 150, 153, 179, 194

T

taste 25, 60, 61, 69, 85, 112, 151, 199
tattoo 22, 33, 36, 159
Thornton, Sarah 9–10, 76
Thrasher, Frederic M. 8, 170, 180

V

veganism 26, 31, 32, 34, 35
violence 35, 48, 193, 201

W

Williams, J. Patrick 96, 98, 118, 170, 174, 184, 199
Willis, Paul 42–44, 178

Z

zine (Including magazine) 59, 63, 80, 103, 112, 129, 150, 151, 165
  e-zine (including webzine, online magazine) 34, 37, 65, 165

www.ingramcontent.com/pod-product-compliance
Lightning Source LLC
Chambersburg PA
CBHW051541020426
42333CB00016B/2041